Arthur Henry Beavan

James and Horace Smith

A Family Narrative

Arthur Henry Beavan

James and Horace Smith
A Family Narrative

ISBN/EAN: 9783744688017

Printed in Europe, USA, Canada, Australia, Japan

Cover: Foto ©Thomas Meinert / pixelio.de

More available books at **www.hansebooks.com**

James
and
Horace Smith

JOINT AUTHORS OF 'REJECTED ADDRESSES'

A Family Narrative

BASED UPON HITHERTO UNPUBLISHED PRIVATE DIARIES, LETTERS,
AND OTHER DOCUMENTS

BY

ARTHUR H. BEAVAN

AUTHOR OF 'MARLBOROUGH HOUSE AND ITS OCCUPANTS,'
'POPULAR ROYALTY,' ETC.

WITH FIVE PORTRAITS

LONDON:
HURST AND BLACKETT, LIMITED,
13, GREAT MARLBOROUGH STREET.
1899

PREFACE

Very many Smithian "footprints on the sands of time" are somewhat faint, but those of James and Horace Smith have left a deep and lasting impression. The brothers' chief work, *Rejected Addresses*, is, in its way, a classic, declared by so high an authority as Lord Jeffrey to indicate a talent to which he "did not know where to look for a parallel."

Why, it may be asked, has not a systematic Life of James and Horace Smith been published before this? The reason is not far to seek: until now, the necessary material has not been available.

Horace penned a brief memoir of James, as preface to a collection of the latter's *Comic Miscellanies*, published in 1840; and after Horace's death in 1849, suggestions were made that a biography of the two eminent brothers should be written. But for various reasons the family discouraged the idea; and without their co-operation, it could not have been accomplished, as the private journals, containing all-important data, would have been inaccessible.

Lapse of time, fortunately, has removed these objections; and through the kindness of a relative of the Smith family—Harry Magnus, Esq., of Stonebridge Park, London—these journals have been placed at my disposal, and are here made use of in the writers' own words, and, as far as possible chronologically.

ARTHUR H. BEAVAN.

CONTENTS

CHAPTER I

1747—1769

PAGE

Introduction—Robert Smith, the father of James and Horace—His birth and parentage—Early recollections—Education—First poetical effort—Meets " Perdita "—Journeys to London—Is articled to an Attorney—Experiences in London—Sets out for the Continent . . 1

CHAPTER II

1769—1779

Robert Smith in Paris—Goes to Compiègne—Sees Louis XV. and Madame du Barry—Sees Louis XV. at supper—Follows the Royal Stag-hunt at Compiègne—Meets the Corsican General, Paoli—Is admitted as an Attorney—His courtship and marriage—Resides at Fen Court—Birth of James Smith—Helps Mr. Hanway to promote philanthropic institutions, and appeals to David Garrick for a Benefit—Attends opening of Free Masons' Hall—Removes from Fen Court to Frederick's Place, Old Jewry 13

CHAPTER III

1779—1787

Birth of Horace Smith—The year 1780—The Lord George Gordon Riots—Robert Smith's personal experi-

CONTENTS

ence of them—He is appointed Assistant-Solicitor to
the Board of Ordnance—Removes to Old Jewry—Visits
the West Indies—Is elected Fellow of the Society of
Antiquaries 28

CHAPTER IV

1787—1790

Association of James and Horace Smith with the City—
Their childhood—James and Horace at Chigwell School 36

CHAPTER V

1790—1791

Sundays at Chigwell—Play days and recreation at
Chigwell—James at New College, Hackney—At Alfred
House Academy, Camberwell—Attends book-keeping
classes—Horace leaves Chigwell, and goes to Alfred
House 46

CHAPTER VI

The eve of the French Revolution—Robert Smith
again in Paris—Sees Louis XVI. and Marie Antoinette
at Versailles—The French Drama—The political agitation in Paris—Robert Smith's providential escape from
the mob—James Smith in France—His narrow escape
from death at Dover 53

CHAPTER VII

1791—1800

James is articled to his father—Goes to Scotland—
Goes to the Isle of Wight—Robert Smith and Sir Joseph
Banks—James visits Dartmouth, the Isle of Thanet, and
"Leasowes" in Shropshire—Goes to various places on
Ordnance Board business—Robert Smith elected Fellow
of the Royal Society—Horace becomes clerk in a City
counting-house—James admitted as an Attorney—The

CONTENTS ix

PAGE

National Thanksgiving at St. Paul's—Patriotism in the City—Robert Smith becomes a member of the Society of Arts—His experiences in Ireland 64

CHAPTER VIII
1800—1804

Earliest literary works of James and Horace Smith—No. 36 Basinghall Street—City Halls and State Lotteries—James dines with the Hon. Spencer Perceval—Family visit to Windsor—Illness and death of Mrs. Robert Smith   78

CHAPTER IX
1804—1812

Robert Smith's second marriage—He visits Cambridge, and there sees Henry Kirke White—Horace Smith becomes a merchant—The City in the first decade of the century—Horace Smith's firm reconstituted—James appointed joint-assistant to the Ordnance Board Solicitor—Robert Smith removes to Austin Friars—Horace Smith becomes a member of the Stock Exchange . . 86

CHAPTER X
1812

Horace Smith's burlesque, *The Highgate Tunnel*, is produced at the Lyceum Theatre—James and Horace Smith's connection with the drama—Destruction of Drury Lane Theatre by fire—Plans for the rebuilding—The new theatre 93

CHAPTER XI
1812

Competition for Address to be spoken at opening of new Drury Lane Theatre—Some of the Addresses—The

PAGE

re-opening of Drury Lane Theatre — How *Rejected Addresses* came to be written—Its publication . . 104

CHAPTER XII

1812—1813

Rejected Addresses and the Reviewers—The effect of its success upon the careers of James and Horace Smith —Their social and literary circle—Horace Smith resides at Knightsbridge—His friend William Heseltine— Horace Smith and the Stock Exchange 117

CHAPTER XIII

1813—1821

Horace Smith's letters to his sister Clara—His second marriage—Removes from Knightsbridge to Fulham— Entertains the poet Keats—Horace Smith's account of his introduction to Shelley and Keats 129

CHAPTER XIV

The Board of Ordnance, its officers and functions— The "Assistant to the Solicitor" and his duties—Emoluments of the office—An Ordnance Parliamentary "preserve"—Retirement of Robert Smith from business, and from the post of "Assistant to the Solicitor"—James Smith appointed "Assistant to the Solicitor" . . 140

CHAPTER XV

1821—1825

Horace Smith and Shelley (*continued*)—Horace Smith's connection with the Scott-Christie duel—Mr. Andrew Lang's remarks thereon—The death of Keats—Horace Smith retires from business, and decides to visit Shelley in Italy—Letter to his sister Clara—Is detained at Paris by ill-health of his wife—Letters to Cyrus Redding . 149

CHAPTER XVI

1821—1825

Horace Smith receives the news of Shelley's death—
His personal recollections of Shelley, and his estimate of
the poet's character 167

CHAPTER XVII

1825—1832

The declining years of Robert Smith—His verse-work
—Family marriages—Death of his second wife—His last
illness and death 178

CHAPTER XVIII

James and Horace Smith as Wits and Humorists . 186

CHAPTER XIX

Horace Smith's recollections of Sir Walter Scott,
Southey, and Thomas Hill of Sydenham . . . 199

CHAPTER XX

Horace Smith's recollections of Charles Mathews and
Theodore Hook 214

CHAPTER XXI

The personal appearance of James Smith—His habits
—His social circle—His clubs—His love of London—
Revisits Chigwell school—His last illness and death . 233

CHAPTER XXII

The later literary works of James and Horace Smith . 249

CHAPTER XXIII

1826—1849

PAGE

Brighton in the "twenties," "thirties," and "forties"
—Horace Smith at Brighton 267

CHAPTER XXIV

The declining years of Horace Smith's life—His last
illness and death—His personal appearance, tastes,
opinions, character, and disposition—The end . . 291

INDEX 307

ILLUSTRATIONS

ROBERT SMITH, ÆTAT 84, THE FATHER OF JAMES AND
HORACE SMITH . . . . *Frontispiece*
From Original Miniature.

MARY SMITH, ÆTAT 25, THE MOTHER OF JAMES AND
HORACE SMITH . . . . . . *To face page* 23
From a Silhouette.

MR. ALDERMAN CADELL, MASTER OF THE STATIONERS'
COMPANY, 1798 115
From a Portrait in Stationers' Hall.

JAMES SMITH, ÆTAT 62 233
From the Portrait by Lonsdale.

HORACE SMITH, ÆTAT 45 291
From the Portrait by Masquerier.
Contributed by the BARONESS BURDETT-COUTTS.

JAMES AND HORACE SMITH

CHAPTER I

1747—1769

Introduction—Robert Smith, the father of James and Horace — His birth and parentage — Early recollections — Education—First poetical effort—Meets " Perdita "—Journeys to London—Is articled to an Attorney—Experiences in London—Sets out for the Continent.

HARD by the Wandle, in the ancient suburb to which the stream has given its name, is All Saints, Wandsworth, an unlovely church of some antiquity, whose flint walls have for many years been hidden beneath a casing of Georgian brickwork. It stands in a small disused churchyard, where, amongst some scores of tombs scattered about in various stages of decay, may be seen a plain headstone, bearing without text or comment this simple inscription :—

𝔈𝔫 𝔐𝔢𝔪𝔬𝔯𝔶 𝔬𝔣

ROBERT SMITH, ESQ.,

OF ST. ANNE'S HILL, IN THIS PARISH,

WHO DIED SEPTEMBER 27, 1832,

AGED 85 YEARS.

Not one person in a thousand, perhaps, would take the trouble to bestow a second thought upon the owner of so common-place a name; but the Robert Smith whose body lies there was no ordinary person, and he was, moreover, the father of the authors of *Rejected Addresses*. His experiences, too, were exceptional. He had gazed upon the features of Louis the Well-Beloved, and of his mistress, Madame du Barry; he had been a witness of the Lord George Gordon riots; he had seen Louis XVI. and Marie Antoinette at Versailles, and had escaped by a mere chance the first outburst of mob-violence that presaged the Reign of Terror.

This plain Robert Smith—a boy of thirteen when George II. died—lived throughout the reigns of George III. and George IV., intelligently observing all the changes of that stirring period, and died just after the passing of the Reform Bill.

Luckily for the biographer, Robert Smith had, from early boyhood, been in the habit of noting down, and afterwards elaborating, his impressions of passing events; and as time went on, this custom led him to keep a systematic diary of family affairs, etc., preserved in two stout closely-written volumes.

I was born [he begins] on the 22nd of November, 1747, O.S., at the dwelling-house belonging to the Custom-House in Castle Street, Bridgwater,[1] and, when between two and three years of age,

[1] Robert Smith's father was at one time Mayor of Bridgwater, and held the post of Deputy Collector of Customs at that port.

was placed at a day-school in the town kept by an old woman of the name of Keene, of whose person, I have still (1818) a clear recollection. There I remained until the latter end of the year 1751, when I was removed to a writing-school kept by Mr. David Webber.

An event of a public nature took place in the year 1752, which was spoken of by everybody, but understood by few. I mean the alteration of the style by Act of Parliament. I was told, among other surprising changes, that I should keep my birthday, not on the anniversary of the day on which it really happened, but on the 4th of December. This puzzled me, as it did others to whom the Julian and Gregorian calendars were alike unknown.

In the summer of 1754, when I was but seven years old, my father indulged me in a jaunt of pleasure to Bath and Bristol, under the charge of my Uncle George. I was mounted on a long-tailed pony, dressed in a new scarlet coat, boots, and a flowing wig. The riding on horse-back so long a journey, and for the first time, I found fatiguing, but the wonders of Bath and a day or two's rest restored me. At Bristol we were met by father and mother, who had gone thither on horseback, she riding behind my father, seated on a blue cloth pillow, and dressed in a " joseph," or brown serge riding-dress, with buttons down to the skirts. We all returned to Bridgwater, when I recounted my adventures with no little pride and satisfaction.

During the same year, the town was a continual scene of riot and disorder, on account of the General Election for members of Parliament. The candidates were John, Earl of Egmont (in Ireland), afterwards created Baron Lovel and Holland (in England), Robert Balch, Esq., of Stowey in Somersetshire, and Bubb Doddington, Esq. (afterwards created Lord

Melcombe-Regis). The two former were elected, and, as usual on such occasions, were "chaired" through the town on men's shoulders, amidst the clamours of the high and low rabble, the ringing of bells, the firing of "chambers," and the rude sneers of the unsuccessful party.

Two circumstances took place in 1755 which made an impression upon my memory—the breaking out of the war with France, and the accounts received of a dreadful earthquake at Lisbon, which happened on the 1st of November; and the year 1760 presented an event of a public nature that made a strong impression upon my mind at the time, viz. the death of his Majesty, George II. It happened on the 25th of October; the account of it was received at Bridgwater on the following day.

Throughout these early years of his life, Robert Smith was receiving a good and sensible education. He was thoroughly well grounded in writing, book-keeping, etc., and the object of his ambition was reached when an opportunity arose for acquiring a knowledge of the classics, by no means easy of attainment in those days at a place like Bridgwater.

The scene now changed [he says]. Holmes' *Latin Grammar* was put in my hands; and the difficulties which first present themselves to a learner being over, I got through my lessons with tolerable credit. If a knowledge of the Latin tongue be a necessary part of education for boys, what harm can it do to girls? So my father reasoned; and he accordingly placed my eldest sister, Molly, at the same school. She went through her exercises regularly with the boys, and had advanced as far as Ovid's epistles, when my father removed her from the school.

Besides Latin and Italian, the boy studied French, in which language he afterwards became proficient; so that he was well qualified for the start in life which presently offered itself in the office of a Mr. John Popham, a London attorney practising in the Court of Common Pleas, who owned a set of chambers on the ground floor of No. 5, New Inn, of which society he was an "Antient," and with whom it was arranged that Robert should be articled on his arrival in the metropolis.

Robert Smith evinced considerable powers of composition at an early age; and it is interesting to record the first literary effort of him from whom James and Horace Smith—the subjects of this biography—inherited the talent of comic versification. He describes it as "a loose imitation of some French verses that he had stumbled upon," in which the leading idea is sustained with humorous effect:

THE BOLD IRRESOLUTE

I.

As on the margin of the flood,
Absorb'd in grief, young Colin stood,
    His hapless fate bewailing,
Rous'd by despair the shepherd swore
Love's torments he'd no more endure,
    So rashly plunged . . . a pail in.

II.

Now, fierce with rage, he maddening flew,
And from its sheath a hanger drew,
    Still o'er destruction brooding;

Before Dorinda's face, the swain,
At one despairing stroke, in twain
    Down cleft, ah me ! . . . a pudding.

III.

" The conflict's o'er—no more I'll flinch,
But in the *poison'd bowl* will quench
    A flame than death more cruel,"
He said—then seizing on the bowl,
To Heav'n commends his parting soul,
    And drank large draughts . . . of gruel.

IV.

With bitter pangs his heart opprest,
Love's tumult boiling in his breast,
    No mortal could abide it ;
Eager he seeks *the halter's* aid
Thick round his neck in order laid,
    He tied, and then . . . untied it.

V.

Now mopish grown, in pensive mood,
Beside his bed the shepherd stood,
    And sigh'd and wept profoundly ;
A *smothering death* he now prefers,
So clos'd his eyes, and said his prayers,
    Then on his bed . . . slept soundly.

VI.

At length the nymph, to ease his pain,
Took pity on the amorous swain,
    Her cruelty relented ;
In mutual love their willing hands
They joined in Hymen's silken bands,
    And lived till both . . . repented.

Shortly before his first journey to London, Robert
and an old school-fellow, John Chubb, seem to have

taken sundry excursions together, one being to Bristol, where they met the historic "Perdita," then an innocent little girl of four years, as unconscious of Florizel, the faithless, as he of his future *innamorata*. Writing of this many years afterwards, Robert Smith says:—

We spent a few days with Captain Derby and his wife, who was a distant relation of the Chubb family. Amongst their children was a most interesting little girl, who, when grown up, married clandestinely at the age of sixteen, and by degrees fell off in her reputation. She became afterwards a "favourite" of the Prince of Wales, and, having made her *debût* on the stage in the character of "Perdita," she was well known to the public by that name. Her person and her manners were pleasing in the highest degree; she lived much among persons of rank and fashion, and her literary talents were not despicable. For several years before her death she lost the use of her lower extremities, so as to be utterly unable to stand.

The morning of Tuesday, the 7th of May, 1765, broke cold and cheerless over the town of Bath, hardly the kind of day one would have chosen for a long journey; but Robert Smith, a tall and sturdy youth of eighteen, who had secured a seat the previous day after a pleasant ride from Bridgwater, was one whom mere physical discomfort would hardly deter from setting forth for London, where he hoped to play no unimportant part. As, however, the cumbersome machine cautiously manœuvred out of the White Lion Inn yard at seven o'clock, few hearts were heavier than his, for he was very fond of his home, and keenly felt the parting from his people.

Travelling in those days was no light thing—uncomfortable at its best, and often full of adventures not infrequently dangerous. It was always expensive, the fare from Bath to London during the summer being twenty-eight shillings, with only fourteen pounds weight of personal luggage allowed, anything extra being charged at the rate of three-halfpence per pound. Then there were the tips to the coachman and guard, and the charges at the various inns were based upon a scale of great liberality towards the landlord.

After leaving Bath, the coach made its way to Trowbridge, whence it leisurely rolled along to Devizes. At this point the serious part of the journey began, as the route lay through the most exposed district of Wiltshire, where the wind blew with frightful violence, not to speak of its being all " collar-work " for the horses.

To beguile the time, the coachman recounted, with ample detail, how, two months before, there had been a most remarkable fall of snow in this part of England—which, indeed, had been general throughout the country—when many lives were lost from exposure, and numerous accidents occurred, the most extraordinary of which was one that happened near Newcastle, where, in the gloom of that storm, two men riding at full gallop in opposite directions met each other with such force that both horses instantly died, and the lives of their riders were despaired of.

But no snow fell on Robert Smith's journey; and, after much laborious struggling over the rugged, hilly road, the travellers reached the inn at Shepherd Shore. Here they rested and had tea.

Invigorated and warmed, horses and men jogged along to Beckhampton Inn, and thence past the famous Silbury Mound, where British warriors once gathered together in battle-array to celebrate King Arthur's second and last great battle of Badon Hill.

On and on, to the George at West Overton, the Swan at Clatford, and—in the failing light—to the Castle at Marlborough; and after skirting Savernake Forest for three miles, a welcome twinkling of lights at Hungerford announced that bed and supper awaited them at the Black Bear, sixty odd miles from London. At daybreak the coach was off again.

The roads were now better, as was also the pace, and there was nothing of interest to note, except that at all the inns at Newbury, at the Angel, at Wool-hampton, and at Reading, the meat-hooks that generally bore a variety of tempting joints sustained nothing but mutton. After passing through Houns-low, the coachman, who had been repeatedly asked for a solution of the mystery, at last admitted that throughout Wilts and Berks, in consequence of the past severe weather, there had been great losses amongst the flocks of sheep, and consequently there was a perfect glut of mutton that had not "inter-viewed the butcher in a constitutional manner," though otherwise perfectly sound. Cart-loads had been brought into the nearest towns, and all the inns along the road had very little else in their larders.

At the Belle Sauvage on Ludgate Hill, where he arrived late on the second day of his journey, Robert Smith tarried not, but at once set out, following a porter who carried his trunk, to Milk Street in the City, where he was to lodge with his uncle Thomas, a wholesale linen-draper.

The following morning, as the youth started westward to present himself to Mr. Popham, it was upon the London of Dr. Johnson, Boswell, Sir Joshua Reynolds, and Garrick that he gazed; a London of picturesque gabled houses flung down apparently at random, with side streets so narrow and tortuous that it was hardly possible to walk or ride in safety, and whose principal thoroughfares, such as the Strand, were so dirty that every morning the apprentices might be seen washing away from the shop-fronts the accumulated filth of the previous day; where pedestrians in long blue coats like dressing-gowns, brown stockings, and red or brown frizzled periwigs, braved all the splashings from passing traffic, as they walked on the narrow *trottoir* of a roadway consisting of rough stones, which rolled and rubbed one against the other on a foundation of nothing but old mud.

Robert Smith was articled for five years to Mr. Popham, by which articles it was agreed that his father should pay down a premium of one hundred guineas, and provide for his son board and lodgings, and " apparel suitable for a clerk," during the period; while Mr. Popham undertook to teach him the law, and so long as he abode with him, and was in his actual service, to pay him each term one guinea as "termage," or term fee. His line of life was now considered settled. His office hours were from 9 a.m. to 9 p.m. during the term time, with an allowance of two hours for dinner; and day after day he valiantly trudged from Milk Street, having besides much walking to the law offices, the courts, etc. He lived frugally, knowing how necessary it was to save his father's purse; and so well did he manage that, from the time of his leaving his father's house until the expiration of his articles, his expenses were not more than £55 per annum, and this at a time when living was comparatively dear.

The neighbourhood soon became quite familiar to the young clerk—his own Inn of Court, with its dingy brick building, high-pitched roof, and clustered chimney-pots, its little hall inside the grass enclosure facing his office, and the archway leading into Wych Street, St. Clement's Church a stone's-throw off, and beyond it, Butcher Row, a decaying remnant of Elizabethan London, whose wood and plaster eaves overhung the street, noted for its shambles and eating-houses.

In one of the last-named Robert Smith used occasionally to see the famous Dr. Johnson, whose acquaintance he subsequently made. Johnson knew the Row well, and rather surprised Boswell, who one day was dining at the Clifton, by coming in and taking his seat like any ordinary mortal intent upon economy.

As years went by Smith became entrusted with more and more of the important business of the office. Diligent as he was, he found time for occasional relaxation. He says :—

Now and then, though sparingly, I went to the theatre, Vauxhall, etc., and I was often entertained, not to say instructed, at the debating society called the " Robin Hood," in Butcher Row, Temple Bar. I attended also at convenient opportunities anatomical lectures, dissections at the hospitals, Martin's lectures on experimental philosophy, and at other places, where I thought a little useful knowledge might be gleaned. At the " Robin Hood," I have seen some of the first characters in point of rank and science ; but the greater part consisted of those who appeared to be attracted by no higher motive than curiosity. The price of admittance was sixpence ; for which sum each person had a right to join in the debates and to a sup at the porter-pot when handed about. The chairman had standing before him a " five-minute " glass, which, when the sand was run out, he turned as a signal for the speaker to draw his arguments to a conclusion. Upon the whole, the business of the evening was conducted with great regularity ; and at the breaking up of the assembly, the chairman, with some of the members of the Society, retired to another room to sup.

In the long vacation of 1769, Robert Smith, instead of paying his customary visit to Bridgwater, decided to travel on the continent, then a somewhat formidable undertaking. On the 3rd of August he left London with his friend, Mr. Atkinson, embarked the same evening from Brighton, and arrived at Dieppe about 11 a.m. on the 5th.

CHAPTER II

1769—1779

Robert Smith in Paris—Goes to Compiègne—Sees Louis
XV. and Mdme. du Barry—Sees Louis XV. at supper—Follows
the Royal Stag-Hunt at Compiègne—Meets the Corsican
General, Paoli—Is admitted as an Attorney—His courtship
and marriage—Resides at Fen Court—Birth of James Smith
—Helps Mr. Hanway to promote philanthropic institutions,
and appeals to David Garrick for a Benefit—Attends opening
of Free Masons' Hall—Removes from Fen Court to Frederick's
Place, Old Jewry.

At Dieppe the two friends engaged a *berline* to
take them to Rouen, and set out the following
morning, not a little entertained by their mode of
conveyance.

The traces of the horses [says Robert Smith]
were of ropes, and the postilion's boots of immense
size and thickness bound round with iron hoops,
into which he thrust his legs without taking off his
shoes. The use of these enormous boots was, however, explained to us. Most of the travelling
carriages in France, we were informed, are of two
wheels only, drawn by three horses abreast. On the
small near horse, or *bidet*, the postilion rides; and
next to the *bidet* is the *limmonier*, or thill-horse

(shaft-horse), which supports the whole weight of the carriage. The unyielding boots, therefore, are meant to protect the postilion's legs from harm, in case of the *bidet* falling, as the carriage could make no impression upon such boots.

From Rouen they travelled in a *chaise à quatre personnes* to Paris, where they put up at the Hôtel de Casignan, Rue Quinquempoix, in the quarter of St. Denis, when the first thing Robert did was to "bespeak a suit of clothes proper to appear in at public places where dress might be required." "I accordingly," he narrates, "ordered a maroon-coloured silk (*soie de la Reine*), a sword, and a hair-bag, as did Mr. Atkinson one of black silk, and each his *chapeau de bras.*"

Meanwhile, the two lost no time in exploring the capital of France, visiting the markets, the Palais Royal, the Palais de Tuileries, the quays, the streets and boulevards, purchasing on their way back to their hotel two knives for their personal use, for they had been told that the *couvert* for each person consisted only of a "large four-pronged silver fork, a silver spoon, a clean napkin, a china plate, and a water-bottle and tumbler," that "every one carried his own knife in his pocket, the same knife serving all purposes of cutting the meat, the fork conveying it to the mouth."

One evening they went to La Comédie Française on the south side of the Seine. The piece performed was *Le Père de l'Orphelin.*

The house [says Robert Smith] not unlike Foote's little theatre in the Haymarket, lamps placed along the front of the stage, no seats in the pit, over which were two chandeliers suspended, and, these being the only lights, the whole had but a sombre appearance. The favourite actor was Mollé, but his action was too violent in parts which did not appear to me to require it. Here, as at the Opera in the Tuileries, the prompter's head is seen rising up through a small opening in the front of the stage.

Their attire being now *en règle*, the friends set out for Compiègne, where the King was at the time, taking with them introductions to certain persons of influence at the Court.

Passing through St. Denis, Ecouen, and Lusarche, we arrived at Chantilly at about seven o'clock in the evening. At this place the Prince of Condé has a superb château, which we visited immediately after our arrival. It is surrounded by a moat full of water, in which were some of the largest carp I ever saw, and so tame that after throwing to them a few bits of bread, they came and nibbled the bread from our hands. Near the village are the Prince's stables, a large uniformly-constructed building, in which we saw a great number of fine English hunters; it is formed to contain two hundred and forty horses. As we walked through the park, we were astonished at the great number of partridges that were running about almost as tame as chickens. I had observed, indeed, in the country we passed through, partridges, pheasants, and hares in great plenty; but this is not to be wondered at when we consider the severity of the game-laws in France; offenders are sent to the army, or even to the

galleys, with very little ceremony. Not far from
the stables, between there and the village, is La
Meute, a superb dog-kennel of three hundred
hounds. Once a year, we were informed, the Prince
treats his tenants, their families, and labourers, with
a great *fête* in the park. Among the diversions is
that of "shooting an arrow" for a silver bowl and a
silver plate given by the Prince. He himself shoots
the first arrow, taking care always to *miss* the mark.
The *fête* lasts three days, during which time dancing-
parties exercise themselves on the lawn, where tents
are erected, as well as in the wood; refreshments are
given out unsparingly, and there are billiards, etc.
etc. It is by these acts of condescension and kindness that princes and all others may recommend
themselves to their dependants and secure their
affections.

The next morning, the Court being then at Compiègne, we dressed ourselves in our silk suits, and
about noon repaired to the château. We readily
gained admittance, and waited with others for nearly
half-an-hour in the King's ante-chamber, when the
King entered it on his way to the chapel. I had
stationed myself so close to the door, that the King
in passing made a short pause and looked steadfastly
at me as if trying to recollect my person. The King
is in stature rather above the middle height, stoops
a little at the shoulders, and his knees turn out a
little. His complexion is rather dark, his hair and
eyebrows nearly black, his nose somewhat aquiline,
and his look altogether majestic, though not the
least severity or haughtiness in his countenance.
Shortly after the King, his sisters, the *mesdames* of
France, passed also through the ante-chamber on
their way to the chapel, whither we ourselves then
went. The chapel is plain and neat, the music soft
and solemn. A little before the service was ended

we returned to the ante-chamber, and then again had a distinct view of the King and his sisters on their way back. We had afterwards another view of him in the court of the palace as he entered his carriage to go a-hunting, a diversion of which the king is said to be passionately fond.

At supper that evening they had, among other things, a dish of fricasséed frogs.

It stood near me [relates Robert Smith]; I tasted and liked it very much. My fellow-traveller tasted too, and thought them larks. The English are strongly prejudiced against frogs as a dish, but the food is delicate, and much prized when the prejudice is overcome. The skin is taken off, and the hind-quarters only are dressed, and when properly cooked with artichoke bottoms, truffles, morels, etc., form a repast of which no Englishman need be ashamed or afraid. What is there in the feeding of frogs more revolting than in that of eels and other pond fish, ducks, hogs, etc. ? Yet all these an Englishman eats without scruple or inquiry.

In the following description given by Robert Smith of Louis XV. and his court, it will be observed that he was not at all impressed by the beauty of Madame du Barry. Voltaire remarked of her likeness that "the original was intended for the gods." Smith writes :—

On the morning of the 27th of August, which was Sunday, we paid another visit to the château. We then again saw the King, the Princess, the King's suite, etc., on their way to and from the chapel, as well as in it. Among the great folks were the

Duchess de Choisie, *embonpoint* and handsome, the Duchess de Chartres, young and pretty. We had a good view also of Madame de Barré, the King's favourite. She is not a beauty, but has an agrecable form and cheerful countenance. That it is the road to preferment in France is well known, and this lady, we observed, had great attention paid to her.

We were afterwards permitted to enter, with others, an apartment in which the King's grandson (the future Louis XVI.), the Comte de Provence, and the Comte d'Artois (afterwards Charles X.), were dining. The former completed his fifteenth year on the 23rd of the present month. He is tall for his years, rather reserved in manner, and of a sallowish complexion. The Comte de Provence has a quick eye, but appears also rather reserved. The Comte d'Artois is handsome, lively, and laughing. From this apartment we went to another, in which the *Mesdames* of France were then at dinner; and here we had a more distinct view of each than before. The eldest, Madame Adelaide, has a genteel figure; the second, Madame Victoire, is a complete brunette, *embonpoint*, and of rather a masculine appearance; the two others, Madame Louison and Madame Sophie, having nothing particular in face or figure. Two of them wore their hair in coloured silk bags, in shape like those of men in full dress, and they were all highly rouged.

In the afternoon we took a regular survey of all the apartments, and upon our going into the gardens, we saw from the terrace the King and his suite returning from his *chasse d'oiseaux*, followed by an immense concourse of people. The day was Sunday, but Sundays in France have their diversions as well as their religious ceremonies. We were told that the King had, on that afternoon, shot with his own hands no less than thirty-seven brace of partridges.

But this is not so surprising when we consider the very great plenty of birds, and the method of a *chasse de fusile Royale.* The King has his *chasseurs* close to him, and the instant he discharges his piece he gives it to one of them, another at the moment clapping a loaded one into his hands, by which he has frequently an opportunity of shooting twice, if not three times, at the same bird or covey.

This being the day on which the King and Royal Family usually go in procession to the Carmelites, we went thither, but were disappointed in our expectations of seeing the ceremony; it did not take place, the King being too much fatigued to attend. In the evening, however, we again saw the King and the *Mesdames* at supper, on which occasion all persons decently dressed are admitted into the apartment. Before the King sat down, he took from his pocket two rolls of bread, which he laid on the table before him. These, we were informed, had been taken by the King from two baskets of bread, baked by different bakers, a practice which had its origin probably from an apprehension of poison. The King ate heartily, taking something from a number of dishes. When he had occasion to drink, he said "*à boire,*" when two of his attendants in full dress, with bags and swords, advanced to the table (which was of semi-circular form), making their obeisances. One of them carried in his hands a gold or silver-gilt salver, on which were two bottles and two goblets of the same metal as the salver. Having poured into one of the goblets some wine from one of the bottles, and water from the other, the other attendant drank it. The two bottles and the other goblet were then presented to the King, who poured from the bottles and drank, when the attendants immediately retiring backwards with similar obeisances, left the room. This ceremony was performed three times during the supper.   What a farce !   As soon as the dessert was finished, the King and his sisters rose from the table and retired to his private apartments, as we did to our *auberge*.

August 28*th*.—On this day was to be a Royal stag-hunt, and we repaired to the rendezvous in a carriage, where the King and his suite shortly afterwards arrived.   Matters had been so arranged by M. Beauvais, that upon our alighting from the carriage we found a couple of English hunters ready for us, most gaily tricked out with crimson and gilt bridles and stirrups.   Upon alighting from their carriages, the King and his suite mounted their horses and proceeded towards a neighbouring wood in which was the stag.   Among others in the King's train was the Field-Marshal, Duke of Richelieu, a little merry-looking old man, mounted on a French *bidet*, and attended by a running footman dressed in a blue satin fancy dress with ornamental cap, holding in his hand a silver staff with a large knob at the top.   As from curiosity we mixed among the King's attendants, one of them politely asked what answer he should return to his Majesty should he make inquiry concerning us, which he usually did upon perceiving strangers.   I told him that we were English individuals who had visited France on a journey of pleasure, and had taken the liberty to attend, that we might have the honour of seeing the King, and the ceremonies of a Royal hunt. The King, it seems, is passionately fond of all field sports.   He conversed freely with those about him, and especially with Madame de Barré, who rode by his side attired in a man's hunting-habit.[1]

[1] This was a favourite dress of hers, usually ornamented with large revers, or facings, trimmed with Honiton lace, which showed off to perfection her bare and faultless neck.

He hummed and whistled several hunting tunes, amongst them the pretty old French ditty *Jean de Nivelle a trois manteaux, Trois palefrois, et trois châteaux*, listening occasionally to the horns of the *chasseurs* in the wood, and the "opening" of the hounds. From there he directed his course, but without attempting to keep in with them. After four or five hours' chase in this fashion, in which he had occasionally a distant view of the stag, the animal took to bay, and was shot to prevent his worrying the hounds. Here all remained until the King and his attendants rode up to the spot, when the principal *chasseur* cut off one of the stag's fore-feet, and on his knees presented it to the King. His Majesty handed it over to one of the attendants that it might be preserved among his other trophies of the chase. All-the horses and dogs were English. We then dismounted, and returned in our carriage to Compiègne, where we again slept.

The friends journeyed home by way of Antwerp, the Hague, and Helvoetsluys, and at the Hague had the good fortune to meet the celebrated Corsican patriot and chief, Paoli (mentioned in Boswell's *Life of Johnson*), who had just escaped from that island, and was proceeding to England by the same packet in company with a young Hanoverian baron. Paoli, it appears, entertained a dismal anticipation that he would be very ill on the passage to Harwich. Says Robert Smith :—

Upon our getting on board the packet, Paoli immediately went below deck and lay down to avoid sickness, but his forebodings were soon realized. I went down occasionally to inquire after him, and found him quite disheartened.   He often exclaimed, half in jest and half in earnest, that he was sure the voyage would kill· him, that he should never live to see England.   The young Hanoverian continued on deck, eating his cold tongue and bread, drinking bottled beer, and capering about, highly rejoiced at the thought of soon seeing England.   Indeed, as soon as the packet had hoisted her sails and put to sea, he said to me with an air of seeming triumph, "Now we are upon English ground!"   I did not understand him at first, and answered, "Oh, no! you must expect some rough weather before you reach England; perhaps you will be ill too, as well as the general."   He immediately replied, with another caper, "I beg your pardon, we are now upon the High Sea; *that* is English *ground.*"

His articles of clerkship having expired, Robert Smith was admitted on the 23rd of June, 1770, as an attorney in the Court of Common Pleas; and he subsequently became a solicitor both of the High Court of Chancery and of the Court of King's Bench, where the celebrated and accomplished Lord Mansfield [1] presided.

And now the most important event in Robert Smith's life was approaching.   The story is best told in his own words:—

During the summer, I attended the Hampstead Assembly, and on the first night danced with Miss

[1] Described by Pope as—

> "Noble and young, who strikes the heart
> With every sprightly, every decent part;
> Equal, the injur'd to defend,
> To charm the Mistress, or to fix the Friend."

MARY SMITH,

THE MOTHER OF JAMES AND HORACE SMITH.

Bogle, daughter of James Bogle French, Esq., a merchant in Swithin's Lane. My partner pleased me. I was struck with her person and manner of behaviour, and was anxious to know who and what she was. The result of my inquiry was satisfactory, and I now began to entertain feelings to which before I was a stranger. On the following ball-night I again danced with her as a partner, slept at a friend's house at Hampstead, and in the morning waited upon my partner to inquire after her health. I was received with great good-humour both by herself and her mother. These circumstances encouraged me, and I danced with her again on the following ball-night. The business was now done so far as respected my own intentions, and on the following morning I waited upon the father in Swithin's Lane, to whom I opened myself fully. He received me with great civility, made the necessary inquiries into my education, family, and prospects, and after a pretty long conversation desired me to call on him again on that day week. I was punctual to the appointment, when Mr. French told me that he had informed himself concerning me, communicated my wishes to his wife and daughter, and that I was at liberty to visit in the family. From this time my visits were constant, and in a month or two our union was considered as fixed.

I now looked out for a home, and at length succeeded in engaging one, No. 1, Fen Court, Fenchurch Street. The house being furnished, and all previous matters arranged, I was married on the 11th of February, 1773, at the Parish Church of St. Swithin's, London-Stone. I had now connected myself with a family who were dissenters from the Established Church, of which Church I considered myself a member, it being that in which I was brought up from my infancy; but, to say the truth, religion, or rather, the difference between one form of Christian worship and another, was a subject that had never engaged my thoughts deeply; and upon now considering it, I found no difficulty in conforming to the mode of a worship adopted by my wife's family."

A daughter, Maria, was born in December of the same year; and in 1775 is recorded the birth at Fen Court of James, his eldest son—one of the future authors of *Rejected Addresses :—*

On the 10th of February, my dear wife presented me with a son. He was baptized by the name of James, in Fen Court, by Mr. Spilsbury on the 9th of March; but his baptism was not registered at Dr. Williams' Library until the 11th of December following, No. 885.[1]

In July [continues the journal] meetings were held by a few individuals, of whose number I was one, for establishing an " Inoculating Dispensary " for the poor. The plan being finally arranged, officers were appointed, and a house was taken in Old Street, opposite St. Luke's Hospital. I acted as their secretary. It went on tolerably well at first, but prejudices and jealousies prevailing too strongly against it, the scheme was abandoned altogether in 1777, and I sat down with the loss of a few pounds.

[1] In the "advertisement" to the 22nd edition of *Rejected Addresses* (John Murray, 1851), it is stated incorrectly that both James and Horace Smith were born at No. 36, Basinghall Street. Robert Smith's family did not remove there until 1790, when James was fifteen, and Horace eleven years of age.

It will be seen that Robert Smith was considerably in advance of his time in his efforts to apply practically the principles of Jenner; and, no doubt, it was the death of King Louis XV. from smallpox that confirmed him in his resolution to do all in his power to mitigate the ravages of the horrible disease in his own country. This, however, was not his first philanthropic work. A charitable institution had been established by the name of the Misericordia Hospital, in Ayliffe Street, Goodman's Fields, for the exclusive reception of contagious diseases of a particular kind. The celebrated philanthropist, Jonas Hanway, best known, perhaps, as having been the first individual who had the temerity to use an umbrella in the streets of London, was the chief promoter of the design, and Robert Smith was the secretary. The latter says :—

In order to help the finances of the hospital, it was thought desirable to obtain a benefit-night for it, if possible, at one of the London theatres, and I was desired to make the necessary application to Mr. Garrick, one of the proprietors, and sole manager of the Drury Lane House. I did so by letter, and received the following answer :—

Adelphi, Dec. 12, 1775.

Sir,

The Theatre Royal in Drury Lane gives two Charity Benefits a year to the Hospitals, and they take their Turn in succession—there are two fix'd for this, and two for the next, and how they go on afterwards I cannot say, not having the Book with me!—if the Committee would be pleas'd to

know the future arrangements of the Benefits, if
they will send their secretary, he shall see what
we have done, what we shall, and what we can do.—
I came from Hampton yesterday, or you should have
had an answer before.

I am, Sir,
Your most obedt Servant,
D. GARRICK.

MR. ROBERT SMITH,
Fen Court, Fenchurch Street.

The following year, Robert Smith was present
when the great actor retired from the boards. He
says :—

On the 10th of June Mr. Garrick took his leave
of the stage, performing the part of Don Felix in
the *Wonder*. After the performance, he addressed
the audience in a composition of his own. The
house was so crowded in all parts, that I had great
difficulty in squeezing myself into a back row of the
front boxes. I never saw plaudits so loudly, liberally,
and deservedly bestowed as on that occasion.

Next year he "assisted" at the function of a
different kind :—

On the 23rd of May, Free Masons' Hall in Great
Queen Street, Lincoln's Inn Fields, was dedicated
with great solemnity. My friend Poole and myself,
we being both of the craft, attended in our appropriate dresses. Strangers were admitted into the
gallery, and among them a number of ladies.

By the end of 1778, another son, Leonard, and
another daughter, Sophia, had been born to him,

and, his business also increasing, he removed at
Michaelmas, 1779, from Fen Court to Frederick's
Place, Old Jewry, where he had taken a twenty-one
years' lease of a roomy house that had been recently
erected on the site of the old Excise Office.

CHAPTER III

1779—1787

Birth of Horace Smith—The year 1780—The Lord George Gordon Riots—Robert Smith's personal experience of them— He is appointed Assistant-Solicitor to the Board of Ordnance —Removes to Old Jewry—Visits the West Indies—Is elected Fellow of the Society of Antiquaries.

ON Friday, the 31st of December, 1779, as the old year lay a-dying, Horace Smith was ushered into the world. Though always called Horace, he was baptized Horatio, on the 18th of February, 1780, by the Rev. Mr. Spilsbury, minister of the dissenting congregation at Salter's Hall; and his baptism, like that of his brother James, was registered at Dr. Williams' Library, in accordance with the wishes of his mother's family, who, as we have seen, were Nonconformists.

The first year of Horace Smith's life was one of stirring historical events. The War of Independence still raged in America, there being ranged against Great Britain, in addition to her rebellious colonies, both France and Spain, while the armed neutrality of Prussia, Russia, Sweden, and Norway, was practically equivalent to open hostility. In far-off Asia,

Warren Hastings was a powerful administrator, fighting against tremendous odds. At home, the year was remarkable for the Lord George Gordon Riots, and the utter failure of the constituted authorities to adequately deal with the disturbance.

James Smith always maintained that he had witnessed the rioting, and humorously posed as an authority on the subject; but cross-examination seldom failed to elicit the fact that, as soon as the first mutterings of the storm reached the city, his nurse, who, in order to see what was going on, had taken him with her into Cheapside, was terrified almost out of her wits by some of the mob insisting upon knowing where her blue cockade was, and so beat a retreat into the haven of Frederick's Place, breathless and exhausted with running all the way from St. Paul's Churchyard.

However, his father has left us a vivid description of his own experience of the riots, which culminated on Wednesday, June the 7th, when the mob attempted to take the Bank of England by storm.

The month of June [says Robert Smith] was distinguished by one of the most atrocious riots that has disgraced the capital for many years. A Bill was then before Parliament for the repeal, or modification, of some of the statutes against Catholics. This measure met with opposition from some of the members, and by many without doors; among others was Lord George Gordon, a half-cracked brother of the Duke of Gordon, who was himself a member, and a furious bigoted " Pro-testant." The cry of " No Popery " was spread pretty generally, and all true Protestants were invited by public hand-bills to assemble on the 2nd of the month, in St. George's Fields, for the purpose of accompanying their leader to the House of Commons with their Petition. A numerous mob assembled, with each a blue ribbon in his hat, and being then arranged in a sort of military array, they were afterwards marched through the City and along the Strand, to the House of Commons. I happened to be coming out of Somerset House as they passed it ; and as the day was hot, and a vulgar, furious zeal marked upon their countenances, I concluded that they would not separate without mischief.

This proved to be the case. I followed them, and witnessed the commencement of the horrid outrages that were committed both on persons and property. The mob stopped the carriages of the members of both Houses, bawling out "No Popery," and chalking these words on the carriages. Such of the members as did not readily return the cry, were grossly insulted, some dragged from their carriages, and others forced to take shelter in the neighbouring houses. After a while, the Horse Guards made their appearance, and rode through the mob, who opened right and left to let them pass, and immediately closed, shouting and hissing, the soldiers flourishing their swords in a menacing attitude, but as they did not otherwise use them, the mob became more insolent, and pelted them with stones and pieces of faggot which they had taken from a neighbouring baker's.

All was now uproar and confusion, and after a while detachments of the mob paraded off to different parts of the town, to execute, as it afterwards appeared, their vengeance upon the places of worship and houses of the Catholics. I thought it now high time to make my retreat, and returned to the city through St. George's Fields, and over Blackfriar's Bridge. In my way back I found that the mob had set fire to Newgate, and were liberating the prisoners. These scenes of lawless uproar continued both by day and by night for above a week, during which time the most savage excesses were committed, the civil power hardly daring to show itself, from a consciousness of its inability to stem the torrent.

Large bodies of troops having at length arrived in London by forced marches, martial law was proclaimed. Houses and shops were kept shut, the military were posted in churches, upon the Royal Exchange, in Guildhall yard, and other places. Regular encampments were also formed in St. James's Park, the gardens of the British Museum, etc. etc. The mob were still daring, committing their ravages in all directions; but at length the soldiery were compelled to act, and many lives were sacrificed!

Robert Smith used to relate how curiously silent Cheapside became as the light began to fail on Wednesday, the 7th of June, when the rioters were expected. Every preparation had been made for them. Warehouses, offices, and shops were close-barred; the usually busy thoroughfare was deserted, and, firmly attached to the stout posts that edged the pavement, great hempen cables had been fixed across the street by the deft hands of sailors, who had brought them up in lighters from Deptford. The same precautions had been observed on the other side of the Bank, in Cornhill. Each soldier had thirty-six rounds of ammunition served out to.

him; and at about sunset the attack began. As
the mob, disconcerted by the barriers in Cheapside,
halted in their impetuous course, and broke up into
small detachments, struggling along the pavement
in their attempt to reach the Poultry, the military
began to fire. At the first discharge some score
of people fell, and were hastily dragged into St.
Mildred's Church. Unfortunately, many innocent
people suffered from the indiscriminate firing in
different parts of the city, as it was very difficult
to distinguish between the rioters and peaceable
citizens. Robert Smith himself had a narrow escape.
from being killed :—

I had [he says] the curiosity to walk out from
Frederick's Place, and to stand at the south-west
corner of the Old Jewry, from whence I could observe
all that passed. Shortly afterwards, four or five
drunken fellows with blue cockades in their hats
came reeling down Cheapside, bawling out "No
Popery." As they approached, the eyes of the
volunteers were intent upon them, and the commanding officer called out "Attention !" All was
silent, and the drunken fellows, without offering any
violence, were about to pass the corps, by walking
on the foot pavement, as if to make towards the
Compter, when the officer told them to "fall back";
and at the same time a few muskets were pointed
towards them to prevent their passing. They re-
treated a few paces to the spot where I stood, and
there made a halt, muttering curses at the soldiery,
when all of a sudden two or three muskets were
discharged at them. One of the balls lodged in the
door-post of the house against which I stood, not

half-a-dozen inches from my right shoulder; another passed between my legs, and shattered the brickwork against the calves of my legs.

I lost no time in making good my retreat down the Old Jewry; and the rioters taking the same direction, the soldiers discharged their pieces plentifully without distinguishing the guilty from the innocent. The balls whistled along by me before I could turn into Frederick's Place, but I providentially escaped; the rioters, too, were all untouched; but a poor fellow who had just come out of Schumaker and Hayman's counting-house with a bill his master had sent him for, was shot through the heart. He fell, gave a convulsive kick or two, and died. Another in crossing the Old Jewry from Dove Court with a plate of oysters in his hand was shot through the wrist. The consternation was so great and general throughout the metropolis, that many of the families removed themselves out of the town, as if to avoid an enemy or the plague. I took mine for a few days to Layton, where they remained until all was quiet. The damage done to property of all descriptions, houses, furniture, and goods, was to an immense amount, and actions were brought by the sufferers, upon the Riot Act (1 Geo. c. 1), for a recovery of their "losses." As attorney to the Hand in Hand Fire Office, which had paid large sums upon their policies, I brought several actions in the names of the assured, and obtained verdicts in all.

Robert Smith often narrated how, on the morning after the attack on the Bank, he visited Lord Mansfield's house in Bloomsbury Square, and saw the *débris* of the unique library and costly furniture smouldering in the road; and how, returning to the City by way of Holborn Hill, he stood aghast before

the burnt-out distillery, and the awful spectacle of
poor wretches lying about, literally roasted to death
in the blazing rum and gin.

In the year 1782 an important change took place
in Robert Smith's fortunes.   He says:—

Upon the Duke of Richmond's coming into office
as Master-General of the Ordnance, he appointed
Mr. Serjeant Adair "Solicitor" to the Ordnance.
Such was the language of the appointment; but the
duties of the situation are exercised by a practising
solicitor, called in office language the "assistant to
the solicitor."   Mr. Serjeant Adair recommended me
as his "assistant"; and this situation I have enjoyed
from that time to the present (1818).

Three years later, Smith received a tempting offer
from his father-in-law to proceed to the West Indies
on important business.

My wife's father [he explains], Mr. Bogle French,
having large balances due to him from some of his
correspondents in the West India Islands, but more
particularly in Granada, he thought it an object that
I should go thither accompanied by his son, in order
to adjust the accounts, and make arrangements for
remittance.   For my own trouble and absence from
my business at home, he offered to pay me £1500,
exclusive of all expenses.   [He was ultimately paid
£2000.]   Knowing the importance of the business
to himself and his family, I readily accepted the
offer.

Meanwhile, both he and his wife thought that the
keeping up of the house in Frederick's Place during
his absence would be an unnecessary expense; and

as the lady preferred to reside altogether at Holloway, where he had taken a small country-house three years before, Smith determined to part with his lease. But he could not do this without proper offices for his business, which was to be conducted during his absence by his managing-clerk. He therefore engaged with his brother-in-law, Mr. Norris, for the building behind his house, No. 21, in the Old Jewry. The lease of the Frederick's Place house he sold for £100.

He set sail from Deal for the West Indies on November the 7th, 1785, and, having successfully accomplished his mission there, returned home, reaching Holloway on July the 1st, 1786. The following year he was elected a Fellow of the Society of Antiquaries of London; and, having paid his admission fee, and the usual composition in lieu of annual payment, he was, on May the 3rd, admitted a Fellow for life.

CHAPTER IV

1787—1790

Association of James and Horace Smith with the City—
Their childhood—James and Horace at Chigwell School.

JAMES and Horace Smith were not only city-born,
but city-bred ; James residing there fifty-eight years,
and Horace thirty-five, until they came to know
every nook and corner of its intricate courts and
alleys, and all worth remembering of its ancient
history.

Fen Court—where James first saw the light—is
still a delightfully shady nook wherein to stray from
Fenchurch Street on some broiling July day. It
retains a fragment of an old churchyard, where
sundry trees contrive to keep up appearances, and
don each spring a new suit of tender green. In
the last century, this scrap of graveyard was hemmed
in by narrow red-brick tenements, where merchants
and lawyers lived, and carried on business, and
were as contented as are their modern descend-
ants in palatial offices and homes in Kent or
Surrey.

As soon as he was able to walk, young James

used to go with his nurse or his mother to all kinds of delightful places close by. There were constant visits to Leadenhall Market, a never-failing source of interest, where the little boy revelled in the sight of live poultry, rabbits, guinea-pigs, and other "small deer" beloved of children. The Tower of London and its menagerie, easily reached down Mincing Lane, was a treat sparingly bestowed and rapturously enjoyed. There was the Monument, across Eastcheap, to be stared up at with wonder and amazement. London Bridge, with its four great wheels for raising water, was easily accessible, and often in the summer James was taken for a stroll through the sheds and pent-houses that then represented Billingsgate, to the river front, or, better still, on the Custom House terrace, where he could watch for hours the noiseless floating traffic. Every day, almost, there was something new to look at, and at every hour of the day there was bustle and excitement in the crowded thoroughfares of the dear old city.

Frederick's Place—where Horace was born—Old Jewry, Basinghall Street, and Austin Friars were not one bit less interesting than Fen Court, and in each of these localities the brothers lived, as from time to time their father shifted his place of abode. Thus while poor, friendless Charles Lamb—born the same year as James Smith—was prowling about the streets, " shivering at cold windows of print-shops to extract a little amusement," James and Horace were joyously exploring the City, until there was hardly an old mansion or hall that they did not know.

By the time James was ten years old, an extensive family of brothers and sisters had sprung up around him. Leonard was nine years of age, Horace six; and there were four sisters, Maria, Sophia, Louisa, and Adelaide. Subsequently, another sister was born, completing Robert Smith's family of three sons and five daughters.

Everything was in favour of the boys starting in life with an exceptionally good education, which began, as it should, at home. All the time that could be spared from the multifarious duties of her household, Mrs. Smith devoted to grounding her children thoroughly in the elements of knowledge; and her sweet, patient disposition, and unaffected but practical piety, effected more by force of example than all the precepts of divines and pedants, in developing their naturally amiable and attractive character.

From their father the boys derived invaluable aid. Tired though he might be after close application to his office-work, Robert Smith was ever ready to devote himself to the lads, teaching them the rudiments of the classics, French, and even Italian, patiently solving the difficulties in the iron rules of grammar, helping them with gentle hands along the stony paths of the three " R's," so that when they went to school, the usual drudgery stage that disgusts all clever boys was quickly surmounted, and they were able to apply unhampered intelligence to the task on hand, and master it with ease.

Their father, who from youth up had been in the

habit of composing what he called "little poetical effusions," encouraged his children to do the same; and both James and Horace soon evinced a special aptitude for rhyming, and such a decided love of punning, as would have been thought remarkable by any family not so accustomed to it.

A particularly sociable man was Robert Smith, and his society was much courted by a large circle of acquaintances, who thoroughly appreciated his wit and conversational powers, which seemed to be rendered more striking because of his singularly handsome face and figure. Besides being a shrewd and close observer of nature, he had made quite a study of mankind, and possessed a deep penetration into character. In this respect, too, his sons were like him, for as mere boys they noted the peculiarities and eccentricities of others, reproducing their idiosyncrasies in neat little verses, all of which have, unluckily, perished.

Several of their father's friends were poetically inclined, and amongst them was Mr. John Chubb, an old Bridgwater playmate, who, during his periodical visits to London, used to stay at the Smiths'. John Chubb possessed also a taste for painting and drawing, which latter art he cultivated with some success as a caricaturist; and nothing more delighted the boys—especially Horace—than to watch him sketch a group of well-known people in all sorts of grotesque attitudes. Sometimes there came to dine with their father various members of literary and scientific societies, and after dinner the boys would creep in to the dining-room, and eagerly listen to the grave dissertations, treasuring up all they could understand for further investigation.

James Smith used to say that the crowning episode in his early years was when, but eight years old, he was taken by his father to Bolt Court and presented to Dr. Johnson, then near his end. The old sage received him very kindly, and told him to be "a good boy, and always obey his father and mother." Another "great event" of his childhood happened one Sunday. As he and his father were leaving Highgate Church, they were met by Lord Chief Justice Mansfield, who, after a somewhat lengthy conversation with Robert Smith, turned to young James, and patting him on the head, inquired if he too intended to be a lawyer, a pleasant smile playing about his firm but kindly mouth. James was too confused to reply; and this, he afterwards explained to his mother, was because he was wondering all the time whether, in order to be a judge, one was obliged to have a big high nose and piercing eyes, in which case *he* had no chance of becoming one.

Every year the young Smiths were taken into the country for change of air. Those were not the days when indulgent parents, aided and abetted by the family doctor, took their boys and girls to the seaside, the Continent, or across the Atlantic, on every possible excuse. Our Georgian forefathers considered country air and country diet all-sufficient for themselves; and if forced to think of sea-air for their little ones, as a rule found it at Gravesend. London, beyond the belt of market-gardens and orchards that encircled it, was surrounded by perfectly rural places—villages as quiet and pleasant as many that are now found five miles from a railway station in Dorsetshire.

Essex was the favourite resort of the London citizen. It was handy, notoriously healthy, and cheap; and for Robert Smith it had other attractions, as many of his friends lived there. Thus in the spring of the year 1775, the family went into furnished lodgings at Layton. The next summer they went to Salter's Buildings near Epping Forest, and the following year a small house with a good garden was taken on lease at Layton for the term of fourteen years, at the rental of £21 per annum. For the greater convenience in going to and from London, and in order to give his wife and young ones an "airing" occasionally, Robert Smith purchased a horse and a "whiskey," a kind of light vehicle.

A twenty-guinea rental does not seem much, but the cheapest bargain Robert Smith ever made in this line—and he seems to have had a craze for taking leases and disposing of them—was at Upper Holloway, then exceedingly rural, where he got a house at the foot of Highgate Hill, with orchard, kitchen-garden, barn, stable, and paddock, for twenty-five guineas per annum, including taxes of every kind !

The day arrived when it became necessary to

select a school for the boys. A kind of family council was held, and, by the advice of his Essex acquaintances, Chigwell School was decided upon. Thither James and Leonard were sent the following term, January 1785; Horace following, at the rather tender age of eight, two years later, there to "learn Latin and Greek, etc."

School-life was then an altogether different affair from what it is now. Parents and boys were more easily satisfied, less fastidious about board and lodging. Pocket-money was sparingly bestowed, the quarterly tip of an ordinary present-day Eton lad probably exceeding the receipts of the eighteenth-century boy's entire school-days.

The staple dietary was: for breakfast, bread and cheese, skimmed milk or porridge; for dinner, plain roast and boiled meat; and for supper, bread and cheese again, with very small beer to wash it down. How would our *jeunesse doré* like it! Yet most of our greatest statesmen, divines, and warriors had to put up with this when they were boys.

The Smiths roughed it with the rest. Their sleeping apartment was decidedly exiguous, neither more nor less than what we should call a large cupboard, with a narrow slit for a window. Still, it had the recommendation of being warm and comfortable in the winter.

An early school anecdote of himself is related by Horace Smith in a letter to his friend, Charles Mathews. Being asked by Mr. Burford, Head

Master, the Latin for the word "cowardice," and having forgotten it, he replied that the Romans "had none." Luckily for Horace, Burford choose to regard this as a *bon-mot*, and he was complimented instead of being awarded the usual penalty for not knowing his lesson.

Burford was a man of considerable ability, a scholar, dignified in manner, and with a kindly and indulgent disposition; a man to be both respected and beloved, and well-deserving the epithet "honoured" bestowed upon him by his favourite pupil, James Smith. In many things he was in advance of his time.

By the ordinance of Archbishop Harsnett, the pious founder, the only Latin and Greek grammars to be used were "Lilly's" and "Cleonard's"; and for "phrase and style" only Tully and Terence were to be studied; the Greek and Latin poets might be read, but "no novelties nor conceited modern writers"! These restrictions, however, did not preclude Burford from giving the brothers Smith a thoroughly good classical education. Unlike most of the boys, they were naturally inclined to be studious, though James was full of animal spirits and fond of practical jokes, for the consequences of which he would have suffered, had he not won the heart of Burford by his cleverness and talent, which always placed him at the top of his class.

He was a capital mimic; and one day, having managed to obtain a cast-off wig of Burford's, he ascended the sacred desk, over which was a sound-ing-board, and, changing the expression of his face with wonderful facility, so exactly imitated his tone and manner that the whole school was in fits of laughter. Burford was at that moment just about to enter, but paused outside the door, enjoying the fun, imagining that the writing-master, Vickary, was being "taken off." He was quickly undeceived, and, hastily entering the room, sternly reprimanded Smith, who was told to report himself in the study after school-hours. But on James promising not to do the like again, he was let off with nothing worse than a good "wigging."

This Vickary, who married into the Burford family, was an exceedingly strict teacher, and, like Dickens's "Mr. Creakle," only too delighted to, have any excuse for rapping the knuckles of some unfortunate boy who was awkward in handling his pen. James Smith held him in such awe that, years afterwards, in his poem on *Chigwell Revisited*, he thus recalls him :—

> Seek we the churchyard, there the yew
> Shades many a swain whom once I knew,
>   Now nameless and forgotten ;
> Here towers Sir Edward's marble bier,
> Here lies stern Vickary, and here
>   My father's friend, Tom Cotton.

James Smith had a very retentive memory for localities, and in the same poem describes the exact position of the ink-bespattered desk where he was initiated into the mysteries of Cornelius Nepos, and of another where he

> fagged hard at Plutarch,
> Found Ovid's mighty pleasant ways,
> While Plato's metaphysic maze
> Appeared like Pluto—too dark !

Nothing was forgotten. He remembered where a certain usher used to sit, and where his school chums—and they were many—had their appointed places, and how one in particular, a boy of chilly temperament and tallowy complexion, always managed to secure the best place near the open hearth :

> Here Usher Ireland sat, and there
> Stood Bolton, Cowel, Parker, Ware,
> Medley, the pert and witty,
> And here—crack station near the fire—
> Sat Roberts, whose Haymarket sire
> Sold oil and spermaceti.

CHAPTER V

1790—1791

Sundays at Chigwell—Playdays and recreation at Chigwell
—James at New College, Hackney—At Alfred House Academy,
Camberwell—Attends book-keeping classes—Horace leaves
Chigwell, and goes to Alfred House.

ON Sundays and Saints'-days, the boys were for-
mally marshalled into the school-rooms, whence they
proceeded in orderly procession, service-books in
hand, to morning-prayers at Chigwell Church, where
good old Archbishop Harsnett sleeps his last sleep
in front of the altar. It was strictly enjoined that
during Divine service they should kneel at the proper
time, " and bow at the name of Jesus," and that those
who were able to do so should take notes of the
sermon, and submit them to the master the following
morning. This was a great trial to the Smiths, as
James, with his keen sense of humour, could hardly
refrain from expounding his notes facetiously ; and
Horace found it difficult to avoid imparting to the
preacher's exordium a romantic and picturesque tone
unwarranted by the solemnity of the subject.

The boys had not far to walk to church. The
quaint little building was almost next door, ap-

proached by an avenue of yew-trees, which met over-head, and were so closely interlaced as to form a living awning of sombre green.

At the west end, opposite the porch, was a small gallery, set apart for the Harsnett boys, and faced by another gallery. A certain village beauty used to walk across the meadows every Sunday to attend the services at Chigwell, in preference to those of her own district, no doubt for good and sufficient reasons. She was dressed very much as we are accustomed to picture the charming Dolly Varden—short frock with tight sleeves, open in front, and drawn through the pocket-holes, long mittens and long white apron, black stockings and the neatest of high-heeled shoes with stout buckles. Unlike Dolly Varden, however, her headgear was a charming white bonnet, which suited her dark complexion to a nicety. Until she arrived at church, the elder boys concentrated their attention upon the door by which she would enter, and afterwards upon herself, while she affected utter indifference to the Harsnett gallery admiration.

This bewitching lass appears to have made a deep impression on James Smith, although it is not on record that he ever so much as spoke to her ; but recalling his school days, and his Sunday in particular, he writes :—

> Yon pew, the gallery below,
> Held Nancy, pride of Chigwell Row,
> Who set all hearts a-dancing :
> In bonnet white, divine brunette,
> O'er Burnet's field, I see thee yet
> To Sunday church advancing.[1]

[1] *Chigwell Revisited.*

Whenever he could get time from his studies, Horace, though in a desultory and sedate fashion, used to join the other boys in games and rambles; but James, a great lover of books, would stroll away alone, mount some old tree, comfortably settle himself between the forked branches, and there revel in any old volume he could procure.

Chigwell consisted of but a few houses, including the old King's Head, immortalized by Charles Dickens in *Barnaby Rudge*. Next to it was a forge round which the boys loved to hover; and there was but one general shop, where sweet-stuff could be obtained. Chigwell was, however, the proud possessor of some parish stocks, though they never seem to have been used, for James observes :—

> I dive not in parochial law,
> Yet this I know—I never saw
> Two legs protruded through 'em.[1]

Adjoining the church lived the village doctor :—

> One Denham, Galen's son, who dealt
> In squills and cream of tartar.[1]

Up the road were some miniature almshouses, where dwelt an old pensioner, " wry-mouthed Martin Hadly," who used to excite the boys' sense of the ridiculous by his queer gesticulations when he talked.

Outdoor games were not elaborated in those days, but swimming, *nolens volens*, they all had to learn in a rough and ready fashion, having to jump into a deep hole formed by the river Roding, and take their chance of sinking or swimming :—

[1] *Chigwell Revisited.*

> Seek we the river's grassy verge,
> Where all were destined to immerge,
> Or willing or abhorrent.[1]

Upon leaving Chigwell in 1789, James Smith was sent to the Nonconformist New College at Hackney, chiefly in deference to the religious principles of his mother, and also because, being a Presbyterian, he was excluded from our universities.

One of the most brilliant of the Presbyterian ministers of that day was the Rev. Dr. Abraham Rees, best known, perhaps, as the compiler of the Encyclopedia which bears his name. Rees was for some years tutor in an academy at Hoxton, and on its dissolution in 1785 he became associated with an institution that had been founded for the purpose of providing a liberal education for dissenting youths, and especially for the training of ministers. The trustees of the institution had purchased a roomy mansion and grounds at Hackney, known as Homerton Hall, or Bond Hopkin's house, and adding two wings, opened the establishment in 1786 as New College, Hackney. Dr. Rees, who occupied the Hebrew and Mathematical chair, was one of the principals, together with Dr. Richard Price and the Rev. Thomas Belsham—all of them eminent for learning and science.

The records of New College are scanty, and have not been preserved with much exactitude; but in an old minute-book there is an entry of a meeting of the committee on the 23rd of July, 1789, Dr. Rees being

---

[1] *Chigwell Revisited.*

present, when it was " resolved that Mr. James Smith of the Old Jewry be admitted as student on his own foundation at the College, Hackney, at the commencement of next session ;" and thither he accordingly went on the 21st of the following September.

In the one year that James Smith remained at New College, young though he was, he derived considerable advantage from the intellectual vigour and clear insight into nearly every subject that characterized " Encyclopedia Rees." His religion was broadened, his latent powers were encouraged into development, and he began to learn the great lesson of self-reliance and independent thought. Had he remained for the whole term, who knows but what he might have evinced a desire to enter the ministry ; in which case we should perhaps have had a second Rowland Hill in the pulpit.

From New College James went to Alfred House Academy, Camberwell. The proprietor of this school, a Mr. Wanostrocht, had been strongly recommended to Robert Smith by his friends in Paris. French was the current language of the school, and Italian, German, and Spanish were taught, together with drawing, fencing, dancing, and music, in addition to the usual course of Latin, Greek, writing, arithmetic, and book-keeping.

Nicholas Wanostrocht seems to have been a kind of prototype of Mr. Barlow in *Sandford and Merton*. His prospectus holds out a delightful prospect to the Sandford and Merton type of boy, and must have been immensely appreciated by the lads in general.

According to the custom of every academy, there are two half-holidays a week, viz. Wednesdays and Saturdays. On these occasions, the master himself always accompanies the young gentlemen, sometimes in the fields ; and by pointing out to them the most useful productions of nature, endeavours to lead their young minds into a habit of observation and attention. In every little country excursion, a variety of objects, both in the vegetable and animal kingdoms, present themselves, and furnish numberless subjects for conversation, and it is the master's employment so to direct his inquiries as to excite the curiosity and improve the understanding of his pupils.

The house, large and airy, was pleasantly situated between Camden Row and Havill's Fields, where the Camberwell House Asylum now stands. The situation was dry and healthy, and the neighbourhood noted for its sylvan beauty. On half-holidays the boys were often taken to the Grove, when moral lessons were inculcated on the identical spot where George Barnwell, the London apprentice, led away by the wiles of a designing and abandoned woman, murdered his rich old uncle, for which crime he reaped his reward at Tyburn.

Amongst James Smith's contributions to *Rejected Addresses* is a ludicrous parody of the story of George Barnwell, in which the writer's school-days evidently rose up before him, as he penned the stanza beginning :—

> A pistol he got from his love—
>   'Twas loaded with powder and bullet ;
> He trudged off to Camberwell Grove,
>   But wanted the courage to pull it.

Both Nicholas Wanostrocht and his school have long since vanished ; but cricketers will recall a work, at one time very popular, that owes its origin to Wanostrocht's son, who wrote under the pseudonym of " N. Felix."   It is called *Felix on the Bat*, and is an able treatise on the national game.

James remained at Alfred House for about a year and a half; after which, being still rather deficient in writing and book-keeping, he went with his brother Leonard to a commercial academy, kept by a Mr. Eaton in Tower Street, where they daily attended the classes, having their meals at home in Basinghall Street, whither Robert Smith had removed from the Old Jewry.

At the same time (midsummer 1791), Horace left Chigwell School, and went to Alfred House, where he stayed for nearly four years, going through the same course of studies as James.

CHAPTER VI

The eve of the French Revolution—Robert Smith again in
Paris—Sees Louis XVI. and Marie Antoinette at Versailles—
The French Drama—The political agitation in Paris—Robert
Smith's providential escape from the mob—James Smith in
France—His narrow escape from death at Dover.

WE must now go back to Robert Smith, who had
returned from the West Indies, and in the summer
of 1788 went again to Paris,—this time on important
legal business,—where he was the subject of some
remarkable experiences. The period was that of
which Hallam writes :—

" An event was now impending which was to shake
Europe to its foundations. To all outward appearance France was in a most prosperous condition.
She was at peace with all Europe ; she had achieved a
triumph over England, her ancient rival, by helping
to emancipate her rebellious colonies ; yet she was
herself on the brink of a terrible convulsion."

Of the preliminary upheavings of this political
and social earthquake, Robert Smith was an eye-
witness.

We put up [he says] at the Hôtel d'York, Rue
Jacob, Fauxbourg St. Germain, kept by one Guillandeau, whose wife was an Englishwoman. A *voiture*

being thought necessary for us during our stay in Paris, or at least convenient, I had desired Monsieur Guillandeau to order one, and this morning a notary waited upon us with a *bail de carrosse* for my signature. An English coachman would have been contented with less ceremony; but here, every instrument to be valid must be entered into *devant notaire.*

August 9, 1788.—Understanding that the ambassadors lately arrived from Tippoo Saib were to be presented in great state to the King and Queen (Louis XVI. and Marie Antoinette) at Versailles to-morrow, we had desired Monsieur Pérégaux to procure us tickets, and this day he sent us two for our admission into the *grands appartements.* In the evening we went to *La Comédie Française*, the performances *Les femmes savantes* of Molière, and *L'École des Maris.*

August 15.—Having procured a *permission* for our *voiture* to Versailles, and ordered an additional pair of horses with a postilion, we set out this morning between 7 and 8 o'clock in our dress-suits for Versailles, where we arrived between 9 and 10, and were set down near the gates of the château or palace. We went immediately to the château, presented our *billets*, and were admitted.

After ascending *Le Grand Escalière*, we went through a suite of rooms, all crowded with well-dressed persons, who, like ourselves, had been admitted by *billets* to the ante-chambers, but were not permitted to enter the presence-chamber. We advanced, however, by degrees to the door of *La Grande Galérie*, where the Swiss Guards stood to prevent the entrance of those who had not been before presented to their Majesties, or who did not come properly introduced. For some time we stood here with others, but at length, by dint of importunity, and telling the guards that it would be a great disappointment to us *as strangers* to return without seeing the ceremony, we were slyly smuggled in, and got at last to the further end next to the Queen's apartment. Here we took our station in the midst of persons of both sexes attired in the most superb court-dress.

After waiting about two hours, the double-door of the Queen's apartment was thrown open, and she came out, attended by her suite of ladies, some of whom held up her train. They passed close to me, her Majesty walking most gracefully and majestically through the gallery to the apartment that leads to the chapel, whither she was going. Very shortly afterwards, the three Indian ambassadors with their suite, all full dressed in the costume of their country, and preceded by a dozen officers of the French court, entered the gallery from the Queen's apartment, and advanced towards the chapel also, as I understood.

In about three-quarters of an hour, the Queen returned in the same dignified manner, and was immediately followed by the ambassadors. They all remained for some time in the Great Gallery, where I had full opportunity of examining their persons. The Queen is tall, fair, of regular features, with a most pleasing smile on her countenance, and moves with great elegance and dignity. She was habited in white silk, embroidered with silver and flowers in the most sumptuous manner, and yet every part of her dress seemed to set easy. I never saw finer men than the three ambassadors; one of them was above six feet high, and well-formed. They were all easy in their behaviour, and every attention was paid to them by the company. Among the persons present was the Count d'Estaing, a character well known to the English during the late war both in the East and West Indies. I never before witnessed so splendid a scene. We remained in the gallery until about three o'clock, when the Queen retired to her apartment, and the company withdrew shortly afterwards. The King did not make his appearance, from what cause I know not.

The ambassadors dined this day at the Prime Minister's, and carriages were ranged along the side of the château in readiness to convey them about the park and gardens. As we were waiting with many others to see them, the Comte d'Artois drove up to the palace, and alighted. In a few minutes the King's carriage also drove up, when he alighted, passed close to us, and ascended a small staircase that leads up to the chapel. His Majesty appeared in high spirits, talking familiarly to the gentlemen who attended him. He is rather inclined to corpulency, has a ruddy complexion, and draws his eyelids together as if short-sighted. He was dressed in scarlet, richly embroidered with gold.

Having gratified our curiosity with a sight of the King, and the day being pretty far spent, we returned in our *voiture* to Paris. In the afternoon of the following day we went to *Les Variétés Amusantes* in the Palais Royal. The entertainment was *L'Anglois à Paris*, and *La Timide*. The latter was a new piece, and was so well received by the audience, that the instant the curtain dropped there was a universal cry throughout the house of *L'Auteur, L'Auteur!* The poor devil of an author then made his appearance, conducted on the stage by one of the performers. The clapping recommenced, the author made a most profound reverence to the house, and seemed as if about to return his thanks for the favourable reception of his piece, but his feelings overpowered him. He clasped his hands together, then opening them, raised his arms above his head, and ran off the stage without saying a word.

A few evenings afterwards we went to see *Les Petits Comédiens* de Monseigneur S.A.S., Le Comte de Beaujolais. The performance was *Alexis and Colin*, preceded by a light *petite pièce*, and followed by *La Belle Esclave*, a musical entertainment. Almost all the performers were young persons from 15 to 20, or 22 years of age, and their manner of acting was new. They come on the stage properly habited for their parts, which they *appear* to perform, moving their lips, adapting their countenances and their motions as the play required; yet not one of them uttered a syllable. The whole of the *speaking* part was performed by persons behind the scenes, as was the *singing*. The deception was so great that it was some time before I discovered it. I am told that the managers of this theatre have no royal license for acting plays, so that they have hit ·upon this expedient to elude the law.

For the last day or two, an *Arrêt du conseil d'état du Roi*, dated the 8th of the present month, has been in circulation, and has been freely commented upon at the coffee-houses. By this *Arrêt* (or decree) his Majesty signifies his intention to convene *Les États Généraux* on the 1st of May next, in order to deliberate on the great and weighty affairs of the nation; and in the meantime, his Majesty *in part* suspends the execution of the late *Arrêt*, which abolished the Parliament, and established *La cour Pléniaire*. This *Arrêt*, so congenial, I understand, to the wishes of the kingdom, cannot fail of giving universal satisfaction.

August 18.—Another *Arrêt* has just come out, dated the 16th of the present month, by which payment of the public debts is in part postponed, and put upon a new footing until the assembling of the *États Généraux* in May next.   A certain class of creditors are to receive entire payment in *Billets du Trésor Royal;* others are to receive part in these bills, and part in money ; and debts under 500 *livres*, as well as the payment of the army and navy, are to be paid wholly in money.   As in the present situation of the kingdom, and of public credit, the King *cannot borrow*, the only alternative which is left to him is, *not to pay.*

The affairs of France, as far as I can judge, seem drawing to a crisis.   No confidence in the present minister (Archbishop Lomenie de Brienne), public credit gone, the administration of justice suspended, and, notwithstanding all this, expensive public buildings are going forwards, and *Les Spectacles* and all other places of public entertainment are crowded to excess.   Who shall pretend to say that France is not a happy nation in spite of the difficulties that threaten her !

August 27.—We drove this forenoon to *Choisy le Roi*, and dined at Saint Nicolas (*au bord de l'eau*), and had at our dinner an excellent *matelotte*, a dish of stewed eels and gudgeon.   This dish alone is a " turtle-feast " to the cockneys of Paris,. and I give them credit for their taste.

Upon our return to Paris, we strolled to *Nôtre Dame*, and on our way back to the hotel we saw an immense multitude of people upon the *Pont Neuf* and in the *Place Dauphiné.*   In the latter place (at the top of which stands Le Palais des Marchands) were illuminations, fireworks, and other demonstrations of joy, on account of the Archbishop's dismissal from office.

August 29.—We drove to *St. Denis*, dined at *Le Pavillon Royal*, and then returned to Paris.   In the evening we took several turns upon the terrace of the *Tuilleries* gardens, and on our return to the hotel we crossed *Pont Royal.* We again observed the illuminations in *Place Dauphiné* and about the *Pont Neuf*, and heard the fireworks. The noise and shouting were louder than before. Surely Necker's friends (who is appointed the new Minister) must have a hand in the furious exultation.

August 30.—Lucky was it for us that we returned from the *Tuilleries* across *Pont Royal.* The noise which we heard proceeded from the most dreadful outrages on the *Pont Neuf, Place Dauphiné, Place de la Grève*, etc. It seems that on the preceding evening, a party of the *Guet-à-pied* (city watch), commanded by Monsieur Le Chevalier du Bois, had been under the necessity of using force to disperse the mob, who had been guilty of great irregularities in and about *Pont Neuf.* The mob resisted, and in the scuffle one of the *Guet* with the butt-end of his musket knocked out the brains of a young lad about seven or eight years old. This so enraged the populace, that last night they attacked the different *Corps de Gardes* (guard-houses), pulled them to the ground, burnt the materials, and routed the *Guets* completely. Every carriage that passed the *Pont Neuf* was stopped, and the passengers and coachmen were made to pull off their hats to the statue of Henry IV., and to bawl out, " *Vivent le roi et Monsieur Necker.*" At length they laid about them with swords and bludgeons, slashing and bruising all without distinction who attempted to pass the bridge. Monsieur le Comte de Nesle, who was returning from Versailles in his *voiture*, was stopped on the *Pont Neuf*, the glasses of his carriage were broken to pieces, and he himself was so much cut and bruised, that he is confined to his bed, and, as I understand, is dangerously ill. In the *Place de Grève* the *Guet* fired upon the mob, who, being possessed of firearms, returned the fire, and fifty or sixty persons were dangerously wounded, five were killed on the spot.

Notwithstanding this disturbed state of things, we returned to those places to view the ravages that had been committed. In the *Place de Grève* we saw against several of the houses marks of the musket balls, the *Corps de Gardes* were everywhere in ruins, not a *Guet* was to be seen; and the mob have now their own way.

Undeterred by the risk he had run in August, Robert Smith again went to Paris in December of the same year, to complete the troublesome piece of legal business he had in hand, taking with him his son James—a great treat for the thirteen-year-old boy. Robert Smith writes:—

December 23, 1788. — At Chantilly, whilst our breakfast was getting ready, we all strolled down to the château and gardens of the Prince de Condé. The moat round the château was frozen over, and several persons were amusing themselves in skating, etc. Among them was the young Duc d'Enghein (son of the Duc de Bourbon, and grandson of the Prince de Condé), who, with a person whom we understood to be his tutor, was entertaining himself in a curious manner. They had each a small *traineau*, or sledge, just large enough to receive one person, with short wooden spikes pointed with iron in their hands. Each *traineau* had in it a low seat, was turned up before and shod with iron. Each withdrew his sledge a short distance from the other, and then, with the assistance of their pointed spikes, advanced towards each other with all the rapidity in their power, just like two rams fighting. The violence with which the prows of the two *traineaux* met each other was *sure* to throw out one or other of the combatants, to the great entertainment of themselves and of the spectators. I could not help observing, however, that the tutor was displaced much oftener than the young duke; perhaps the etiquette required that he should be.

Arrived at Paris, the Smiths put up at their old hotel, the York, and in the evening young James made his first acquaintance with a French Variety Theatre in the Palais Royal. His father took him to Astley's, where they were entertained with feats of English horsemanship, some of which "made the French spectators stare with astonishment." They went everywhere, and appear to have seen every phase of Parisian life, even going to several of the *guinguettes* in the Faubourg Montmartre, where they saw the lower orders of people in high glee, eating, drinking, dancing, and waltzing, of which latter amusement Robert Smith evidently did not approve, for he remarks, "This species of dance I understand to be German, but to me it appears wanton and indecent ! "

At last the wished-for day arrived, when the business that had detained Robert Smith three weeks, "doing little more than kicking up his heels," was completed, and he was free to return home.

Being anxious to be gone [he says] I set off with my son in a cabriolet, but owing to the ruggedness of the roads and the darkness of the evening, we proceeded no further than St. Denis. We left there at six o'clock this morning (January 16). We breakfasted at Chantilly, dined in our cabriolet on a cold *langue de bœuf de Flandres*, which I had laid in at Paris, and at half-past eight o'clock in the evening had reached Amiens. Continuing to Montreuil, we left that place early in the morning. Upon our arrival at Calais (January 18), I found that the wind had been so boisterous, none of the boats could venture out, so that all my hurry in getting away from Paris, and on the road, is likely to prove of little avail, the wind still continuing to blow strong.

January 23.—The wind still blows strong, but Captain Oakley of the *Royal Charlotte*, with whom I had agreed to sail when the weather should moderate, telling us that he might now venture out, we went on board, and soon afterwards sailed with a rough sea and a high wind. After beating up some time to the westward, the captain stretched across the channel, but before our arrival off Dover we perceived the flag on the pier-head was taken down, as a signal that there was not water sufficient over the bar. Captain Oakley paused for a few minutes, then whispering something to the man at the helm, he told us that he must either make the attempt to get in, or return to mid-channel, and there lie-to until the morning tide. He dashed therefore for the mouth of the harbour, notwithstanding the waving of hats on the pier for him to keep out. He persisted, and just as we got upon the bar, the vessel struck, and immediately laid down on her beam-ends. The mainyard almost instantly came upon deck, giving me a smart blow on the shoulder in its fall, but I held fast to the pump, and saved myself from being carried overboard with the boat. My son James had fortunately slipped into the cabin, and by that means escaped the danger. The sailors on the pier, perceiving the mischief, bawled out to the captain with their speaking-trumpets to "keep all taut," meaning not to let go a single sail, lest the ship should be struck backwards and forwards by the waves and dashed to pieces against the pier. A boat made the attempt to toss a rope to us, but the sea washed so powerfully into the mouth of the harbour that she could not get near enough. The bustle on the shore, and the confusion on board, were not a little alarming. However, after a few seas had broken over us, a most tremendous one came, took the ship's bottom as she lay on her side, and canted her over the bar into deeper water, when she righted, and was moored in the harbour as fast as possible. We all scrambled on shore, taking with us our luggage, without the ceremony of its being taken to the Custom House. The danger was certainly great, and our escape ought to call forth all our gratitude!

Having taken a hearty dinner, I set off with my son in a chaise and four horses for Canterbury, and from thence we went on to Sittingbourne, where we supped and slept. We proceeded in the same manner next morning, breakfasted at Rochester, changed horses at Dartford, and arrived safely at London. From thence, after a short stay, I went to my family at Holloway.

CHAPTER VII

1791—1800

James is articled to his father—Goes to Scotland—Goes to
the Isle of Wight—Robert Smith and Sir Joseph Banks—
James visits Dartmouth, the Isle of Thanet, and " Leasowes "
in Shropshire—Goes to various places on Ordnance Board
business—Robert Smith elected Fellow of the Royal Society
—Horace becomes clerk in a City counting-house—James
admitted as an Attorney—The National Thanksgiving at
St. Paul's—Patriotism in the City—Robert Smith becomes
a member of the Society of Arts—His experiences in Ireland.

ROBERT SMITH was keenly in favour of boys seeing, as soon as possible, all of the world that they
could, regarding it as a most important part of
their education that they should learn from personal
observation what kind of a country they lived in.
He therefore never lost an opportunity of taking
them on his journeys. As to James, who was
destined for the law, it was deemed essential that
he should go with his father on his professional
tours, especially on those of Ordnance Board
business, in order to familiarize him with the dock-
yards and forts under its control.

Consequently we find that in their holidays, or whenever leave of absence could be obtained, the boys paid visits to various parts of the kingdom; the deliberate mode of travelling then in vogue affording them capital opportunity for their favourite study of humanity. Their experiences and adventures proved of the greatest use to them, for their memories were wonderfully retentive; nothing, however trivial, escaped their keen powers of observation; and, of course, every humorous incident was treasured up as a jewel of great price. By the time they had arrived at manhood, the two young Smiths were looked upon as experienced travellers, and probably knew Great Britain better than we, at the close of the nineteenth century, who, in our rush of travelling from London to distant centres, ignore the interesting districts that lie between.

On March the 9th, 1791, James, at the age of seventeen, was articled to his father for five years as attorney's clerk.

In August of the same year, James went on a tour to the North with his father, his grandfather French, and his sister Sophia, a man-servant accompanying them. The party set out on Sunday in their " glass-coach and four," and with the usual changing of horses, breakfasting, dining, and supping on the road, arrived at Carlisle in five days, by way of Greta Bridge—the destined scene of Sir Walter Scott's *Rokeby*—which Robert Smith describes as " a romantic little spot."

F

On Sunday morning, the 12th of August, they entered Scotland at the river Sark, the incident being thus recorded in the Journal :—

A little beyond the river is Gretna Green, a place well-known to many a young couple, some of whom, no doubt, have heartily repented of their folly. Upon our entering the village, our post-boys, out of mere fun, began smacking their whips, and driving at a furious rate. From a house on the left hand, we perceived a man come hastily to the door and stare at us ; but the drivers went on, shaking their heads at him and laughing. This man, they told us, was the famous blacksmith, Joseph Paisley.

Two days later the party arrived at Glasgow, putting up at the Tontine.

Citizens of Glasgow, and others who are acquainted with its wonderful progress, and with the marvellous transformation of the river Clyde, will be amused at Robert Smith's account :—

Over the river [he says] are thrown two stone bridges, the " Old Bridge " and the " New Bridge." Just above the Old Bridge is a meadow of good size, called the " Green," which belongs to the town, and is rented by one Smith, at £120 per annum. Upon it is erected a large building or wash-house, fitted up with a number of coppers, and provided with tubs. A number of women we saw at the tubs, busily employed, and many hundreds were scattered about on the banks of the river, washing their linen and spreading it out on the Green to dry. Smith furnishes tubs and coal ; the women, soap and starch ; and from each washerwoman in the

"House" he receives sixpence per day for the hot water, and threepence more for the tub!

The travellers reached Edinburgh from Glasgow in about seven hours, and drove to Walker's Hotel in Princes' Street in the new town.

Like any tourist of to-day, they "did" all the sights: the Register Office, the Castle, Holyrood, the old town, St. Giles's Church (four places of worship under one roof), etc. etc. Robert Smith naïvely remarks :—

Edinburgh has many religious establishments, of which the supreme is the "General Assembly of the Church of Scotland." It meets annually in the month of May, in an aisle of St. Giles's Church, which is fitted up for the purpose. The "Throne" on such occasions is filled by a "commissioner" from the Crown; but he neither debates nor votes. *He* calls them together, and dissolves them in the name of the "King"; but *they* call and dissolve *themselves* in the name of the Lord Jesus Christ.

The return home, by way of Berwick, Newcastle, Carlisle, Doncaster, Grantham, and Barnet, occupied ten days, and "all arrived in safety at London after a journey of more than 800 miles."

In January 1793 Robert Smith went to Liverpool. He appears not to have formed a very favourable opinion of the future industry of Lancashire. He writes :—

On this occasion I saw the whole process of cotton manufacture. The machinery is curious, and

the whole acted upon by the power of a steam-
engine.   The throwing together, however, of so
many men, women, and children of both sexes, from
what little I saw, and by the information I received,
is highly injurious both to their health and their
morals!

The following July the three boys set out on a
"jaunt of pleasure" with their father to Portsmouth
and the Isle of Wight.

From Cowes in a post-chaise and a whiskey, we
drove to Newport, and viewed the interior of Caris-
brook Castle. Upon our return to the outer gate
of the castle, the person who had conducted us
through the apartments, turned to me and asked
whether I had ever seen him before? I answered,
"Not that I recollected."—"Sir," said he, "you have
seen, I dare say, Mr. West's famous print of the
death of General Wolfe?"—"Yes, everybody has
seen that."—"Do you recollect the figure of the
Grenadier serjeant who is running up to the General
with his hat off, to bring the account of the French
having run?"—"Yes, I do."—"Sir, I am that
serjeant. I sat to Mr. West for the likeness, which
was then thought a good one. But I am grown old
now, sir; I don't wonder at your not recollecting
me."

In August James went on a little tour to Gravesend, Tilbury Fort, Upnor Castle, etc., and viewed
the Ordnance Board lands, picking up much valuable information respecting his future official duties.

In the year 1794 there is a curious entry in
Robert Smith's journal. It appears that a friend
had given him a small Chinese book, of whose con-

tents both were utterly ignorant, so it was sent to
Sir Joseph Banks with a letter desiring his acceptance of the volume. The following was received in
reply :—

Sir Joseph Banks presents his compliments to
Mr. Smith, and returns him many thanks for the
present of a Chinese book, which he will carefully
deposit in his library, in hopes at some future time
he may meet with a Chinese man who will inform
him of the nature of the contents, of which he
confesses himself just as ignorant as Mr. Smith.

Soho Square, Jan. 25th, 1794.

In September James accompanied his father to
Dartmouth on important Ordnance business, when
the land required for the erection of forts on Berry
Head, near Brixham, was arranged to be purchased
by the Government.

It is worthy of remark, that although Robert
Smith travelled about so much, he was never
attacked by highwaymen, probably owing to his
great personal strength and activity, which had
become known, and also to the fact that he always
carried firearms, and was ready to use them.

Not long after the West of England trip, James
and his father went to Ramsgate and Margate in
search of lodgings for the family, when they managed to see a good deal of the Isle of Thanet, and
in Margate Churchyard were struck with the
quaintness of an epitaph, the subject of which was
a girl-child, aged four years and six months :—

> " With flowing sail and easy gale
>   Kidd brought her to the pier ;
> Though safe in port, her time was short,
>   T' enjoy the pleasures here.
> Seager, 'tis true, restored her to
>   Her former health and charms,
> But Christ did say, ' Come, haste away,'
>   And clasp'd her in His arms."

They ascertained that the said Kidd was master of one of the Margate hoys, and Seager an apothecary of the town, but could not so easily discover what the " pleasures " of Margate could have been to a mere infant !

Robert Smith was always keen on epitaphs, and particularly partial to one he had seen in the church-yard of Frampton on Severn, relating to a humble imitator of Henry VIII.   It ran thus :—

𝔈𝔫 𝔐𝔢𝔪𝔬𝔯𝔶 𝔬𝔣

JOHN GRIFFIN,

HIS SIX WIVES, AND FOUR CHILDREN.
He was lay clerk of this church
for upwards of 59 years.
Died, February 13th, 1788. Aet. 84.

" This short inscription let it bear,
The Clerk, etc., lies quiet here."

James's next journey was a delightful one, made in company with his father to " Leasowes " in Shropshire, immortalized as the residence of the poet Shenstone—author of *The Schoolmistress*, etc.— whom Horace Walpole used to call the " water-gruel bard," and of Hugh Miller, the prince of landscape gardeners. "Leasowes" had been sold for £17,000 by its owner, Captain J. Halliday, R.N., and the Smiths had to give formal possession to the purchaser.

On their way back to London they passed through Oxford, when James took the opportunity of going through the colleges; and when, a year later, business calling them to Landguard Fort, Harwich, and Ipswich, they explored the rival University town of Cambridge—James regretted that he had not been "baptized a Churchman!"

We next find James at Lewes, at the trial and conviction of certain artillery-men who had been embezzling Ordnance stores; then followed his first visit to Brighton, a place of which both he and Horace were destined to see much in after years.

On the 24th of November, 1796, Robert Smith was elected a Fellow of the Royal Society, Sir Joseph Banks being the president; and on the 8th of December he was admitted as a Fellow for life, his certificate being immediately preceded by that of Samuel Rogers, who had been elected a week earlier.

The same year Horace left Alfred House Academy, and became a clerk in the counting-house of Mr. Robert Kingston, a merchant, of 39 Coleman Street. Owing to Robert Smith's great influence as a solicitor to the Hand-in-Hand Insurance Company, and his connection with the African Company, which ensured his nomination being accepted, no premium was paid; but, on the other hand, Horace received no salary.

On the 9th of March, 1797, James's articles expired; but it was not until February 1798 that he was admitted as an Attorney of the Court of King's Bench.

The year closed by the Smiths being spectators of a " very solemn and impressive scene."

Their Majesties [writes Robert Smith], with the whole of the Family and a numerous suite of the nobility and gentry, followed by an immense populace, attended a National Thanksgiving at St. Paul's, on account of the three great victories that were obtained over the enemy by the British fleet. These were, by Lord Howe over the French, on June the 1st, 1794 ; by Sir John Jarvis over the Spaniards, on February the 14th last; and by Admiral Duncan over the Dutch, on the 11th of October last. The sight was truly grand. All the shops were shut in the line of procession, the front windows of most of the houses taken out, and the rooms fitted up with seats for company. We stationed ourselves in the crowd at the corner of the Old Bailey, and had a very fair view of the procession as it passed.

England, threatened by an invasion, was then in the midst of her tremendous struggle with Bonaparte, fighting the French by sea and land; and the City, as ever, was not behindhand in patriotism. Says Robert Smith :—

February, 1798.—On the 9th of this month, a public meeting of the bankers, merchants, and tradesmen of London, was held by advertisement at the Royal Exchange. The object of the meeting was to raise by voluntary contribution a sum of money for the public service, and many resolutions were entered into, calculated to inspire confidence and ardour in the public cause. The Exchange was crowded in every part.

May 1*st.*—On this day, ward-meetings assembled, and other meetings were held of the inhabitants of London for forming an " Armed Association," which the threatening aspect of the French had rendered a prudent measure.

November 21*st.*—On this day I was admitted a member of the Society of Arts, Manufactures, and Commerce in the Adelphi. I paid my annual subscription of two guineas, and have continued to do so to the present time (1818).

In the first year of the nineteenth century James Smith had attained his twenty-fifth year, and was considered sufficiently experienced to be left in charge of the office while his father went to Dublin on one of the most interesting of his numerous journeys. Robert Smith writes :—

The commercial house in London, of French and Burrowes, having become contractors for the Irish $2\frac{1}{2}$ million loan of this year, it was thought advisable to concert a plan of executing it, so as to render the stock marketable in both countries. I prepared the draft of a Trust deed for carrying it into effect, and, the deed being settled by counsel, Mr. Burrowes wished me to accompany him to Dublin. I consented, and we left London together in the mail-coach on the 16th of June, Mr. Burrowes taking with him in the inside of the coach a leather trunk well secured, in which were guineas and banknotes to the amount of £70,000! This sum was intended to make good the first deposit upon the loan.

At 10 p.m. on the 19th we embarked for Holy-head on board the *Leiccster* packet, with a fresh breeze at S.W., and squally appearance of the sky. The breeze had increased, and at about three o'clock in morning the wind chopped to the west, which obliged the packet to work her way close-hauled. After about twelve hours' tossing and tacking, we arrived at the "Hill of Houth." Standing on towards the point of land on the left, the Wicklow mountains rising in the background, we worked our way into the Bay of Dublin. Here the prospect is delightful. Crossing the bar, we entered the Liffey, and at the "Pigeon House Dock" we took the Post-Office wherry to the Watch House on Rogerson's Quay, whence we proceeded in a hackney coach to Kearns's hotel in Kildare Street. After breakfast, we strolled out to see the "lions," Trinity College, the Four Courts, Merrion Square, and St. Stephen's Greens, etc., etc. A meeting was held in connection with the Irish Loan, and a plan was finally adopted calculated to make it a success.

When the meeting broke up, Mr. Burrowes and myself went to dine with his brother, and in the evening we all went to the Theatre Royal in Crow Street. The play was Cumberland's comedy of *The Wheel of Fortune*, in which John Kemble (who is over here for a time) performed the part of "Penruddock." The entertainment was, "No song, no supper." The theatre itself is neat and commodious, the approach to it by no means convenient or agreeable.

Next day we went to view the interiors of the Houses of Lords and Commons, just by Trinity College. The walls of the House of Lords are hung with tapestry, on which are represented the Battle of the Boyne and the Siege of Londonderry, two well-known events in Irish history; the chair of state is covered with crimson velvet; the woodwork of burnished gold, and over it is a handsome canopy; the woolsack, the table, and the seats are all covered with scarlet cloth, and disposed in much the same manner as those in the House of Lords at Westminster. The whole produces a very pleasing effect. In the same building is the House of Commons, which is of a circular form; the seats for the members are circular stools or chairs, the bottoms covered with black leather, the backs of solid mahogany. Facing the Speaker's chair in the body of the House are two boxes, one for the Serjeant-at-Arms, the other for the Chaplain of the House; a large gilt chandelier of wood hangs from the centre of the dome, and round the House is a circular gallery for strangers.

At three o'clock Mr. Nevill and Mr. Roper, a barrister, did me the favour to call at our hotel, in order to introduce me into the Gallery of the House of Commons. I remained in the gallery until the House broke up at a quarter before six o'clock. There happened to be no interesting debate, the time of the House being chiefly occupied in Committee upon matters of revenue.

A day or two afterwards I had an opportunity of seeing the House of Lords during a sitting. Their Lordships had under consideration a Bill for making compensation to corporations, and to individuals who would lose their situations, or sustain a loss, by the approaching Union.

Lord Farnham spoke violently against the Bill, animadverting upon the preamble, the clauses, the conduct of the House in passing it through its different stages in the manner in which it had to be done, not forgetting that of the Commons. He was called to order two or three times by the Lord Chancellor, but soon relapsing into the same strain.

the Marquis of Drogheda (who is well-disposed to Government and the Union) rose to speak to " order," and in a dry, arch manner, said he thought it would very much " shorten the debate " if the House were cleared of strangers. He moved it, and we were all obliged to depart. His meaning was, that Lord Farnham, in the violent language he was using, addressed himself more to the strangers below the Bar, and through them to the newspapers, than to their Lordships.

In the evening Mr. Burrowes and myself dined by invitation with the directors of the two Assurance Companies of Dublin at Atwell's Tavern. The conversation after dinner turned principally upon the new loan, the trade of Ireland, the advantages and disadvantages to Ireland, particularly to Dublin, of the approaching union of the two countries. The topics were well handled, but I could clearly perceive great difference of sentiment among the directors touching the latter. Dublin, they said, would suffer immense loss by the removal of the Parliament; which would be felt in a particular manner by the proprietors of houses and lodgings, by tradesmen of all descriptions, by the theatres and other places of public resort, by the professors of the law, and by the numerous dependents upon all these. A certain description of persons, it was admitted, would receive compensation, but it was fifty chances to one whether any of them would deem the compensation adequate. There appeared to be much good sense in the remarks, but they are unavailing; the measure, I believe, is already determined upon.

January 25th.—In my rambles this morning I walked to the Four Courts. Mr. Justice Finucane was then sitting at Nisi Prius in the Court of Common Pleas. The forms of proceeding are much the same as in England, except that, after the summing up by the Judge, a copy of the issue is handed up to the jury, who confer together; and when agreed on their verdict, the foreman writes it on the paper, subscribes his name, and returns it to the officer, who files the written verdict as his voucher. There is no witness-box, but the witness sits on a chair that is placed on the table of the Court. I stayed here for nearly a couple of hours, and was particularly entertained in hearing Mr. Curran, the facetious Irish barrister. It was some squabble about a duel, or rather, a challenge; and it was to the interest of his client that he should turn the whole into ridicule, which he did most completely. " My Lords, the Judges laugh, and you're dismissed."

By the bye, the style of pleading at the Irish Bar is different from what it is with us. The counsel indulge more in digression, in oratorical flourishes, and give a greater rein to the fancy. An English barrister sticks more to his instructions, to the matter of fact, and to the law.

The object of our journey being now completed, we left Dublin about midnight on the 27th of June, and arrived safely at the General Post-Office in Lombard Street at five o'clock on the morning of the 1st of July.

CHAPTER VIII

1800—1804

ABOUT the period 1799—1800, just as he was coming of age, Horace Smith made his first essay in literature. It was not for want of example and encouragement that he had not begun still earlier, for his father spent most of his spare moments in literary work of one kind or another, constantly contributing papers on weighty subjects to the *Gentleman's Magazine* and the *European Magazine*, and to the learned societies of which he was a member; and sometimes indulging in lighter articles, one of which, burlesquing the etymology of the word "danger," as given by J. P. Andrews in his anecdotes, appeared in the *European Magazine*.

Horace, uncertain how his first novel (for such it was), entitled, *A Family Story*, would be received by his father, who considered that kind of writing frivolous and inconsistent with his son's position as clerk in a city counting-house, brought it out under the convenient name of "Mr. Smith." [1] It dealt with the felicities of domestic life in a highly moral and improving manner, after the fashion of the day. It must have had a *succès d'estime*; for, the following year, the same publishers issued "Mr. Smith's" second novel, *The Runaway, or the Seat of Benevolence*, in four volumes, the scene of which entertaining production—a "novel with a purpose"—is laid at Cliffdown Lodge on the banks of the Avon in Gloucestershire, where the owner, Mr. Somers, a rich recluse, receives the penniless and ragged Theodore, a perfect stranger to him, and is so touched by his artless story of distress, and of his willingness to work as a clerk, or "even as a gardener," that he instantly closes with the offer of his services in the latter capacity, as follows :—

" It fortunately happens at this time I am making some improvements in my pleasure-garden; if you will assist me in the design by giving your opinion and instruction, I shall consider it a favour; in return for which, my house, table, and purse are at your service." .... Theodore was grateful, and was preparing to thank him, but Somers insisted that the obligation was on his side, and therefore requested he would say no more on the subject He next furnished him with a change of linen and various other articles he had immediate occasion for, and then threw down his purse on the table, desiring he would supply himself with sufficient to procure other necessaries.

[1] Published by Crosby and Letterman of Stationer's Court, in three small volumes, at the price of half-a-guinea.

"Mr. Smith's" style was much appreciated in certain circles, and *The Runaway* was quickly followed (in 1801) by *Trevanion, or Matrimonial Errors* (published by Earle and Hermit, 47 Albemarle Street), prefaced by these lines:

> 'Tis an important point to know,
> There's no perfection here below ;
> Man's an odd compound after all,
> And ever has been since the Fall !

Trevanion is, perhaps, even more stilted than *The Runaway*. It treats of secret marriages generally, and the mischief arising therefrom, and, in a kind of epilogue, propounds some exceedingly virtuous sentiments. This work was followed in 1807 by *Horatio, or Memoirs of the Davenport Family*.

James, while quite a youngster, started his literary career by sending to the *Gentleman's Magazine* a series of characteristic letters, detailing the most extraordinary discoveries in natural history and antiquity. They were pure hoaxes, and the brothers, with all but irrepressible feelings of mirth, used to watch their unsuspecting father as he gravely read the pages of "Mr. Sylvanus Urban's" ultra-respectable periodical, in which their contributions appeared anonymously.

Together with Horace, James contributed in 1802 to the *Pic Nic and Cabinet Weekly*, an ephemeral publication started by Colonel Henry Greville, of whom Lord Byron wrote :—

> "Or hail at once the patron and the pile
> Of vice and folly, Greville and Argyle."

In 1809 James was a contributor to *The London Review*, which proved a failure, and was soon discontinued. With Horace, he wrote several of the prefaces to *Bell's British Theatre*, published under the sanction of Mr. Richard Cumberland, the well-known dramatic author. From 1807 to 1810 James was a constant writer for the *Monthly Mirror*, the property of the eccentric Mr. Thomas Hill of Sydenham. It was in this periodical that the poetical imitations called *Horace in London*—subsequently published in the first edition of *Rejected Addresses*—first appeared.

It will be seen that the brothers were accustomed to the wielding of the pen, and, in fact, were experienced writers, when (in 1812) their literary masterpiece was conceived and brought forth.

In the year 1800 the Smith family were living at 36 Basinghall Street, whither they had removed from Old Jewry in 1790. The house was old-fashioned and roomy, of red-brick, and hidden away behind one of the ugly warehouses abounding in that narrow and tortuous thoroughfare, which connected Catcaton Street with London Wall. It had a long garden at the back, reaching almost to Coleman Street, where, in the heart of the city, all kinds of hardy shrubs flourished, and well-known herbaceous favourites appeared in the narrow borders, with each changing season.

This garden adjoined that of the old Girdler's Hall, famous for a venerable mulberry-tree, said to have escaped the devouring flames of the Great Fire of London, which, raging all around, destroyed the parish-church of St. Michael's just across the street.

There was much in the locality to feed the imaginations of such lovers of the past as James and Horace Smith. Improvements had not yet begun. London—at any rate the City—was to a great extent "old and picturesque London" still. The age of ugliness had not arrived, and designs for the dismal "bald street" yet slumbered in the brain of Nash, the architect, and his Royal patron. Quaint little casements, framed by projecting eaves and peaked gables, gazed into the street below with a look of hospitable invitation.

Close by the church in Basinghall Street was Coopers' Hall, whose members made casks for the packing of dry goods, and of goods the reverse of "dry." For some years the State lotteries were held here, the tickets being arranged at Somerset House, and afterwards conveyed to Coopers' Hall on sledges, escorted by a detachment of Life Guards; the drawings (which James and Horace used frequently to witness) being conducted by boys from Christ's Hospital.

Whatever may be said against the morality of the State lotteries, the temptation to an impecunious Government to raise money by this means was too great to be resisted, and all classes were bitten by the insane hope of making a fortune by the turn of a lucky number.

Even such a high-minded man as the Right Honourable William Windham was not above trying his luck, and seems to have regarded it as a perfectly legitimate investment.

Robert Smith occasionally ventured his money, and, when verging upon his eightieth year, took a chance in the last public lottery in England, which he thus briefly records :—

October 17, 1826.—I went to London in the stage. The drawing of the State lottery closing to-morrow, I was disposed to *try my luck*, and purchased a ticket. It came up a blank.

James was now his father's partner in all but name, and industriously attended to his legal duties. Leonard, to whom it is not necessary to refer at length in this narrative, was completing his seven years' clerkship at Downs, Thornton, and Free, the Bankers, in Bartholomew Lane. Horace, as we have seen, was a clerk in a Coleman Street counting-house, literally round the corner, just at the back of his house in Basinghall Street, where he joined the family at meal-times.

James went a good deal into society even at this period; and on January 2nd, 1801, we find him dining at Bellsise House, Hampstead, with the Hon. Spencer Perceval and Mrs. Perceval, a daughter of Sir Thomas Wilson of Charlton.[1]

In the summer of 1803 James and Horace went

---

[1] On March 11 of the following year, James Smith's sister, Sophia, was married at the church of St. Michael's, Bassishaw, to Mr. Thomas Cadell, only son of Mr. Alderman Cadell, the well-known publisher in the Strand.

with their father and mother to the Royal Borough, when they had the gratification of having a good look at King George and the Royal Family. Says the Journal :—

On the 19th of July, Mrs. Smith and myself and our young folks took a little excursion to Windsor. We dined, supped, and slept at the Windmill Inn, at Salt Hill, and the following day (Sunday) drove in a glass coach to Windsor that we might see the Royal Family. We had the first view of them on their going to Chapel, and afterwards during the service. We dined at the inn at Windsor, and in the evening walked to the Terrace. Upon the King, Queen, and Family entering the Terrace. from the Queen's Palace, we all ranged ourselves against the wall of the castle, myself and my sons with our hats off. The King and Queen on passing looked at us, paused for a moment, and smiled as if pleased at the sight.

King George and his consort, at sight of the Smiths and their eight children, were probably reminded only too forcibly of their own extensive family.

This, unhappily, was the last excursion which Mrs. Robert Smith was permitted to take with the whole of her family. Up to this period her children had been spared that saddest of all experiences— personal bereavement; but they were soon to realize it in its acutest form. For some time Mrs. Robert Smith's health had been declining, owing to constitutional weakness of the heart, which increased as she grew older, and suddenly developed alarming symptoms in the form of most distressing spasms. After a temporary recovery, the doctors advised her removal to Worthing, a place she much liked.

She returned to Basinghall Street on the 24th of the month in better spirits, and improved in her general appearance; but her husband's heart was " full of anxiety and forebodings," alas! only too well-founded, for one Saturday—the 3rd of November— she died suddenly, from the effects of sudden excitement caused by unexpected noise and fear of fire.

CHAPTER IX

1804—1812

Robert Smith's second marriage—He visits Cambridge, and there sees Henry Kirke White—Horace Smith becomes a merchant—The City in the first decade of the century—Horace Smith's firm reconstituted—James appointed joint-assistant to the Ordnance Board Solicitor—Robert Smith removes to Austin Friars—Horace Smith becomes a member of the Stock Exchange.

MRS. ROBERT SMITH'S death left a dismal void in the family life at 36 Basinghall Street.

Though many years elapsed before James and Horace set up establishments of their own, their lives gradually became more and more independent and self-contained, until with the second marriage of their father an entirely new order of things prevailed. For, in spite of the loving attention of sons and daughters, Robert Smith, now verging on sixty, sorely felt his loneliness. Essentially a domestic man, he shrank from the idea of having to face old age without the companionship and comfort of a wife, and his thoughts turned involuntarily to his old friend Poole's widow, then about fifty-six.

I had been intimately acquainted with Mrs. Poole

[he says] for more than thirty years; and to her, after much consideration on the fitness of the measure, I made an offer of my hand. After a while the offer was accepted, and matters were arranged for our future union. On Friday, the 17th of January, 1806, the marriage took place at the chapel in Queen Square, Bath.

The couple went to reside at Woodford, in Essex —the late Mr. Poole's residence—the house in Basinghall Street being still maintained as a town-house. Before settling down they made several excursions into the country, and amongst other places went to Cambridge, where they saw the poet, Kirke White, shortly before his death.

Early in August [says Robert Smith] I set out in our coach with Mrs. Smith and my two daughters on a little excursion to Cambridge. We slept the first night at Hockerill, called on the following day at Little Shelford, and dined, supped, and slept at Cambridge. The next day was spent in viewing the several colleges, the Senate House, the Library, etc. Coming out of the gardens of one of the colleges, St. John's, we met Kirke White,[1] a young student, of whom the Rev. Thomas Thomason spoke highly for his piety, talents, and general good conduct. He is a young man, about one-and-twenty, of good appearance, but of consumptive habit.

The same year (1806) Horace Smith left the counting-house of Mr. Robert Kingston, the mer-

---

[1] Henry Kirke White died (from overwork) at St. John's College, Cambridge, Oct. 19, 1806, aged twenty-one years and seven months.

chant in Coleman Street, where he had been a probationer for ten years, and, with his father's aid, went into partnership with a Mr. Chesmer, under the title of "Smith & Chesmer," Merchants and Insurance Brokers, 3 Copthall Chambers. His brother Leonard, the following year, became a partner in the firm of "Bogle, French, Borrowes, and Canning," West-India merchants, reconstituted under the name of "Bogle, French, Warren, and Smith."

The times were hardly propitious for entering into mercantile partnership, and yet, if the risk were great, the gains were proportionally large; and in those stirring days, before the invention of the telegraph had brought all the world to the same dead level, and reduced profit to a mere fraction, individuals with cool heads, possessed of exceptional means of information, were almost certain of acquiring fortunes. Business was a fascinating and exciting pursuit, when at any moment intelligence might arrive of engagements won or lost by the British. Although the year 1805 had seen Napoleon's gigantic efforts on land everywhere crowned with success, it had been immortalized by Nelson's victory at Trafalgar; and consols, though they had once touched 58¾, had been remarkably even throughout the year.

In the spring of 1806, the great Pitt, worn out with cares and anxieties, died at the age of forty-six. Lord Grenville and all the "Talents" succeeded, and made themselves specially unpopular in mercantile circles by the imposition of a property-tax of ten per cent. The celebrated Berlin Decrees, intended to cripple, if not to destory, British commerce, were promulgated by Napoleon, and added still more to the intense uneasiness and anxiety that prevailed in the City. Distrust abounded; yet the most extraordinary frauds were concocted, and successfully carried out.

In those days business was transacted with deliberation and dignity; not in the " life or death " manner of the present day. As regards costume, it was the era of top-boots and knee-breeches; and we can picture the future author of *Rejected Addresses* standing in front of the bow-windows of old Lloyd's coffee-house in Lombard Street, or on the flagstones of the Royal Exchange, clad in snuff-coloured coat, grey trousers, yellow-topped bluchers, and low hat, or in black coat, white cravat, and gaiters, according to the season, bargaining in the market for West Indian produce.

Horace Smith exhibited in business a shrewdness and clearness of judgment for which his literary friends in after life never could give him credit. They quite overlooked the nature of his early training, and his constant association with a father who possessed business qualifications of a high order. Moreover, as has been observed, the possession of exceptional information was in those days more important even than now. Robert Smith's position in the Ordnance Office enabled him to receive the earliest and most accurate intimation of the movements of the British forces, upon whom all eyes were fixed; and the purport of many an important Government dispatch from the seat of war, privately reaching his ears some time before it was generally known in the City, was communicated by him to Horace.

Horace Smith's firm prospered, inspiring so much confidence that three years after its formation Mr. John Down, a son of Robert Smith's banker (of the firm of Down, Thornton, Free, and Cornwall), joined the concern, and put into it the sum of £10,000, after which it was designated " Smith, Chesmer, and Down." Horace now began to make money; and a pleasant side-light is thrown upon his disposition by a fact which his father records with great satisfaction. He says :—

On this day (October 17th) my son Horace, in consideration of the heavy payments which I have made for himself and his brothers, very kindly presented me with £500. I received it as a token of affection from a dutiful son, and shall retain the remembrance of it as long as I live.

James Smith pursued his calling with no less diligence than his brother, making himself more and more indispensable in his father's office, and qualifying for the important post of Joint-Assistant to the Solicitor of the Ordnance. He met with all kinds of curious experience, both in the ordinary course of business as a solicitor, and in that of the Government Department with which he was connected.

In the year 1812, memorable for the dastardly

assassination of Mr. Perceval, the Chancellor of the Exchequer, by Bellingham in the lobby of the House of Commons, Robert Smith, who for some time had been endeavouring to get his son James appointed as his joint-assistant—with a view, no doubt, to his eventually succeeding him—renewed his application as soon as the Earl of Mulgrave became Master-General of the Ordnance, in place of the Earl of Chatham. His request was granted, and the following letters were received from the Board's secretary :—

The Master-General and Board, having been pleased to acquiesce in the request you have preferred, that the name of your son, Mr. James Smith, may be added to your own in the appointment of "Assistant to the Ordnance Solicitor," I am directed to state the same for your information, and that you and your son will accordingly be termed " Joint-Assistants to the Solicitor."

Having returned his thanks to the Master-General, Robert Smith received the following reply :—

Sir,—The result of the inquiries which I made in consequence of your application, has rendered it highly satisfactory to comply with your request for the appointment of your son as assistant to the Ordnance Solicitor.

I am, sir,
You most obedient humble servant,
Mulgrave.

Robert Smith, Esq.

Finding that his means would not admit of his keeping up both the large expensive house in

Basinghall Street and the one at Woodford, and also that his wife preferred to live in the country, Robert Smith determined to make new arrangements. The lease of the Basinghall Street premises was therefore disposed of; rooms were taken at No. 18 Austin Friars, and thither the office papers were removed, and the business thenceforth carried on; while he and his wife, with his unmarried daughters, went to live at Woodford.

Horace Smith, who had severed his connection with the mercantile firm in which he was a partner, about this period became a member of the Stock Exchange, his place of business being in Shorter's Court, Throgmorton Street; and he and his brothers lived together in rooms attached to the office in Austin Friars.

CHAPTER X

In the year 1810, a private Act of Parliament was applied for, empowering a Company [1] to carry out a laudable scheme, whose object was to divert the traffic entirely from the difficult and often dangerous ascent of Highgate Hill, by the creation of a new and easily accessible route.

It was proposed to effect this object by the construction of a tunnel of considerable length ; but Mr. John Rennie, the famous engineer, having pointed out the great inconvenience of this, a shorter one with open approaches was agreed upon. The Act, in spite of the decided unpopularity of the project, was passed, and the work began.

In this age of steel and iron, the idea of a petty little culvert, 211 yards in length, being regarded as a wonderful piece of engineering, seems incredible.

[1] This Company eventually built the well-known Highgate Archway, now in course of re-construction by the London County Council.

But the good folk of 1810, innocent of modern modes of steam and electricity, thought a good deal of it, and watched its progress with deep interest.

Early on the morning of April 15th, 1812, when the work was about half finished, and luckily before any of the workmen had arrived, a tremendous slip occurred, the whole of the excavation collapsed, and the tunnel was filled up with earth.

This accident caused an immense sensation in London, where the idea had from the first been regarded as chimerical and ridiculous; so much so that the wits had at once produced a satirical prospectus for getting rid of the difficult ascent by the summary process of removing the hill itself.

"It is intended," they said, "by means of a mechanical slide, to remove the whole of the hill into the vale behind Caen Wood, where the seven ponds now are, thereby forming a junction with Hampstead, and inviting the approach of the two hamlets in a more sociable manner. On the spot where Highgate now stands, it is intended to form a large lake of salt water of two miles over or thereabouts, beginning at the north end of Kentish Town, and reaching to the spot where the White Lion at Finchley now stands."

The prospectus went on to say, that the said lake was to be supplied with sea-water from the Essex coast by means of pipes, and to be stocked with all kinds of sea-fish except sharks, "there being plenty of these to be had in the neighbourhood." Further, it was intended, it said, to erect a large building in the centre of the wood on the north side of the lake,

which building was to be used for insane surveyors
and attorneys who had lately infested the neighbourhood of Highgate, to the annoyance of the ordinary
inhabitants.

Horace Smith seized the opportunity, and under
the pseudonym of " Momus Medlar, Esq.," produced
a burlesque operatic tragedy in two acts, called
The Highgate Tunnel, or, the Secret Arch, which
was accepted by John Miller, the dramatic publisher
of 25 Bow Street, was produced at the Lyceum
Theatre on Thursday, the 2nd of July, 1812, and had
what was then considered " quite a *run* " of twenty-
four nights.

Robert Smith, to whom the secret of the author's
real name had been confided, was proud enough of
his son's success, though tradition and professional
etiquette forbade him openly to approve. The
following bald entry appears in his Journal :—

October, 1812.—A few months ago, my son Horace
wrote a little after-piece for the stage, called *The
Highgate Tunnel*, which was brought out at the
Lyceum Theatre in the Strand, and had a run.

There was, of course, after the fashion of the day,
a Prelude to this production, termed *An Ode to
Fortune*, when Momus Medlar, Esq., one of the
characters, and " Author of the New Tragedy,"
invokes the fickle Goddess :—

<blockquote>
Kick down (and welcome) Highgate Arch,
  But be content with one ill,
When from the Gallery Ruin nods,
'Oh ! whisper silence to the gods,
  And spare the Muses' Tunnel !
</blockquote>

The gods were pleased, and the critics favourable. Even the leading journal, the *Times* (July 4, 1812), condescended to bestow upon the piece the following remarks :—

It is a burlesque, and a not unamusing one, on some of the late Covent Garden melodramas. The *Secret Mine* is treated with ridicule, if not very dexterous, at least very allowable ; and by the help of some popular melodies, the piece proceeds to its conclusion without any violent offence to criticism. Ridicule has been long since disallowed as the test of truth, and it must not rise into a test of dramatic merit ; but whatever makes some of the later productions of the melodrame manufacture hide their diminished heads renders a general service to public taste. The plot of the present piece is founded on the terrors of the Highgate publicans of losing their trade by the change of the road. The principal sufferer has " a daughter fair," who has won the heart of a youthful miner. He is promised her hand on betraying the key-stone of the arch. The publicans project a general attack ; they are discomfited ; they attack again on horseback ; the battle is joined with fierceness, till, like Virgil's bees, *exigui pulveris jactu*, the battle is stilled by a cloud of dust from above,—the arch gives way,—and the combatants all fall instantly dead. This is sustained with some lively dialogue, and some parodies of favourite passages. The music is tolerably well selected ; and the piece, without admitting of much praise from the nature of the thing, is sufficiently well-conceived for its object.

One of the parodies here referred to was recited by Jerry Grout, described in the play-bill as " an honourable bricklayer, lover, and tunnelleer," who soliloquizes thus :—

'Tis all the same—
All the World's a stable,
And all the men and women ride on horses ;
Youth has its field-horse ; age its chamber-horse ;
And one man in his time mounts many hobbies,
To travel many stages.—First, the rocking-horse,
See-saw succeeding to the nurse's arms :—
And then the braying donkey with his driver,
Mounted by Margate Miss in shining spencer,
Trotting to Dandelion.[1]   Then the hack
By priggish cockney guided, prime, bang up,
Whose threaten'd lash is all my eye, like that,
Beneath his Mistress's eyebrow :—Then the palfrey
Bearing an Actress feather'd like shuttlecock,
Seeking the bubble reputation
Even in the Secret Mine.—Last scene of all,
That ends this jockey, groomish history,
Is second childishness, and neighing Actors,
Whose dull horse-play can raise a dull horse-laugh,
Sans wit, sans speech, sans taste, sans everything.—
And now, my Mum, what say'st thou to a glass ?

The musical portion of the burlesque included another amusing parody set to Dr. Arne's noble air, "The soldier, tir'd of war's alarms."   It was sung by Tom Trowel, "a vocal labourer," to the words—

The bricklayer, tir'd of bearing hods,
Deserts his gang, exhausted nods,
And snores both loud and clear ;
But if the penny trumpet sound,
He jumps, transported, from the ground,
And claims his pot of beer.

From early youth Horace, like his brother James, was an intense admirer of the drama, particularly of the plays of Richard Cumberland.   These had

---

[1] A place of amusement near Margate.

fallen out of fashion; and in the year 1805, while Horace was still in a city counting-house, his conviction that this neglect was utterly unwarranted became so strong, that he wrote a poem deploring the lamentable absence of taste on the part of the theatre-going public in preferring the dramatic works of other writers to those of Cumberland.

This effusion fell into Cumberland's hands, and he was so pleased that he quickly made the author's acquaintance, and introduced him into his own literary circle, and, to Horace's great delight, to most of the notable actors of the day.

Thus James and Horace Smith soon came to know everybody in any way connected with the stage, and amongst them Miller, the dramatic publisher of Bow Street, and Charles William Ward, both of whom were destined to influence very considerably the lives of the brothers.

Ward was of good family and well-connected, and had married Jane Linley, a younger sister of Brinsley Sheridan's first wife. He possessed a versatile talent, social tact, and easy manners, and had, besides, considerable judgment in business matters, so that he was well fitted for the responsible position of secretary to the Theatre Royal, Drury Lane.

Ward was of a convivial disposition, as were most of the popular men of his day, and an excellent judge of port, the frequent imbibing of which generous liquor had set its sign and seal on his nose. Hence the sobriquet of " Portsoken [1]

____
[1] One of the City wards.

Ward," privately bestowed upon him by Horace Smith.

It was really the Smiths' acquaintance with Ward that led to their writing *Rejected Addresses*. But here it is necessary that I should diverge slightly from the chronological order which I have endeavoured to maintain in this family narrative.

On the 20th of September, 1808, a great sensation was created in London by the total destruction of Covent Garden Theatre, attended by sad loss of life.

The recollection of this catastrophe was fresh in people's memories, when the town was startled (January 1809) by the intelligence that the entire east wing of St. James's Palace, including their Majesties' private apartments, and those of the Duke of Cambridge, had been burnt down, and the rest of the Palace saved only with great difficulty.

An epidemic of terrible fires seemed to have set in. At the Theatre Royal, Drury Lane, the *Circassian Bride* was running; and on the 24th of February, 1809,—the first Friday in Lent,—the theatre, according to custom throughout that season of mortification and fasting, was closed until the following day, and left in charge of the usual watchmen and caretakers. About eleven o'clock that night, a gentleman named Kent, residing in Tavistock Street, Covent Garden, happened to be passing, and noticed a strong light in one of the second-floor windows of the theatre facing Little Russell Street. He watched it for a few minutes, and deciding that it betokened nothing more unusual than workmen busy upon an urgent piece of repairs or alterations, passed on.

In twenty minutes, however, the light had increased, and tongues of fire began to make their appearance at the window. Alarm was given, and messengers were dispatched in every direction for the fire-engines. At that time there was no Fire Brigade, but each of the Insurance Companies (and there were sixteen) maintained a number of engines, with a staff of firemen in distinctive costume.

The engines were only manuals, and incapable of forcing the water to any great distance or in anything like an adequate quantity for a large fire. By the time the " Hand-in-Hand," quickly followed by the " Phœnix " and the " Sun," had reached the spot, the entire upper portion of the great edifice was in a blaze, at an elevation that would have severely taxed the powers of even a modern "steamer."

As it was, the manuals confined their attention to the surrounding houses, and, the supply of water being plentiful, managed to keep them from catching alight. The sight was splendid; an unbroken mass of flame enwrapped the whole building from Brydges [1] (now Catherine Street) Street to Drury Lane, a distance of one hundred and fifty yards. By midnight the roof had fallen in, and with it the gigantic wooden figure of Apollo that had stood on the summit; and soon afterwards, a portion of the

[1] Catherine Street formerly ended at Exeter Street, whence to Little Russell Street it was called Brydges Street.

outer walls in Russell Street and Vinegar Yard fell down, completely blocking up the passage.

By three o'clock the flames had nearly subsided, and at five o'clock a.m. all was over, and nothing but the mere shell remained of the structure that eighteen years before had been re-built by Holland, when Garrick's Drury Lane—styled by Mrs. Siddons, from the magnitude of its dimensions, the " Wilderness "—was pulled down.

An enormous crowd, kept well in check by a strong detachment from the Horse Guards and Foot Guards, and estimated to number at least a hundred thousand souls, quickly assembled, as, from the central position of the fire, the reflection of the flames was visible for miles. [1]

> Far and wide
> Across red Thames's gleaming tide,
> To distant fields the blaze was borne,
> And daisy white and hoary thorn
> In borrow'd lustre seem'd to shame
> The rose or red sweet Wil-li-am.
> To those who on the hills around
> Behold the flames from Drury's mound,
>   As from a lofty altar rise,
> It seem'd that nations did conspire
> To offer to the god of fire
>   Some vast stupendous sacrifice ! [2]

In all directions the tops of the houses were covered with people, and from those that commanded

[1] Now that a large open space has been created by the pulling down of part of Catherine Street near Russell Court, a fine view can be obtained of Drury Lane Theatre, and it is easy to realize what a commanding site the great building occupies.

[2] *Rejected Addresses.*

a view of the river it was possible to distinguish every person crossing Westminster and Blackfriars' Bridges, so bright was the light that played upon the water.   And so great was the heat given out by the conflagration that it was distinctly felt across Covent Garden Market, at the portico of St. Paul's Church.

A considerable time elapsed before arrangements could be made for the re-erection of the theatre. There were many questions to decide, and money was slow to come in.   But by July of 1811, the Committee—appointed under the Act of Parliament, which authorized the formation of a Joint-Stock Company for the re-building by shares of £100 each—met under the presidency of Mr. Samuel Whitbread, M.P., the celebrated brewer, and were able to report that subscriptions were flowing in freely.

Various designs for the new building were considered, and, finally, Mr. Benjamin Wyatt was appointed architect; and his plan, accompanied by a lucid explanatory tract, was freely circulated in the papers, and on the whole approved of by the public.

A certain kind of provision was made against possible future conflagrations, by means of an aqueduct of considerable depth, ingeniously designed by Colonel Congreve, to furnish the house with an ample supply of water, should accident occur from fire.   It was to be effected by an engine that would play from the stage into every box in the house!   This is referred to by Horace Smith in the *Rejected Addresses* :—

> Again should it burst in a blaze,
>   In vain would they ply Congreve's plug,
> For nought could extinguish the rays
>   From the glance of divine Lady Mugg.

CHAPTER XI

1812

Competition for Address to be spoken at opening of new Drury Lane Theatre—Some of the Addresses—The re-opening of Drury Lane Theatre—How *Rejected Addresses* came to be written—Its publication.

IT was arranged by the Committee that the opening night of the new theatre should be on the 10th of October, 1812 ; and on the 12th of August preceding, there appeared the following announcement in the leading daily paper :—

"REBUILDING OF DRURY LANE THEATRE.

" The Committee are desirous of promoting a free and fair competition for an Address to be spoken upon the opening of the Theatre, which will take place on the 10th of October next. They have, therefore, thought fit to announce to the public, that they will be glad to receive any such compositions, addressed to their Secretary, at the Treasury Office in Drury Lane, on or before the 10th of September, sealed up, with a distinguishing word, number, or motto on the cover, corresponding with the inscription on a separate sealed paper, containing the name of the author, which will not be opened unless containing the name of the successful candidate."

The brothers Smith had previously been made aware by their friend, Mr. Ward, that such a competition would be promoted, and Horace, taking advantage of this information, prepared a *genuine* address, which was sent up with the others, and shared the same fate of rejection. It was incorporated in his volume of *Rejected Addresses* as " An Address without a Phœnix," and concludes thus :—

> Oh ! may we still, to sense and nature true,
> Delight the many, nor offend the few.
> Though varying tastes our changeful Drama claim,
> Still be its moral tendency the same—
> To win by precept, by example warn,
> To brand the front of Vice with pointed scorn,
> And Virtue's smiling brows with votive wreaths adorn.

As many as one hundred and twelve Addresses were sent in to the Committee, who heroically sat and patiently listened while each one in turn was recited before them. Some were brief, others of inordinate length ; in fifteen, the poet " flashes his maiden sword." In general they bore a close resemblance to each other; thirty contained complimentary allusions to Wellington, and to Whitbread, the brewer ; and in no fewer than sixty-nine, the fabled *Phœnix* was invoked. Even Whitbread, who himself sent in an Address, had a Phœnix, but, according to Sheridan, he made more of the bird than his rivals had done, entering into particulars, and describing its wings, beak, tail, etc. ; in short, it was " a poulterer's description of a Phœnix."

Some few of the Addresses were manifestly not seriously meant to be spoken ; and the professionals in the poetical world studiously abstained from competing.

Bravely the Committee struggled through their thankless task.   One Address, abounding in pathos, from the pen of the well-known W. T. Fitzgerald, of whom Lord Byron wrote—

> "Shall hoarse Fitzgerald bawl
> His creaking couplets in a tavern hall—"

tried their "staying" powers very severely. Six hours were spent in discussing the merits of this lengthy and elaborate elegiac, until at last it was decided, *nem. con.*, that, as it was confessedly by far the *longest*, it should be referred to the prompter to report, whether, with that superior merit, it might not, in his opinion, prove also the *fittest*, as giving the scene-shifters more time to arrange matters before the rising of the curtain.

Eventually the Committee, sadly puzzled what to do, since none came up to their expectations, decided to reject them all, and in their dilemma applied to Lord Byron, who acceded to their request, and provided them with an Address which was duly recited at the re-opening.

All London was astir, and, as the hour of opening approached, the streets leading to Drury Lane were crowded with sight-seers, patiently waiting in the pouring rain, up to their knees in mud. Soldiers guarded the entrances to the theatre, and admitted

the company so gradually that there was no crushing
or confusion.

The house was rapidly filled with an enthusiastic,
well-behaved audience, who considerately abstained
from hanging their shawls and coats over the front of
the boxes, thus leaving the splendid decorations open
to the sight of all.

When the curtain drew up at half-past six o'clock,
the entire company came forward and sang "God
Save the King" and "Rule, Britannia," received with
the loudest applause.[1]   Then came Lord Byron's
Address, spoken by Elliston dressed as Hamlet.   It
began thus—

> "In one dread night, our city saw and sighed,
>   Bowed to the dust, the Drama's tower of pride,
>   In one short hour beheld the blazing fane,
>   Apollo sink, and Shakspeare cease to reign,"

and finished—after more than sixty lines—with the
following—

> "The curtain rises—may our stage unfold
>   Scenes not unworthy Drury's days of old !
>   Britons our judges, Nature for our guide,
>   Still may *we* please, long, long—may *you* preside."

A touching incident occurred before the performance began.   As Mrs. Garrick entered the box
specially reserved for her, the audience rose, and
welcomed her with three such hearty cheers, in
memory of her incomparable husband, that the poor
old lady, deeply moved by this exhibition of popular
affection, shed tears.

[1] The leader of the band was Sir George Smart.

The play[1] then proceeded, followed by the farce, *The Devil to Pay*. The audience was full of good-humour, and " all went merry as a marriage-bell."

Finally, it was said that the sum taken that night at the doors amounted to £859.

So passed the memorable performance, at which (it need hardly be said) James and Horace Smith were present, the former relating to his friends his personal recollection of the opening of the former Drury Lane Theatre, when, between the play and the farce, an epilogue, written by George Colman, had been " excellently spoken " by Miss Farren.

Of course a good deal of discontent was felt among the one hundred and twelve " rejected," from the fact of Byron not having *competed ;* but only one of the number tried publicly to air his grievance. This was a certain Dr. Busby, who, soon after the re-opening, created considerable disturbance by addressing the audience from one of the boxes, and, after much interruption and confusion, prevailed upon the good-natured audience to allow him to recite his own rejected Address from the stage. His voice, however, was so weak as to be almost inaudible; the public had given him a chance, and he had failed. Dr. Busby, politely handed from the stage by the stage-manager, bowed respectfully to the audience, and disappeared.[2]

---

[1] *Hamlet*—Elliston in the title rôle, Mrs. Mountain as Ophelia, and Mr. Pope as the Ghost.

[2] In the British Museum, on the title-page of a book containing some " *Genuine* Rejected Addresses," the Library authori-

On the 21st of August—just six weeks before the re-opening—James Smith was dining with the general secretary, C. W. Ward, at the Piarra Coffee House, Covent Garden. Ward had been telling Smith of the large number of Addresses that within a fortnight after the issue of the advertisement had come to hand, and of his opinion that the bulk of them would turn out to be inferior and absurd compositions; whereupon, James improvised some verses that sent Ward, who had by this time consumed the greater part of a magnum of fine old port, into fits of laughter. Suddenly he exclaimed, "But what about all the rejected ones, my boy! Won't there be a d——d row when the award is given! They'll be wanting the rejected Addresses published, just to show the public what they were like. Now, I have an idea; why shouldn't *you* try and make fun of them all, and write *your* idea of the rejected ones!"—" Well, I don't know," said James, " perhaps I may try;" and nothing more was said upon the subject. But the hint thrown out was not forgotten; James repeated it to Horace, who caught at the idea, and together they concocted a plan of action.

It was, of course, impossible for them to know for a certainty who had or who had not sent in Addresses, or who were likely to do so; but from some casual

---

ties have thought it prudent to append a pencilled note, to the effect that they were *not* written by James and Horace Smith.

remarks made by Ward, they were almost sure that William Thomas Fitzgerald would be in the list, and also Dr. Thomas Busby, Mus. Doc., notorious for his classical translation of Lucretius; but whether the great lights in the literary firmament would show on this occasion was a matter of surmise. Another and grave difficulty stood in the way, which Horace shall explain in his own words.

No sooner was the idea of our work conceived [says he] than it was about to be abandoned in embryo, from the apprehension that we had no time to mature and bring it forth, as it was indispensable that it should be written, printed, and published by the opening of Drury Lane Theatre, which would only allow us an interval of six weeks, and we had both of us other avocations that precluded us from the full command of even that limited period. Encouraged, however, by the conviction that the thought was a good one, and by the hope of making a lucky hit, we set to work, *con amore*, our very hurry not improbably enabling us to strike out at a heat what we might have failed to produce so well, had we possessed time enough to hammer it into more careful and elaborate form.

Our first difficulty, that of selection, was by no means a light one. . . . We had to confine ourselves to writers whose style and habit of thought, being more marked and peculiar, was more capable of exaggeration and distraction. To avoid politics and personality, to imitate the turn of mind as well as the phraseology of our originals, and at all events to raise a harmless laugh, were our main objects; in the attainment of which united aims we were sometimes hurried into extravagance, by attaching much more importance to the last than to the first.

The *Rejected Addresses* consist of twenty-one effusions in prose and verse, supposed to have been sent in to the Committee and rejected as unsuitable ; they are also supposed to have fallen into the hands of the authors, and to have been published by them as fair samples of the state of poetry in Great Britain. In reality, they are clever imitations of well-known poets and writers ; but, strictly speaking, they are not so much parodies as distinct literary compositions. "A Tale of Drury Lane" so exactly imitated Sir Walter Scott that the "Wizard of the North" was himself deceived, and said to James Smith, "I certainly must have written this myself, although I forget upon what occasion." Well might he have thought so. Compare the genuine coin with the counterfeit—

MARMION.

CANTO V, STANZA XX.

At night, in secret, there they came,
The Palmer and the holy Dame.
The moon among the clouds rose high,
And all the city hum was by.
Upon the street, where late before
Did din of war and warrior roar,
    You might have heard a pebble fall,
A beetle hum, a cricket sing,
An owlet flap his boding wing
    On Giles's steeple tall.

CANTO VI, STANZA XI.

That night, upon the rocks and bay,
The midnight moonbeam slumbering lay,
And pour'd its silver light, and pure,
Through loop-hole, and through embrazure,
    Upon Tantallon tower and hall ;

> But chief where arched windows wide
> Illuminate the chapel's pride,
>   The sober glances fall.

REJECTED ADDRESSES.

"A TALE OF DRURY LANE," BY HORACE SMITH.

> On fair Augusta's[1] towers and trees
> Flitted the silent midnight breeze,
> Curling the foliage as it pass'd,
> Which from the moon-tipp'd plumage cast
> A spangled light, like dancing spray,
> Then re-assumed its still array ;
> When, as night's lamp unclouded hung,
> And down its full effulgence flung,
> It shed such soft and balmy power
> That cot and castle, hall and bower,
> And spire and dome and turret height,
> Appeared to slumber in the light.
> From Henry's chapel, Rufus' hall,
> To Savoy, Temple, and St. Paul ;
> From Knightsbridge, Pancras, Camden Town,
> To Redriffe,[2] Shadwell, Horsleydown,
> No voice was heard, no eye unclosed,
> But all in deepest sleep reposed.

No wonder that an old matter-of-fact Leicestershire clergyman, after reading the *Rejected Addresses*, remarked, "I do not see why they should have been rejected. I think some of them very good!"

Perhaps the very best of all is the parody of Southey's *Curse of Kehama :—*

THE FUNERAL.

> Midnight, and yet no eye
> Through all the Imperial city closed in sleep !
> Behold her streets ablaze

---

[1] One of the old names for London.   [2] Rotherhithe.

With light, that seems to kindle the red sky,
Her myriads swarming thro' the crowded ways.
Master and slave, old age and infancy,
All, all abroad to gaze :
House-top and balcony
Clustered with women, who throw back their veils,
With unimpeded and insatiate sight
To view the funeral pomp which passes by,
As if the mournful rite
Were but to them a scene of joyaunce and delight.

REJECTED ADDRESSES.

"The Rebuilding," by James Smith.

Midnight, yet not a nose
From Tower Hill to Piccadilly snored !
Midnight, yet not a nose
From India drew the essence of repose !
See with what crimson fury,
By Indra fann'd, the god of fire ascends the walls of Drury !
Tops of houses, blue with lead
Bend beneath the landlord's tread,
Master and 'prentice, serving-man and lord,
Nailor and tailor
Grazier and brazier,
Through streets and alleys pour'd—
All, all abroad to gaze,
And wonder at the blaze.
Thick calf, fat foot, and slim knee
Mounted on roof and chimney,[1]
The mighty roast, the mighty stew
To see ;
As if the dismal view
Were but to them a Brentford jubilee.

A general favourite in the *Rejected Addresses* is "The Theatre," by James Smith,—in the opinion of the *Edinburgh Review* the best piece of the collection. It begins :—

[1] This couplet was introduced in answer to one who alleged that the English language contained no rhyme to "chimney."

> 'Tis sweet to view, from half-past five to six,
> Our long wax-candles, with short cotton wicks,
> Touch'd by the lamplighter's Promethean art,
> Start into light, and make the lighter start ;
> To see red Phœbus through the gallery-pane
> Tinge with his beam the beams of Drury Lane ;
> While gradual parties fill our widen'd pit,
> And gape, and gaze, and wonder, ere they sit.

"The Theatre" is more than a masterly imitation of George Crabbe. One can picture the interior of Drury Lane and the expectant audience, and can watch with deepest interest the successful efforts of Pat Jennings, the red-haired youth, who, to recover his hat, let down a "motley cable" composed of borrowed handkerchiefs—

> Starr'd, striped, and spotted, yellow, red, and blue,
> Old calico, torn silk, and muslin new,

and thus

> Regain'd the felt, and felt what he regain'd ;
> While to the applauding galleries grateful Pat
> Made a low bow, and touch'd the ransom'd hat.

The "Hampshire Farmer's Address," a parody of William Cobbett, also by James Smith, is considered by many excellent judges to be among the very best of the imitations.

On the completion of *Rejected Addresses*, the authors sent their MS. to some of the leading publishers, but in every case it was perused and " returned with thanks." The Smiths did not care to pay for its publication out of their own pocket, for, as Horace says, " We had no objection to raise a laugh at the expense of others, but to do it at our own cost, uncertain

MR. ALDERMAN CADELL.

as we were to what extent we might be involved, had never entered our contemplation."

Amongst others, they had communicated with Mr. John Murray, but before sending him the MS. had inquired if he would entertain the idea of publishing it, in which case he might have the copyright for the modest sum of £20. Mr. Murray refused the offer, and subsequently stated that he did so because he had taken it for granted that, as Mr. Cadell was related to the Smiths, they had previously offered the MS. to him, and that he had declined it.

The feeling of clanship is rarely so strong south of the Tweed as to lead people to be particularly anxious to do business with relations or connections, as such ; and Cadell was the last man in the world to be influenced by these considerations. This the Smiths well knew ; but there was also another reason for their not offering the work to him. On the death of Alderman Cadell in 1802, the business, which had fallen into a state of comparative decrepitude, required that the closest economy should be practised, and that for many years no financial risks, however small, should be run. This had become a fixed principle of the firm, and Cadell—an excellent " man of affairs " —was well known among authors as " close," and little disposed to deal on the basis of cash down if he could avoid it.[1]

---

[1] As Thomas Cadell's grandson, the author may be allowed to make the above statement with some authority. Thomas Cadell, by dint of steady application, and ably assisted by his partner, Wm. Davies, and a particularly capable chief clerk,

However, as Mr. Murray had blindly rejected their *Rejected Addresses*, the question was, what were they to do?   At this point their good angel, C. W. Ward, reminded Horace that John Miller, the dramatic publisher of Bow Street, having already fathered the *Highgate Tunnel*, would be the most likely person to apply to.

No sooner had this gentleman looked over our manuscript [says Horace] than he immediately offered to take upon himself all the risk of publication, and to give us half the profit, *should there be any*—a liberal proposition with which we gladly closed.

The success of the book was immediate and re-markable; and as new editions were called for in quick succession, the lucky authors were by and by able to dispose of their half copyright to Mr. Miller for £1000.

In Robert Smith's Journal we find this terse entry :—

October 11*th*, 1812.—My two sons, James and Horace, jointly composed a little *jeu d'esprit* of a satirical nature, called *Rejected Addresses, or the New Theatrum Poetarum.*   It hit the fancy of the public, and went through several editions in a short time.

---

named Mutlow, slowly but surely restored the firm's prosperity, and died in 1836, leaving a handsome fortune to his family.

CHAPTER XII

1812—1813

Rejected Addresses and the Reviewers—The effect of its success upon the careers of James and Horace Smith—Their social and literary circle—Horace Smith resides at Knightsbridge—His friend William Heseltine—Horace Smith and the Stock Exchange.

Rejected Addresses was published on the day Drury Lane Theatre was re-opened.

Lord Byron, alluding to the success of *Childe Harold*, says, " I awoke, and found myself famous " (which Horace Smith tells us was thus parodied by a witty, runaway wife—" I awoke," said she, " and found myself *infamous !*").

The authors of *Rejected Addresses* had reason to be quite as exultant as Byron.   Within a week, reviews and newspapers of all shades and complexions were praising their production, and speculating on the identity of the authors; and the moment this was revealed, their acquaintance was eagerly courted by the notabilities of the day.   Amongst many others, the Dowager Countess of Cork—the first lady of rank who threw open her house to literature, and made intellectual distinction a recognized passport to society — was anxious to have them at her *soirées*.

Many of the writers who were parodied hastened to bear testimony to the accuracy of the imitations, and joined heartily in the laugh.   On the whole, the only discontented persons were the poets who were left out.   Campbell ventured a remonstrance, and was told that it was as impossible to parody the finished elegance of his poetry as the handsome features of his face.   "That's all very well," he replied, "but I should have liked to have been among them for all that."

The Press was all but unanimous in praising the work.   The *Edinburgh Review* for November 1812 devoted to it no fewer than eighteen pages, and the *Quarterly* gave five pages to a most favourable notice of the little volume ; while, across the Atlantic, the *Analectic Magazine* (1813), published in Philadelphia, allotted ten of its pages to the work.   It long continued a favourite in the United States, where three editions—1844, 1859, and 1871—were published.

How many copies of *Rejected Addresses* were sold on its first appearance it is difficult to conjecture ; but the book ultimately ran into more than thirty editions.   Mr. Murray had to wait seven years before he could secure the copyright for £131, and thousands of the little volume must have been since disposed of by the noted firm in Albemarle Street. By the time the third edition was exhausted the brothers Smith had realized from *Rejected Addresses* the sum of £1000.

In the prime of life,—thirty-seven and thirty-three years of age respectively,—of eminently gentlemanly manners and bearing, and of remarkably handsome personal appearance, highly educated, and possessed of an inexhaustible fund of literary knowledge, James and Horace Smith were exactly fitted to shine in the presence of the highest and most learned.

Mr. S. C. Hall, in his *Book of Memories*, writing of James and Horace Smith, says he thinks it "surprising that a stockbroker and a solicitor should have become poetical and literary;" an observation resembling that of the *Times* reviewer of *In Memoriam*, who seemed to think it an absurdity that Tennyson should have wasted his poetic sentiment over the death of Arthur Henry Hallam, "a mere barrister at the Chancery Bar!" Neither romance nor emotion, forsooth, may dwell in the tents of a professional man, nor in the fastnesses of the money-grubbing city and the Stock Exchange. If, as the Rev. F. W. Robertson indignantly says, "the Chancery Bar, or any other accident of a man's environment, destroys the real poetry of life, then the human soul has no worth but that which comes from its trappings—an idea which I reckon about the most decisive proof of a vulgar soul which can be found."

The Smiths had now the *entrée* into West-End salons, inaccessible to all but the most distinguished men and women of the period; and amongst their many friends were Lady Salisbury, Lady Jersey,

and Lady Albina Buckinghamshire, at one time
prominent members of the " Pic Nic Club." [1] The
brothers were admitted into the sacred circle of
Almacks' by the high-priestesses who ruled over the
establishment. The Earl of Mulgrave was their
close and faithful friend ; also Lord Abinger, Lord
Denman, Lord Hartington, Lady Blessington, Count
d'Orsay, Mrs. Verschoyle, John Wilson Croker of
Moulsey, The Countess Guiccioli, Sir E. L. Bulwer,
Lord Hertford, General Phipps, Lord Essex, Miss
Burdett Coutts, Mrs. Lane Fox, and a host of others.
They came into close contact with the galaxy of
famous poets and authors that bedecked the literary
firmament—Byron, Campbell, Coleridge, Hood (born
in the Poultry, not far from their own home in Old
Jewry), Keats, Thomas Moore, Samuel Rogers,
Shelley, Sir Walter Scott, Southey, Wordsworth,
Jane Austen, Harrison Ainsworth, the Rev. Thomas
Barham, Mrs. Barbauld, William Cobbett, George
Crabbe, Miss Edgeworth, De Quincey, William
Hazlitt, Leigh Hunt, Theodore Hook (a friend of
James Smith in his youthful days), Jesse (the writer
on Natural History), Charles Lamb, W. S. Landor,
Captain Marryat, the Rev. T. R. Malthus, Lady
Morgan, Miss Jane Porter, Sydney Smith, John
Horne Tooke, Sharon Turner. Of artists they knew
Benjamin West (President of the Royal Academy),
Henry Fuseli, Turner, Stothard, Sir Thomas
Laurence, Robert Smirke, Sir Francis Chantry (then
a rising sculptor), Flaxman (in his zenith), and

[1] *Vide* Chapter VIII.

Westmacott (who had been made an A.R.A. some years before the appearance of *Rejected Addresses*).

As to actors, the Smiths lived in a fortunate period of the Drama. They had seen Kemble, Munden, Bannister, Dowton, Elliston, Liston, Mrs. Siddons, Fawcett, Johnston, Miss Farren, Charles Young, and Edmund Kean, and, later on, his talented son Charles. They had heard Mrs. Billington, Mdlle. Mara, Incledon, and Braham sing the sweet music of Arnold, Callcott, Shield, Stevens, and Clementi.

With many of the above the Smiths had for years been intimately associated, but their circle of dramatic acquaintances kept extending. Their heads were not in the least turned by their notoriety. In their daily vocations they "kept the noiseless tenor of their way;" James in his father's office, Horace on the Stock Exchange, making money in a very prosaic fashion.

James Smith used to illustrate the limited and ephemeral nature of fame by an incident that happened to himself in a Brighton coach. One of the passengers, an old lady, struck with his extraordinary familiarity with things and people, suddenly exclaimed—"And pray, sir,—you who seem to know everybody—pray, may I ask who you are?"—"James Smith, ma'am." This reply evidently conveying nothing to her mind, a fellow-passenger added, "One of the authors of *Rejected Addresses*." The old lady stared at them by turns, and quietly said, "I never heard of the gentleman or the book before."

James Smith was content to rest himself upon
the reputation secured by his share in the production
of *Rejected Addresses*, and laid down a maxim, to
which he adhered, if not to the exact letter, at all
events in spirit, that, when a man had once made a
good hit, he should not attempt another.

Horace, on the other hand, fired by greater
ambition, and being, perhaps, of a more active mental temperament, decided to embark in a literary
career—a decision which he successfully carried out
some years later, when he had obtained an independency, and leisure.

As was not unnatural, the brothers were immensely
popular with women. To the blandishments of the
fair sex individually James always seemed to exhibit
a stoical indifference; yet Horace tells a wicked
story of his brother, who, being made free of the
green-room in a certain theatre, was thus addressed
one night by an actress of note—" Mr. Smith, you are
constantly here, but you do not appear to attach
yourself to any of our ladies." " Oh, Madam," was
the reply, " that proves my discretion; you little
know what is going on in private between me and
some of you."

With Horace it was different. He was thoroughly
domesticated, and, longing for the felicity of a home
of his own, had in 1810 contracted a matrimonial
alliance, which, unfortunately, failed to obtain the
approbation of his father. There thus arose between
them a coolness which it took years to remove.
Horace became the tenant of a modest dwelling, No.

3 Knightsbridge Terrace, in the Kensington Road, on a site locally known as "the island," and opposite the present Wellington Court; but the old buildings have long ago disappeared, and have been replaced by little shops. Knightsbridge was then but a hamlet, and quite rural. The "Green" was unbuilt over, and Tattersall's was still in Grosvenor Place. Nursery grounds and market-gardens occupied the site of Belgravia, and Lowndes Square was a kind of Vauxhall Gardens.

No. 3 Knightsbridge Terrace was convenient for a city man, as he could go to and from business in any of the stages. At a pinch, he could take a hackney-coach to the Bank for 4s. 6d., or drive himself in a whiskey, which it was Horace Smith's custom to do. It was quiet enough, but from the front windows there was always something to be seen, as the main road was crowded with traffic throughout the day and far into the small hours of the morning. Four-horse coaches were seldom out of sight, lumbering wagons crawled along incessantly to the pleasant music of horse-bells, and every now and again post-chaises, glass-coaches, and at intervals the equipages of Royalty, dashed past along this, the approach to the famous Bath road.

The children born to Horace from this union were Eliza (Tizey) and Horatio Shakespeare; the former still living at Brighton, and known far and wide as "Miss Horace Smith," a truly grand old lady in mental powers and intelligence, whose memory is prodigious, and whose conversation, though increasing infirmities forbid its continuance for long at a time, still flashes with wit and humour like that of her father.   Horatio Shakespeare died when a school-boy at Boulogne-sur-Mer.   He was a sprightly lad, full of oddity and fun; and when, some little time before his death, his intellect suddenly became somewhat dulled, the French tutors attributed the fact to stupidity, not suspecting that a growing disease—water on the brain—was the cause of the poor boy's inability to learn.

Among Horace Smith's many friends on the Stock Exchange was William Heseltine, whose office in Throgmorton Street adjoined his own, and whose private residence was Turret House, Lambeth.

It would very much surprise us now-a-days, if we learned that any of the gentlemen clad in irreproach-able frock-coats and hats always glossy and new, who every day in the week may be seen issuing from their comfortable offices in Austin Friars, Draper's Gardens, Throgmorton Avenue, or Copthall Court, and wending their way to the " House," were living " over the water " at Lambeth.   But in Horace Smith's time there were no Pullman-car trains to convey successful dealers in stocks and shares, when their arduous toil was over, to luxurious homes anywhere within a radius of sixty miles from town; and they thought themselves fortunate indeed if they could secure the lease of one of the fine mansions in Bloomsbury, which was still a fashionable quarter of London.

Turret House, in the South Lambeth Road, however, was one that the noblest of families might have been proud to dwell in. Standing in its own beautiful grounds of some four acres in extent, the picturesque old mansion, rich in association of the Tudor and early Stuart epochs, was celebrated as the home of Sir John Tradescant, and of his son and grandson, who were successively gardeners to Queen Elizabeth, James I., and Charles I., and to whom posterity is indebted for the introduction of the study of botany as a science into this country.

The wonderful collection of curiosities and rarities. gathered together by this enterprising Dutch family from every part of the then known world, passed into the keeping of their personal friend, the famous Elias Ashmole, and was by him presented to the University of Oxford, where it constituted the Ashmolean Museum.

The first mulberry-tree planted in England grew in the garden of Turret House, where also the rarest of plants had been introduced by the Tradescants after their numerous and extensive travels. No home, in fact, could have been better suited to feed the romantic instincts of Horace Smith; and in *Brambletye House*, the most popular of his romances, he makes special reference to the ancient mansion he knew so well.

It has been said that every man has an *alter ego.* If so, William Heseltine certainly occupied that position in relation to Horace Smith. In Stock Exchange transactions, though no formal partnership existed between them, the one was *fidus Achates* to the other. William Heseltine was a man of large experience and great shrewdness, and under his fostering wing Horace Smith, never too proud to learn from others, made but few mistakes in his transactions.

Horace Smith happened to become a stockbroker at a period (1812) when everybody possessed of a certain amount of shrewdness had a good chance of making money; but he had the immense advantage —call it good luck—of being well-advised, and of possessing the rare qualification of readiness to act upon advice when offered disinterestedly. He had, besides, a large and influential connection of relatives and friends, who, when stock had to be transferred, investments made or re-made, brought their transactions to him. Thus he soon came to possess the more legitimate, if less remunerative, conventional business of a stockbroker. Eminently a prudent man, he was not given to extremes in his speculations; and he could usually learn, either from his father or his brother James, through the Ordnance Office, the truth of the innumerable rumours constantly disturbing the Stock markets.

Horace Smith had the good fortune to be amongst those who were " on the right side " and early buyers of " Omnium," when the period of uncertainty that succeeded the escape of Napoleon from Elba terminated on receipt of the news of Waterloo in this country.

Miss Frances Williams Wynn relates in her *Diaries* how a spy from the house of Rothschild, who had

for many days been on the watch at Ghent, where
Louis XVIII. and his little court resided while the
fate of his dynasty was in the balance, observed on
the morning of Monday, the 19th of June, that
the Royal party, breakfasting in an apartment whose
French windows were wide open, suddenly commenced to embrace one another with every sign of
rejoicing. This was quite enough to apprise him
that unusually good news had arrived from the field
of battle, so without waiting an instant he started
off for London, arriving there shortly before the
official and accredited messenger.

This may, or may not, account for Rothschild's
early information; the probability points rather to
the employment of carrier pigeons, which would have
reached the office much quicker than an *employé.*
Anyhow, he had the news first; and his recognized
agents on the Stock Exchange instantly began the
old game by professing to *sell* "Omnium," while he
was in reality secretly *buying* largely through other
brokers. The device succeeded for a short time,
but many of the more wary speculators were not
thus to be deceived. Heseltine quickly conjectured
that something serious was in the wind, and that
probably a grand success had been scored by the
allies. He communicated his theory to Horace
Smith, who was only too ready to believe that the
" Corsican tyrant " had met with a decisive reverse.
Horace slipped away to Austin Friars, and was
privately told by James that, so far as information
had reached their Department, he had good reason

for conjecturing that victory was on the side of Wellington.

Both Heseltine and Horace Smith were purchasers of Omnium, and when, on the 21st, it rose to 6 per cent, premium, their prudence was rewarded, and a good many thousand pounds went into their pockets.

Spanish, for some reason or other, always a fascinating security to dabble in during those piping days of rash speculation, was never approved of by Horace Smith; and in his *Midsummer Medley* for 1830 he thus condemns these risky securities—

> Others, the dupes of Ferdinand,
> By royal roguery trepann'd,
>   Find all their treasure vanish,
> Leaving a warning to the rash,
> That the best way to keep their cash
>   Is *not* to touch the Spanish.

In William Heseltine, Smith found not only a firm business friend but a kindred spirit. Heseltine was imaginative and of a literary and antiquarian turn of mind; and Smith's visits to the old Turret House, continued until long after he had left the Stock Exchange, no doubt helped to foster his love of the Carolian period of history.

Heseltine, a kind and most unostentatious man, was, like Smith, an author, and subsequently produced *The Last of the Plantagenets*, an historical narrative dedicated to the Earl of Winchelsea and Nottingham. Amongst his other works were *Some Reflections at the Grave*, written after having been present at the interment (August 8th, 1836) of the famous N. M. Rothschild.

CHAPTER XIII

1813—1821

Horace Smith's letters to his sister Clara—His second marriage—Removes from Knightsbridge to Fulham—Entertains the poet Keats—Horace Smith's account of his introduction to Shelley and Keats.

FROM Ryde, Isle of Wight, where he had taken a house, Horace Smith dates the following letter to his youngest and favourite sister Clara, a very attractive girl, who in 1813 had married Mr. Dodson, "second Assistant-Collector Inwards" at the Custom-House, and to whose grandson, Mr. Harry Magnus, the journals of Robert Smith have descended.[1]

July 22, 1817.

Bating the intense and bitter cold, I had a pleasant ride yesterday outside the coach, reaching Portsmouth about half-past seven, but as old Neptune look'd rather scrowling and sulky I did not cross till this morning, when a stiff breeze (which owes me thirty shillings for spoiling my hat with the spray) conveyed me hither in an hour and a half.

I found my vermin quite well, and Eliza mani-

---

[1] *Vide* Preface.

festly improved, as her bones no longer rattle as she walks, nor does her back look so much like a rabbit before it is smothered in onions.

Ryde stands where it did, and as I have gathered no scandal, I have of course nothing interesting to send you.

Walking by myself in the fields this beautiful evening, I bethought myself of your brats, when my reflections *involuntarily arranged themselves* (as the novels have it) with the annexed sonnet, which I venture to send, because I'm sure the subject will bribe the judge to give a verdict of acquittal.

Your affectionate brother,

HORACE SMITH.

SONNET TO CLARA'S BRATS

Thou laughing Julia and Selina grave,
  Of azure eye and stout athletic limb,
Ye whom one birth to our embraces gave,
  Not like the race of Twins deformed and slim,
  But rather those Latona bore to him
Who wields the thunder—may ye live to brave
  The storms of fate, and in the sparkling brim
Of joy's full cup, your lips for ever lave.
O may the morning of each life be bright
As parents' wishes in their fondest flight.
  And may its evening be as calm a scene
As that which smiles around me while I write,
  Where Ocean by a cloudless sky made green
  Awaits the night unruffled and serene !

If Jupiter was not the father of Latona's twins it is not my fault, for it rhymes; but you had better look, as I have no means of reference here, and cut the lines according to pattern; only let Dodson get the best god he can to be compared to himself. Were it my case, I should select Vulcan, for all the world knows he was a *Smith*.

Ryde, Isle of Wight,
Thursday, the somethingth of August, 1817.

DEAR CLARA,

We seem to have commenced a regular Sewardian correspondence with an interchange of sonnets and poetical pretties, which it now comes to my turn to contribute, and which I should have done sooner, but that I have been running up to London for some days, leaving Parnassus for the Stock Exchange, and only returned here on Wednesday night. Many thanks for your verses, which I perused with very great pleasure, and, as in duty bound, return you a sonnet, inscribed among others, though of *course*, inferior scribblings in the porch of Binstead Church. . . . As a punishment for my sins, I came off by the Cowes packet at seven o'clock *without breakfast*, and it soon fell so dead a calm that the captain proposed taking to the boat, into which accordingly about twenty were stowed, but as Mr. Parker, who accompanied me, and who is a sea-faring man, thought her over-laden and unsafe, and refused to go on board, we remained with four others on board the packet. Not a drop, not a crumb, not a boat left, not a breath of wind, the tide left us long before we got to Caldishot [Calshot] Castle, and in this plight, like a log on the water, and no boat to be hailed to our assistance, we remained till *half-past two*, when a wherry from Cowes came to deliver us from thraldom at an expense of twelve shillings. . . .

In the last week the arrivals have been numerous, and all the large houses are now occupied. Croker and his family are in George Street. I met him on the pier last night and had a chat with him, and was introduced to his wife. Mr. Cooper, the brewer, has drowned himself in one of his own vats, and a gig last Tuesday bolted over the cliff close to Shanklin Chine, owing to the horse taking fright, but the

lady and gentleman were at the time walking up the
hill; so nobody was killed but horse and gig.   This
is all our news.

Yours affectionately,
H. SMITH.

SONNET INSCRIBED IN THE PORCH OF BINSTEAD CHURCH

Farewell, sweet Binstead, take a fond farewell
　From one unused to sight of Woods and Seas,
Amid the strife of Cities doomed to dwell,
　Yet roused to extacy by scenes like these :—
　Who could for ever sit beneath thy trees
Inhaling fragrance from the flowery dell ;
　Or, listening to the murmur of the breeze,
Gaze with delight on Ocean's awful swell.

Once more adieu ! nor deem that I profane
Thy sacred Porch, for while the Sabbath strain
　May fail to turn the Sinner from his ways,
There are impressions none can feel in vain,
　These are the wonders which perforce must raise
　The soul to God in silent faith and praise.

ANNA SEWARD.

In his matrimonial affairs Horace Smith seems
to have been fated not to please his father.   It is an
acknowledged axiom that people seldom practise
what they preach ; and Horace Smith, who at the
age of twenty-two had written a novel to illustrate
the evils of clandestine marriages,[1] was no exception
to this rule, for in the year 1818 he contracted a
second alliance, the circumstances of which did not
tend to heal the breach between him and his father,
who thus enters the fact in his journal :—

---

[1] *Trevanion, or Matrimonial Errors* (1801).

March 17th.—My son Horace was married this day (unknown to me at the time) to Miss Ford, a young lady originally from Devonshire. The first intimation given me of this marriage was by a letter from Horace dated from Cheltenham, for which place the young married couple set out immediately after the ceremony. I sincerely hope that the connection will prove a source of happiness to both! Horace has good understanding, and many amiable qualities: all of which, I have no doubt, he will continue to make a proper use. My two other sons still remain bachelors! I am sorry for it.

Miss Ford was a real west country beauty, with dark hair and eyes and lovely complexion, and her children inherited no small share of her personal attractions. Her three sisters were equally famed for their beauty, and one of them became the mother of the well-known E. M. Ward, R.A.

On this his second marriage, Horace Smith removed from Knightsbridge, and went still further away from town—to Elysium Row, Fulham, where he lived until the year 1821.

Pleasure-seeking denizens of Belgravia, driving *viâ* the King's road, Chelsea, towards Barn Elms or Ranelagh, to be present at a polo-match or other fashionable gathering, after passing Parson's Green along what is called the New King's Road, will notice an unpretending one-storied house with stone eagles guarding the entrance-gates, upon which are inscribed the words " Draycott Lodge." Here lives one of England's greatest painters, Mr. Holman Hunt. The ugly arches of the District Railway to

Putney cut diagonally through the western boundary of his grounds, and also through what was once a garden of some one and a half acres belonging to a comfortable three-storied tenement at the corner of an isolated terrace of about a dozen old-fashioned houses which constitute Elysium Row, Fulham, and date back to the year 1738. This corner house was Horace Smith's home from 1818 to 1821; and though now there seems little justification for its alluring title of "Elysium," in the "twenties" and "thirties" the Row was most prettily located with gardens, nursery grounds, and orchards in every direction, while for absolute retirement it might have been miles away in the country.

To this little retreat, with its pleasant old-fashioned garden, Horace Smith used to invite his intimate friends to "come down and rusticate;" and his eldest daughter remembers that, when she was a child, she was solemnly led into the garden by her father one lovely afternoon in July to take a peep at a fragile-looking and rather ill-dressed gentleman sitting "immantled in ambrosial dark," beneath a wide-spreading ilex. "Do you see that man?" said her father; "that's a poet." It was poor Keats, then fast nearing his end, whom Smith had enticed from Wentworth Place, Hampstead, to dine and spend a long day with him.

Dinner—at which James and Leonard Smith, Thomas Hill, "the literary city drysalter," [1] and one or two other kindred spirits, were also guests—was

[1] See Chapter VIII.

served earlier than usual to lengthen the exquisite
evening, and everything that could be thought of
to tempt the poet's feeble appetite was there. As
the Rev. Thomas Barham relates in *Ingoldsby
Legends* :—

> —in due time a banquet was placed on the board
> In the very best style, which implies in a word
> All the dainties the season (and King) could afford.
> Fricandeau, fricassées, Ducks and green peas,
> Cotelottes à l'Indienne, and chops à la Soubise.
>
> .   .   .   .
>
> Then the wines—round the circle how swiftly they went !
> Canary, Sack, Malaga, Malvoisie, Tent ;
> Old Hock from the Rhine, wine remarkably fine,
> Of the Champagne vintage, of seven ninety-nine ;
> Five cen'tries in bottle had made it divine !

Hill, as a special favour, had been allowed to send
over from his well-filled cellars at Sydenham a dozen
of Keats' favourite beverage, some quite undeniable
Chateau Margeaux ; and it was unanimously voted
that the company should drink their wine in the
open air.

In the course of a letter quoted in the *Life and
Letters of John Keats*, by Lord Houghton, the poet
says :—

I dined with Haydon the Sunday after you left,
and had a very pleasant day. I dined too (for I
have been out much lately) with Horace Smith, and
met his two brothers, with Hill and Kingston, and
one Du Bois. They only served to convince me
how superior humour is to wit in respect to enjoyment. These men say things which make one start
without making one feel ; they all know fashion-

ables; they have all a mannerism in their very eating and drinking, in their mere handling of a decanter. They talked of Kean and his low company. "Would I were with that company instead of yours," said I to myself! I know such like acquaintance will never do for me, and yet I am going to Reynolds' on Wednesday.

The Smiths had made both Shelley's and Keats' acquaintance at Leigh Hunt's house at Hampstead.

In the year 1816 [says Horace Smith] at the house of our mutual friend, Leigh Hunt, then residing at Hampstead, I made my first personal acquaintance with this remarkable man [Shelley]. Punishments disproportionately severe always excite sympathy for their victim, rather than condemnation of his offence. In the midst of all the reckless enthusiasm that prompted Shelley, like a moral Quixote, to run atilt at whatever he considered an abuse, I felt convinced that his aims were pure and lofty, that he was solely animated by an impassioned philanthropy in the prosecution of which he was ready to sacrifice his life ; and such being his motives, I thought it most cruel and unjust that he should be proscribed as a reprobate, and be made the butt of the most malignant invectives. Having long compassionated him as a grievously over-punished man, and having recently read his poems with a profound admiration of his genius, I had looked forward to our first meeting with no common interest. He was not in the cottage when I arrived, but I was introduced to another young poet of no common talent—Keats, who was destined, alas! ere many years had flown, to meet the same premature death, and to lie in the same cemetery with Shelley beneath the ruined walls of Rome. Keats has been described by Coleridge in his *Table Talk* as a "loose, slack, not well-dressed youth," and to an observant eye his looks and his attenuated frame already foreshadowed the consumption that had marked him for its prey.

In a short time Shelley was announced, and I beheld a fair, freckled, blue-eyed, light-haired, delicate-looking person, whose countenance was serious and thoughtful; whose stature would have been rather tall had he carried himself upright; whose earnest voice, though never loud, was somewhat unmusical. Manifest as it was that his pre-occupied mind had no thought to spare for the modish adjustment of his fashionably-made clothes, it was impossible to doubt, even for a moment, that you were gazing upon a *gentleman*; a first impression which subsequent observation never failed to confirm, even in the most exalted acceptation of the term, as indicating one that is gentle, generous, accomplished, brave. "Never did a more finished gentleman than Shelley step across a drawing-room," was the remark of Lord Byron ; and Captain Medwin, writing after several years' acquaintance with Shelley, and an extensive intercourse with the polite world, thus expresses a similar opinion :—" I can affirm that Shelley was almost the only example I have yet found that was never wanting, even to the most minute particular, in the infinite and various observances of pure, entire, and perfect gentility."

Two or three more friends presently arriving, the discourse, under the inspiration of our facetious host, assumed a playful and bantering character, which Shelley by his smiles appeared to enjoy, but in which he took no part ; and I then surmised, as I found afterwards, that it might be said of him, as of Demosthenes, *Non displicuisse illi jocos sed non contigisse.* Young as he was, a mind so deeply impressed with the sense of his own wrongs, and sobered by his solemn vow to redress, if possible, the wrongs of his fellow-creatures, was naturally more disposed to seriousness than to levity. The weather being fine, the whole party sallied forth to stroll upon the Heath, where I attached myself to Shelley, and gradually drawing him apart, enjoyed with him a long and uninterrupted conversation. Well may I say enjoyed, for to talk with a man of extensive reading and undoubted genius, who felt such a devout reverence for what he believed to be the truth, and was so fearless in its assertion that he laid his whole many-thoughted mind bare before you, was indeed a treat to one whose chief social intercourse had been with minds all stamped in the same established educational mould, or conforming to it with that plastic conventional hypocrisy which the worldly-wise find so exceedingly convenient. My companion, who, as he became interested in his subjects, talked much and eagerly, seemed to me a psychological curiosity, infinitely more curious than Coleridge's Kubla Khan, to which strange vision he made reference. His principal discourse, however, was of Plato, for whose character, writings, and philosophy he expressed an unbounded admiration, dwelling much on the similarity of portions of his doctrines to those of the New Testament, and on the singular accordance between the scriptural narrative of the birth of Christ and the miraculous nativity attributed to Plato, 420 years before our era. On my confession that I could not manage so subtle a thinker in the original Greek, but that I possessed Dacier's translation, Shelley replied, " Then you have seen him by moonlight, instead of in the sunshine ; the closeness of his logic and the splendour of his diction cannot be transferred into another language."

The friendship between Shelley and Horace Smith

was very sincere. "For the author of *Rejected Addresses*," says Lady Shelley, "Shelley had the most affectionate regard, a regard fully deserved by that excellent and warmed-hearted wit." This feeling was thoroughly reciprocated, and when Shelley left England in 1818, never to return, he, with the utmost confidence in Smith's integrity and discretion, placed his pecuniary affairs in his hands.

But before dealing with this interesting period of Horace Smith's life, it is necessary to revert to his brother James.

CHAPTER XIV

The Board of Ordnance, its officers and functions—The
"Assistant to the Solicitor" and his duties—Emoluments of
the office—On Ordnance Parliamentary "preserve"—Retirement of Robert Smith from business, and from the post of
"Assistant to the Solicitor"—James Smith appointed "Assistant to the Solicitor."

THE important State Department with which
James Smith and his father were intimately associated for periods of twenty-seven and thirty-seven
years respectively, deserves more than a passing
notice.

As its title implies, the special function of the
Ordnance has always been the construction, provision, and charge of every kind of projectile imple-
ment of war. The splendidly equipped workshops
of Woolwich, Enfield, Birmingham, and Waltham
Abbey, attest the modern development of a system
that has lasted since artillery and small arms came
into use; but in the Smiths' time the Board looked
after other important matters, now in the province
of the Royal Engineers; viz. the acquisition of lands,
and the construction of forts, for the defence of the
nation during times of war.

The original "Instructions" for the government of the Office of Ordnance were entered in an old folio book of Charles II.'s time, and kept in the Ordnance Office. Robert Smith had a copy of this book made for his own private use, soon after he became "Assistant to the Solicitor" of the Ordnance; and it was from this source, not accessible to any outsider, that he was able to give the following account of the Board and of his own official duties, which I believe will be new to most of my readers.

The Office of Ordnance [he says] is governed by a Master-General and a Board under him, all separately appointed by Letters Patent, to hold during pleasure. The Board consists of five "Principal Officers"—the Lieutenant-General, the Surveyor-General, the Clerk of the Ordnance, the Store-Keeper, and the Clerk of the Deliveries, any three of whom form a "Board." The Master-General and Lieutenant-General are each by virtue of his office in two capacities — the · one military, the other civil.

In their military capacity, the Master-General is Commander-in-Chief; and the Lieutenant-General second in command over the artillery and engineers.

In his civil capacity the Master-General is entrusted with the entire management and control over the whole Ordnance Department. He can do alone any act, which can otherwise, if he does not interpose, be done by the Board. The Board make contracts and agreements for the purchase of stores and performance of services, and direct the issue of money and stores. They also order, sign, execute, transact, and perform every other matter incident to the office of the Ordnance.

What these " matters " were may be learnt from Robert Smith's account.

The solicitor to the Ordnance [he says] receives his appointment from the Master-General by warrant, and is borne upon the " Establishment " at a salary of £300 per annum. Properly speaking, he is the " Counsel " of the Ordnance, and is always a Barrister-at-Law, and although in official proceedings he is styled the " Solicitor," the duties of that situation are executed by a practising solicitor, called in office language the " Assistant to the Solicitor." He also is appointed by the Master-General, though not by warrant, but by a minute of the Board. He is not upon the " Establishment," neither does he receive a salary, and he is removable at the pleasure of the Master-General or the Board. His duties are various. He prepares all contracts, agreements, and other instruments that are directed by the Master-General or the Board. He solicits all Acts of Parliament for the purchase or exchange of lands for the use of the Ordnance, and for making compensation to the proprietors and occupiers of the lands taken, and then makes out and transmits to the Surveyor-General's office, the several bills for the sums awarded to each proprietor. He likewise conducts all prosecutions of whatever kind, and brings and defends all such actions and suits as are previously directed by the Master-General or Board, conferring with the " Solicitor " on all necessary occasions. He makes written reports to the Master-General and Board upon a variety of subjects, such as the Crown's title to houses and lands placed under the charge of the Ordnance; the boundaries of such lands, and all trespasses and encroachments made upon any of them; the liability of Ordnance lands and buildings to the payment of tithes, taxes, etc.; the liability of the several officers of the Ordnance who occupy such lands to the payment of personal taxes, etc.; the liability of Ordnance wagons and carriages to the payment of turnpike and other tolls; as also the artillery horses whether attached or not attached to guns and carriages; or whether proceeding under march routes, or otherwise; questions arising out of the Mutiny, or other Act of Parliament, relative to fraud, embezzlement, the enlistment, desertion, pay, subsistence, etc., of the privates of the artillery, etc. etc.

To enable himself to perform these and the other duties attached to his situation, he must be possessed of a tolerable law library, particularly of the statutes at large. He keeps plans or copies of plans whenever he is able of the Ordnance lands and fortifications throughout the kingdom and abroad. He keeps abstracts of or references to the several Acts of Parliament, and deeds under which the lands are purchased. He makes a digest of the whole, and of the laws relative to Ordnance matters for his own particular use. By means of this digest, and of an alphabetical list of former references and reports, arranged according to place and subject-matter, he furnishes himself with ready information upon the several points that are brought under his notice. For his attendance on the Master-General and Board as the "Solicitor" at the office at Westminster and at the Tower, he is allowed the yearly sum of £100, which he charges in his half-yearly bills. For preparing deeds and contracts, conducting prosecutions and actions, and transacting all other law business, he charges in the ordinary manner of solicitors, and for travelling he is allowed 1s. 3d. per mile for chaise hire, and £1 1s. 0d. per day during his attendance from London when ordered by the Master-General or Board.

These charges, "in the ordinary manner of solicitors," during the course of Robert Smith's tenancy of his office came to a notable sum. In his journal he says : "As a matter of private curiosity, I have given the annual amount of my Ordnance bills from the time I first entered upon my office in 1782[1] down to the end of the present year, 1818." "The profits," he naïvely adds, "have not been inconsiderable."

For the thirty-seven years the total was £62,000, and from 1805 to 1818—the war years—the bills averaged £3,400 per annum.

Not long after James Smith had been admitted as an attorney, he was made acquainted by personal experience with the system of "close boroughs" that prevailed before the Reform Bill of 1832. Queenborough was considered a strict Government "preserve," and its representatives were usually *recommended* to the voters by the Ordnance and Admiralty Department turn and turn about. On the occasion referred to, it was the turn of Robert Smith's office to recommend a candidate, and as the Duke of Richmond, the then Master-General, desired Mr. Rogers, the Secretary to the Board, to get in, that gentleman offered himself, and Robert Smith was requested to be on the spot, to give his professional advice should it be deemed necessary.

Accordingly, he proceeded to Sheerness with his son James, and put himself in contact with the Ordnance officers there, who were thoroughly ac-

---

[1] See Chapter III.

quainted with the political ground. The whole
affair was delightfully simple, as no other candidate
dreamed of offering himself; and Mr. Secretary
Rogers was without opposition elected as the repre-
sentative of the free and enlightened burgesses of
Queenborough.

The termination of war after the battle of
Waterloo brought about an important change in
Robert Smith's affairs, and hastened his determina-
tion to retire altogether from business.

The late peace [he says], though a blessing in
itself, must produce a great diminution of my
Ordnance and other business, which has occasioned
me to think of quitting business entirely in favour
of my son James. This I shall probably do at the
end of the present year [1818] should both our lives
be spared. When the measure shall be finally
determined on, James must endeavour to prevail
on the Master-General, Lord Mulgrave (who has for
some time honoured him with his particular notice)
to consent to my son being *sole* assistant to the
Ordnance Solicitor.[1] This will fix him in the
situation. . . . My intention with respect to my son
James cannot be accomplished for the present. On
account of declining years and health, the Earl of
Mulgrave signified his wish to resign his office of
Master-General of the Ordnance. This he shortly
afterwards did; and in December, Field-Marshal
the Duke of Wellington was gazetted in his room.

But though all application on the subject of
changing must be postponed until the new Master-
General shall have completed his office arrangements
(whatever they may be), the other part of our

---

[1] See Chapter IX.

L

design, that of my relinquishing business,[1] has been arranged between me and my son—my son, however, to receive the *whole profits*.

On this day, therefore, December 31st, 1818, my son provided himself with a new set of books; and my name was withdrawn from the office doors.

In the course of the following year, the Duke of Wellington having done me the honour to ask my opinion upon some point of law that was connected with his official character of Master-General, I conceived this a favourable opportunity to make known to his Grace my wishes concerning my son.

To these applications I received a favourable answer; that from the Duke's private secretary was as follows :—

Office of Ordnance,
July 20th, 1819.

Sir,

I am directed by the Master-General to acknowledge the receipt of your letter of the 11th instant, and to acquaint you that his Grace has given orders that the name of your son may be allowed to stand singly, as Assistant to the Ordnance Solicitor, agreeably with your request.

I am, Sir,
Your most obedient,
Humble servant,
F. B. HERVEY.

ROBERT SMITH, ESQ.,
   18 *Austin Friars.*

Thus my wishes in this respect are now accomplished, and I rejoice at it. The situation of "Assistant to the Solicitor" of so distinguished a public Board as that of the Ordnance, besides being

---

[1] Robert Smith was then seventy-one years of age.

honourable to a professional man, is the source of emolument, especially in time of war, as the amounts of my bills for a number of years will show. But it is one that requires attention, and in that attention I hope my son will not be wanting.

James Smith did not belie the confidence reposed in him by his father. His literary work was never allowed to interfere with his official duties. Until almost the day of his death, in 1839, as grave as a judge, and looking as if a joke or witty saying were an impossible perpetration on his part, he sat in his office at No. 18 Austin Friars, and subsequently at 27 Craven Street, Strand, surrounded by tin boxes, heavy volumes of statutes, and all the dusty " properties " of a solicitor's office, as if sticking to business were the one and only aim of life.

His situation as Assistant to the Solicitor, in course of time, became a purely nominal one. Long years of peace followed his appointment.

> " No war or battle's sound
> Was heard the world around."

Martello Towers began to fall into a state of dilapidation; luxuriant growths of herbage sprang up on ramparts that once echoed with the tread of watchful sentinels; the few pieces of artillery that were suffered to remain slowly rusted and sank to the ground from their rotting carriages; lambs gambolled at the muzzles of the harmless cannon; and all along our coasts Landseer's *Peace* became a living reality. From Tilbury to distant Berry

Head, and yet more remote Pendennis Castle, the sites of our national defences became peaceful pastures for cattle or the resort of picnickers.

Yet James Smith remained at his post in a State Department which was once essential to the safety of the nation, but whose *raison d'être* had disappeared.

CHAPTER XV

1821—1825

Horace Smith and Shelley (*continued*)—Horace Smith's connection with the Scott-Christie duel—Mr. Andrew Lang's remarks thereon—The death of Keats—Horace Smith retires from business, and decides to visit Shelley in Italy—Letter to his sister Clara—Is detained at Paris by ill-health of his wife —Letters to Cyrus Redding.

Horace Smith, at the opening of the year 1818, met Shelley for the last time, when the poet was in London making arrangements for his departure from England—a step determined upon, partly for the purpose of finding a milder climate in the south of Europe, and also because of his dread that Lord Chancellor Eldon might give effect to some hints he had thrown out in Court respecting the custody of Shelley's infant son by his second wife.

Under a Chancery decree, Shelley had already been bereft of the offspring of his earlier marriage, and had been compelled to set aside £200 for their maintenance out of the £1000 per annum allowed him by his father, Sir Timothy Shelley. This income was regularly paid until March 1821, when, to the astonishment of Horace Smith—his financial agent at that period—it was abruptly stopped. Horace at once wrote to his friend in Italy as follows :—

March 28*th*, 1821.

My dear Shelley,

I called to-day at Brookes and Co. for your money as usual, and was not a little surprised to be told that they had received notice *not to advance anything more on your account, as the payment to them would in future be discontinued;* but they could give me no information why the alteration had occurred, or whether you were apprised of it. Perhaps you have been, though you could hardly have failed to mention it to me.   But I will call again, and endeavour to get some solution of the apparent mystery.   Meantime, if you are in any straits you had better draw on me at the Stock Exchange for what you want.   I would remit you, but that, knowing that you are not over regular in matters of business, you may, perhaps, have made new arrangements for your money, and, through inadvertency, omitted to apprise me. . . .[1]

Burning with indignation at what he conceived to be a conspiracy against poor Shelley, Horace Smith, restraining himself with great effort, wrote, amongst many other letters, a very temperate one to Sir Timothy (whom he felt sure had no participation in the plot), asking for an explanation ; and, receiving a courteous reply, wrote to his friend :—

London, April 19*th*, 1821.

Dear Shelley,

I wrote you on the 17th inst., with a budget of letters relative to this lawsuit; and

[1] *Shelley Memorials*, by Lady Shelley.

annexed I hand you a copy of Sir Timothy's reply, received yesterday. I am most glad that I wrote to him, for it turns out that my conjecture that he was unacquainted with the affair is correct, and that the law proceedings were literally *cooked up* by the lawyers. It appears a most scandalous liberty in Mr. Whitton, not only to make your father a party without his privity, but actually to stop your money on his own authority. I have this day written a few lines to Sir Timothy, stating that I had seen a letter at Wright's from Whitton, certainly *implying* that he *had* communicated with Sir T., and I leave the lawyer to get out of this dilemma as well as he can. Of Whitton I know nothing; but I seem to dislike him by instinct. Having written you so many letters lately, I have nothing further to say, than to repeat the pleasant assurance that I shall this summer or autumn take you by the hand, when we can talk over all these matters.

I am, my dear Shelley,
Ever yours,
HORATIO SMITH.

If the Fates had permitted the " taking in hand," the man of business might have succeeded in keeping the poet's money matters in order, and have saved him much worry and petty annoyance. Horace Smith always did what he could to help Shelley in the way of temporary advances and loans, which substantial proof of friendship was fully appreciated.

" It's odd," Shelley once remarked, " that the only truly generous person I ever knew who had money to be generous with, should be a stockbroker." And when Horace Smith sent him a copy of his book, entitled *Amarynthus the Nympholet, a Pastoral Drama,*

With other Poems, Shelley exclaimed, " And he writes poetry too ; he writes poetry and pastoral dramas, and yet knows how to make money, and does make it, and is still generous."

In his letter to Shelley of March the 28th, 1821, Horace Smith thus refers to the Scott duel :—

Poor Scott ! what a melancholy termination ! and how perfectly unnecessary ! Christie and the two seconds will surrender and take their trial at the Old Bailey Session next month. We are raising a subscription for Scott's family.

John Scott was the editor of the *London Magazine*, and in the November number of 1820 there appeared a long article written by himself, bringing forward serious charges against the managers of *Blackwood's Magazine*,[1] and this was followed up in the December number by a more vigorous onslaught, entitled *The Mohawk Magazine*. Naturally, the result was retaliation on the part of *Blackwood's*, which took the form of anonymous attacks on Scott, who, by guess-work only, attributed their authorship to John Gibson Lockhart. A bitter controversy ensued, and finally merged into an acrimonious dispute between Scott and Lockhart's friend, Mr. Christie. Scott challenged Christie, and a duel by moonlight was fought on Friday night, February the 16th, 1821, at Chalk Farm, when, after an interchange of shots without effect, there was a second encounter, and

[1] Dubbed by Sir Walter Scott, " The Mother of Mischief."

poor Scott received a wound to which he succumbed in a few days.

Scott had asked Horace Smith to act as his second, in case a personal encounter with Lockhart or Christie should take place. So one night, he called upon him at No. 1 Elysium Row, Fulham, to discuss the subject. Horace Smith did his best to dissuade his bellicose friend from resorting to physical force, and made him plainly understand that under no circumstances would he bo a party to a duel. His views on duelling are here set forth in his own words :—

A duellist is a moral coward, seeking to hide the pusillanimity of his mind by affecting a corporeal courage. Instead of discharging a pistol, the resort of bullies and bravoes, the really brave soul will dare to discharge its duty to God and man by refusing to break the laws of both. He is the true hero who can exclaim in the sublime language of Voltaire, *Je crains Dieu, cher Abner, et je n'ai d'autre crainte.*

Scott could not have applied to a more unsuitable man than Horace Smith, as the latter was quite unacquainted with the rules and nice points of etiquette connected with duelling, and at no stage of the squabble did he give Scott any warrant for stating that he had consented to act as his second. He published in 1821 an explanation of his own part in this sad transaction, and in 1847 he referred to it in his *Recollections of John Scott.*

Mr. Andrew Lang, the Universal Provider of the

literary world, seeking, like the busy bee, to gather honey from every opening flower, must needs alight on the grave of Horace Smith. To quit metaphor, Mr. Lang, in several bewildering passages in his *Life and Letters of John Gibson Lockhart*,[1] referring to these explanations of Horace Smith, goes out of his way to accuse him of a gross misstatement of facts, because he—Mr. Lang—*imagines* he has discovered some inconsistencies in Smith's statements, one of which was made six-and-twenty years after the other!

Keats once wrote:—" The Scotch cannot manage themselves at all; they want imagination, and that is why they are so fond of Hogg, who has so little of it."

Mr. Andrew Lang is gifted with the supposed missing faculty in an unusual degree; but, in his arraignment of Horace Smith, it has led him astray. Surely the eulogy of a Lockhart does not necessitate the calumniation of a most honourable man, who has been dead for the last fifty years! Such conduct is hardly worthy of one who hails from the " Borders," where of old " life was held of light account, but honour was highly reckoned."

On the night of February the 23rd, 1821, Keats died of consumption at Rome, where he had been tenderly nursed by Mr. Severn, the artist. The news was published in London on the 25th of March; and it is supposed that Shelley first heard of it by a letter from Horace Smith, which, dating from Fulham, March 28th, 1821, contains the following :—

[1] 1896-97.

You never said anything of Keats, who I see (in *The Examiner*, March 25th) died at Rome under lamentable circumstances.

But as Shelley at the time of Keats's death was living at Pisa, barely two hundred miles distant from Rome, it seems incredible that he should obtain his first intelligence of the sad event from England. Shelley's letter to Severn, dated November the 29th, 1821, proves nothing either one way or the other.

Shelley sent a copy of *Adonais* to Horace Smith, who, in acknowledging it, says :—

He (Mr. Gisborne) handed me also your poem on Keats's death, which I like, with the exception of the *Cenci*, better than anything you have written, finding in it a great deal of fancy, feeling, and beautiful language, with none of the metaphysical abstraction which is so apt to puzzle the uninitiated in your productions. It reminded me of *Lycidas*, more from the similarity of the subject than anything in the mode of treatment.

Shelley made a point of sending a copy of each of his works to Horace Smith as they came out. He writes from Leghorn to Mr. Ollier, his publisher— “Whenever I publish, send copies of my books to the following people for me—Mr. Hunt, Mr. Godwin, Mr. Hogg, Mr. Peacock, Mr. Keats, Mr. Thomas Moore, Mr. Horace Smith, and Lord Byron ” (at Murray's); and again, from Pisa, he writes to him— “ Allow me particularly to request you to send copies of whatever I publish to Horace Smith.”

In a letter, September 4th, 1820, Horace Smith

expresses to Shelley his opinion of two of his works :—

I got from Ollier last week a copy of the *Prometheus Unbound*, which is a most original, grand, and occasionally sublime work, evincing, in my opinion, a higher order of talent than any of your previous productions; and yet, contrary to your own estimation, I must say I prefer the *Cenci*, because it contains a deep and sustained human interest, of which we feel a want in the other. Prometheus himself certainly touches us nearly; but we see very little of him after his liberation; and, though I have no doubt it will be more admired than anything you have written, I question whether it will be so much read as the *Cenci*. . . .

On the 6th of April, 1821, a daughter was born to Horace Smith at Fulham. She was christened Rosalind, after the heroine of Shelley's beautiful poem *Rosalind and Helen*, which had been begun at Marlow, and completed at the baths of Lucca at the special request of Mrs. Shelley. The next day Horace Smith wrote to Shelley at Pisa :—

As affairs (political) seem all settling in Italy, I resume my intention of taking you by the hand. My wife has a daughter, and is doing perfectly well. I expect we shall be ready to start in July or August. Will that be too hot, and would you preferably recommend October ?

Horace Smith's ambition was to make literature a profession, and about this time he, with wonderful self-restraint, carried into effect a resolution he had

made to retire from the Stock Exchange, however
great the temptation to the contrary might be, as
soon as he had amassed a fortune sufficient to ensure
him a modest independency.   On the very day that
he considered this aspiration was reached, he sent in
his resignation to the committee without a moment's
hesitation.   His retirement turned out to be a lucky
thing, for in the panic period of 1825–1826, when
no fewer than 770 banks stopped payment, the fruit
of all his labours might, like that of thousands, have
been swept away.

Before settling down, however, he determined to
visit Italy.   We read in his father's journal :—

June 12*th*, 1821.—My son Horace has been for
some time desirous of visiting Florence for a couple
of years, and on this day, he, his wife, three children,[1]
and a female servant, came to town preparatory to
their setting out for Dover.   His reasons for the
measure are, economy, pleasure, and the acquisition
of French and Italian literature.   I wish he may
not be disappointed in any of these views; but I
cannot say that I like the scheme.

Arrived at Paris, Horace wrote the following letter
to his sister Clara :—

36 *Chautereine, Chaussée d'Antin, Paris,*
July 22nd, 1821.

My dear Clara,
          I should have written to you sooner, but
that I doubted whether they would forward letters
to you at the Isle of Wight, where I suppose you

---

[1] Eliza, Horatio, and Rosalind.

are enjoying walks and woods and solitude, while I am rambling amid the bustle of the crowded Boulevards, or the classical retreats of the Champs Elysées. I am delighted with Paris, and have hardly been a day without encountering some English acquaintance. On board the packet, I heard a gentleman laying down the law somewhat authoritatively, and informing us that, owing to the high wind when he last crossed, he lost a *gnat* (no great loss thought I), and in talking of the inns at Boulogne, he depreciated all the understandings of the place, by maintaining stoutly that there was not *a nous* in the town. This proved to be Adelaide's [1] quondam neighbour, Mr. Prestwidge, with whom I renewed my acquaintance, and from whom we experienced the greatest civility, both on board the packet and in Paris, where he was sufficiently at home to be enabled to show us some of the lions.

We stayed at Calais two or three days to recruit, and posted hither, sleeping at Abbeville and Beauvais, passing through dull, desolate, moated, and drawbridged towns, all obviously built before the Flood ; and a flat, treeless, hedgeless, uninteresting country, with here and there a shabby, wild, grass-grown château, looking very prison-like or mad-housey, and now and then a scarecrow straggling village, or cluster of mud-hovels, till we got into an apple country, where there were plenty of trees, but not a single apple, the crop having utterly failed. Little variations occurred in these features till we got to the very barriers of Paris, when all at once we seemed to have leapt forward about a thousand years, the houses presenting modern classical elevations, all built of white stone, extremely lofty, magnificent, and impressive, the streets wide and handsome, gay carriages flitting about, and a smart,

---

[1] His sister.

numerous, and noisy population succeeding to the
stagnation of life through which we had passed.
We went to the Hôtel Maurice, an immense place
(140 bedrooms), so full of English that we could
only get accommodated by putting up a temporary
bed for Horace. Next day we put the children to
school with a friend of Sophia's settled here, and
most happy we were to get rid of Horace, who kept
us in perpetual fear of his being lost or run over, or
both, as he was perfectly wild with the novelty of
the scene.

Opposite to the back of our hotel is the Tuilleries
and Louvre, with all its far-famed contents—the
gardens with their Frenchified but very grand
succession of statues, ponds, shady walks, gates and
arches leading to the Bois de Boulogne and the
Champs Elysées, where you may fancy yourself in
Abyssinia—and on the other side of our street we
walked to the Palais Royal, with its noble square
surrounded with innumerable shops, and refreshed
with trees and a handsome *jet d'eau* in the centre.
To see all this within five minutes' walk of our
residence, in the midst of Paris, certainly struck us
all of a heap. But what pleases me most is the
abundance of gardens and flowers, all as green and
fresh as a pickled herring; artificial flowers inside
the house, and real ones outside, seems to be a
passion with the French, and I like them for it.

We went one day to dine at Grignon's, a famous
restaurateur, but Sophia could not be reconciled to
the dishes or the publicity, and we sat down once or
twice at the *table d'hôte* at Maurice's, generally from
thirty to forty, and all English; but the place was
so expensive and noisy that we have moved into
these lodgings, small but comfortable, for which
we pay 200 f. a month, and where, to the amazement of those who know it, we have determined on

dining at home occasionally, which to a Parisian seems perfectly ridiculous.   We have bought a *batterie de cuisine* for three or four francs, and enjoyed to-day some stewed veal and peas, *au naturel*, as the Frenchman says with a sneer when you decline kickshaws; and for wine, I am quite content with the lowest price, which is 15 sous or $7\frac{1}{2}d.$ per bottle. I like all their wines except champagne.

We spent a most delightful morning at the *Cimetière* of Père la Chaise (whither I must go again), and the sight of which, with its exquisitely tasteful and picturesque tombs, embowered in trees, shrubs, and flowers, with their simple and feeling inscriptions, was quite sufficient in my mind to disprove the assertion that the French are deficient in sentiment and affection. They come constantly to hang garlands and crosses on the tombs of their relations, and to refresh the flowers with which they are planted, for which purpose water-pots are left in many of the enclosures ;—not a flower was picked— not a stone scribbled—not a figure defaced, and inside most of the railings are chairs for the friends to come occasionally and weep in, an office in which we saw more than one engaged, and the day after our visit a man blew out his brains on the tomb of his wife ! There may be some parade in all this, but I am convinced there is a good deal of feeling, and I am glad I came here, were it only on account of Père la Chaise.

About five minutes' walk from our present lodgings are Tivoli Gardens, where we have been roaming, and of which some parts are perfectly secluded and rural. I think I shall subscribe for the morning walks. We have warm baths in the building for fifteen-pence, and are near all the gaiety if we like, but have yet been to no theatre. Once we have walked through the Louvre, and to-morrow we are going to the Luxembourg. . . . I shall stay here two months longer, and shall write to you again.

Your affectionate brother,

H. SMITH.

Horace Smith's plans, however, received an unwelcome upheaval. He had intended joining Shelley in Italy, and had, in fact, sent on all his heavy luggage to Leghorn by sea; but the weather in Paris became intensely hot, and his wife, who was singularly intolerant of warm weather, became so ill that she could not travel further. It was a great disappointment to Horace Smith, who wrote to his friend as follows :—

Paris, August 30th, 1821.

MY DEAR SHELLEY,

The disappointment and vexation by the sudden overthrow of all my long-cherished plans is not less painful to me than the cause of it is distressing. I have also to regret the trouble I have unnecessarily given you, and the disappointment (for I have vanity enough to believe you will think it such) to which I have exposed you.

In the midst of these more serious annoyances, I have hardly time to attend to the petty inconveniences to which we must be subjected by wintering here without any of our clothes, books, or comforts, all of which have been shipped to Leghorn. I think of taking a house at Versailles, but at present I am quite unsettled in everything. When I have arranged my plans I shall write to you again, till when, and always,

I am, my dear Shelley,

Your very sincere and disappointed friend,

HORATIO SMITH.

Eventually, Horace Smith took an *appartement* in the Hôtel des Reservoirs, Versailles, which he furnished, and from which he dates some very interesting letters to his friend, Cyrus Redding.[1]

15 Rue des Reservoirs,
Versailles, 1821.

DEAR SIR,

I have been a good deal occupied in changing and furnishing my lodgings, and have had but little time for writing, and I have no access to books, as mine have not yet been returned from Italy, but they are on the route, and I hope to keep you supplied with admissible matter. Your account of the sale is gratifying, and I should think must be satisfactory to Mr. Colburn, even should it not advance further, though his heavy expenses must demand a wide circulation.

That you should not receive much novelty is natural enough, for who the deuce can hit upon anything new, when half the world are racking their brains to do the same? The magazine certainly improves, and as far as I can judge from those who see it here and at Galignani's, gives great satisfaction.

I had heard of poor Leigh Hunt's adventure. I hope to heaven he will get out to Italy somehow, for this is the very crisis of his fate, not only as it may remove him from all the devilry with which he has been so long beleaguered, but that it may place him within the powerful influence of Lord Byron. His non-arrival has occasioned a whole chapter of embarrassments at Pisa, where his lordship has

---

[1] Cyrus Redding's *Fifty Years' Recollections*. From 1821 to 1830 Redding was the working editor of the *New Monthly Magazine*, of which Campbell, the poet, was the nominal chief. He was also the author of several works.

appropriated a part of his palace for his reception, and has matured the other plans for which he was wanted. What these are I do not exactly know, but Shelley is only interested as an occasional contributor, and none of the party will dream of heretical, still less of atheistical theories, in a periodical publication which would be inevitably suppressed. Though Shelley is my most particular friend, I regret the imprudence of his early publications on more points than one, but as I know him to possess the most exalted virtues, and find in others who promulgate the most startling theories most amiable traits, I learn to be liberal towards abstract speculations, which, not exercising any baneful influence on their authors' lives, are still less likely to corrupt others. Truth is great, and will prevail—that is my motto, and I would, therefore, leave everything unshackled —what is true will stand, and what is false ought to fall, whatever be the consequences. Ought we not to feel ashamed that Lucretius could publish his book in the teeth of an established religion, while martyrs are groaning in perpetual imprisonment for expressing a conscientious dissent from Christianity?

Human punishments and rewards will generally be found sufficient for human control, so far as it can really be controlled. Jack Ketch is the most effectual devil, and the gallows the most practical hell; the theoretical ones, which could not deter from crime, are seldom much thought of by the rogue, until these most tangible ones are about to punish him.

John Hunt is a fine-spirited fellow, and I beg to be kindly remembered to him.

I am delighted with France, particularly Versailles, and do not think of an immediate return. There is very good English society here.

I never look at the magazine without wondering

how you get through the labour, which I fear is too heavy to allow you any trip to this side, where I should be most happy to see you. I have taken apartments and furnished them myself, which I find a much cheaper plan.

I am always, Dear Sir,
Yours very faithfully,
HORATIO SMITH.

15 Rue des Reservoirs,
Versailles, 1822.

Many thanks, my dear Sir, for your acceptable letter of the 21st July, handed to me by Mr. Crowe, who passed a day with me, very agreeably on my part, and to whom I should have been happy to show further civilities, but that the shortness of his stay prevented it. He seems a very intelligent, unassuming man, and I should much like to join him in his excursion, as I still hope to visit the classic regions if I can get my wife's health re-established.

I understand the paragraph to which you allude in *Blackwood* is an ill-natured one towards me, and it does not contain an atom of truth, as I knew nothing of the projected work at Pisa, and certainly shall not contribute a line, even were I requested, which I have never been, so that if you have an opportunity of contradicting the assertion, I will thank you to do so. Even Shelley, the only one of the party with whom I am in communication, has no share in the domiciliation of Hunt, nor has he pledged himself to any literary participation in the plans, whatever they may be. From him I have lately heard of Hunt's arrival at Genoa on his way to Leghorn, Lord Byron's present residence, where he is amusing himself with a beautiful yacht, which he has just had built at Genoa.

Two more cantos of *Don Juan* are finished, at

which I for one feel little pleasure, for I hate all productions, whatever be their talent, which present disheartening and degrading views of human nature. This is, in my opinion, worse than impiety, though it is the latter imputation which will destroy its popularity in England, almost the only country existing in Europe where bigotry retains its omnipotence.   You did well, however, to strike out anything in any contribution calculated to give offence, even to particular professions, for what Johnson said of the drama is applicable to magazines:—"Those who live to please, must please to live."

I suppose a similar feeling suppressed my final journal of a tourist, where my summary of the French national character is probably deemed too favourable, though I do think the English might be benefited by hearing something about the virtues of their neighbours, instead of having their blind hostility aggravated by lying diatribes.   A man of four or five hundred a year keeps a cabriolet and horse which would be hooted and pelted in England, but they answer his purpose, convey him to his friends, and give him air, pleasure, and variety.   All these an Englishman foregoes if he cannot do it in style, and mount a lacky behind in a blue jacket with gold lace.   Pride, filthy pride!—pride is the besetting sin of England, and, like most other sins, brings its own punishment, by converting existence into a struggle, and environing it with gloom and heart-burning.

I am exactly of your feeling—I can live comfortably under an arbitrary foreign government, while I was perpetually annoyed at home by the tyranny and mismanagement of men whose talents were despicable. I felt as if I was constantly kicked by jackasses— here I do not trouble my head about the French, and only endeavour to forget the English ministers.

Your information about a paper will be most valuable if we get permission to establish one, of which I have no expectation. We have a Paris English magazine, to which Galignani has started an opposition. I occasionally give it a lift with my pen, but neither of the works answer, nor do I much expect they will.   Adieu.

My dear Sir,
Yours very faithfully,
HORATIO SMITH.

CHAPTER XVI

1821—1825

Horace Smith receives the news of Shelley's death—His
personal recollections of Shelley, and his estimate of the poet's
character.

It was when residing at Versailles that the intelligence of Shelley's death reached Horace Smith.
It was a terrible blow to him, and for years afterwards he could hardly speak of it without emotion.
I think I cannot do better than devote this chapter
to Horace Smith's recollections of his poet-friend.[1]

The fatal catastrophe [he says] was made known
to me by the following letter from a mutual friend[2]
then residing in Italy:—

'Pisa, July 25th, 1822.

'I trust that the first news of the dreadful calamity
which has befallen us here will have been broken to
you by report, otherwise I shall come upon you with
a most painful abruptness; but Shelley, my divine-
minded friend—the friend of the universe—he has
perished at sea! He was in a boat with his friend
Captain Williams, going from Leghorn to Lerici,

[1] *A Greybeard's Gossip about his Literary Acquaintances.*

[2] Leigh Hunt.

when a storm arose, and it is supposed the boat
must have foundered. . . . God bless him ! I cannot help thinking of him as if he were still alive, so
unearthly he always appeared to me, and so seraph-
ical a thing of the elements; and this is what all his
friends say. But what we all feel your own heart
will tell you. . . . Our dear friend was passionately
fond of the sea, and has been heard to say he should
like it to be his death-bed.'

And in a subsequent letter from Albaro, near
Genoa, the same party wrote to me :—

'I am sure you will think the maxim of " Better
late than never " a very good one, when you see the
enclosed lock of hair. You will know whose it is.
I cannot bear yet to put his name down upon paper
more than I can help ; and this is my best excuse for
not having written sooner. With regard to himself,
who left me so far behind in this as well as in other
qualities, I am confident he must have written to you
on the subject to which you refer. I have a strong
recollection that he mentioned it to me. I know
that you were one of the last persons he spoke of, and
in a way full of kindness and acknowledgment.'

Though I had occasional interviews with Shelley
after this commencement of our acquaintance,[1] his
wandering life prevented my seeing much of him
until the year 1817, when I gladly accepted an
invitation to pass a few days with him at Marlow in
Buckinghamshire, where he was settled.

Since his first arrival in London, his circumstances
had materially altered. He was now united to his
second wife, whose talents justified her illustrious
descent as the daughter of Godwin and Mary Wol-
stencroft, while her virtues and her amiability, bless-

---

[1] At Leigh Hunt's house.

ing their union with a domestic happiness which
suffered no intermission up to the moment of her
husband's death, infused a reconciling sweetness into
the grievously bitter cup of his life. At one time
he had been reduced to such extremity of destitution
as to be in danger of actual starvation; but by con-
senting to cut off a portion of the entail on the
estate to which he was entitled, he secured to himself an income of a thousand a-year, which would
have been more than competent had his all-loving
heart and ever-open hand allowed him to limit his
charities. Denying himself all luxuries, and scarcely
ever tasting any other food than bread, vegetables,
and water, this good Samaritan wandered to the
various prisons for debtors, and to the obscure
haunts of poverty, to seek deserving objects for the
exercise of his unwearied and lavish charity.

> In Misery's darkest caverns known,
>   His ready help was ever nigh,
> Where helpless anguish pour'd the groan,
>   And lonely want retired to die.

Captain Medwin has related an affecting instance
of his youthful generosity, in pawning his beautiful
solar microscope to raise five pounds for the relief of
a poor old man; but the time had now arrived when,
for the purposes of his unbounded benevolence, the
strictest economizing of his liberal income proved
insufficient, and he had recourse to the ruinous
expedient of raising money upon post obits. I can
speak with certainty to his having bestowed upwards of five thousand pounds on eminent and
deserving men of letters, gracing his munificence by
the delicacy and tact with which he conferred it.
And this large sum was exclusive of innumerable
smaller donations to less distinguished writers, and
of his regular alms to miscellaneous claimants and

established pensioners. He loved to recount the rich legacies bequeathed to Cicero and to Pliny the younger, by strangers whom their writings had delighted or instructed, as evidencing a prevailing literary taste among the ancients much more liberal than our own ; but, he added, that as no one could be sure of surviving the parties whom he wished to benefit, and still less certain that the latter could afford to wait, it was much better that such intentions should be carried into immediate execution. "*Solas quas dederis semper habebis opes,*" what you have given away is the only wealth you will always keep, seemed to be the motto of his life. No wonder that among such a nation of Mammonites as the English, a man so utterly self-denying and unworldly should be viewed as a sort of *lusus naturæ*. No wonder that rich curmudgeons maligned him, for there was a daily beauty in his life that made theirs ugly. No wonder that the writer of this record, educated in the sordid school of mercantile life, could hardly trust the evidence of his senses when he saw this extraordinary being living like the austerest anchorite, denying himself all the luxuries appropriate to his birth and station, that he might appropriate his savings to the relief of his fellow-creatures; and silently showing, for he never made a proclamation of his bounties, that, despising riches on his own account, he only valued them so far as they enabled him to minister to the relief of others.

For several years Shelley had scrupulously refrained from the use of animal food, not upon the Pythagorean or Brahminical doctrine that such a diet necessitates a wanton, and, therefore, a cruel destruction of God's creatures, but from an impression that to kill the native "burghers of the wood," or tenants of the flood and sky, that we may chew their flesh and drink their blood, tends to fiercen and animalize both the slaughterer and devourer. This morbid sensibility, and the mistaken conclusion to which it led, did not permanently condemn him to an ascetical Lent; but he was ever jealous of his body, ever anxious to preserve the supremacy of his mind, ever solicitous to keep the temple pure and holy and undefiled by any taint of grossness that might debase the soul enshrined within it. Zealously devout and loyal was the worship that he tendered to the majesty of intellect.

Though the least effeminate of men, so far as personal and moral courage were concerned, the mind of Shelley was essentially feminine, some would say fastidious, in its delicacy; an innate purity which not even the licence of college habits and society could corrupt. A fellow-collegian thus writes of him:—" Shelley was actually offended, and, indeed, more indignant than would appear to be consistent with the singular mildness of his nature, at a coarse and awkward jest, especially if it were immodest or uncleanly; in the latter case, his anger was unbounded, and his uneasiness pre-eminent."

During one of our rambles in the noble woods near Marlow, we encountered two boys driving a squirrel from bough to bough by pelting it with stones. My companion, who was remarkably fond of children (guess how his affectionate heart must have been lacerated by the forcible abstraction of his own), and who could not bear to see any sentient creature ill-used, reasoned so mildly with the urchins on their cruelty, that they threw down their missiles and slunk away. On my expressing a hope that they would not soon forget a lesson so lovingly given, he shook his head, observing that before they got home, they would probably encounter some of those who ought to set them a better example, amusing themselves by what are unfeelingly termed the *sports* of the field,

and he congratulated himself that he had never
been one of those amateur butchers—had never
found a pleasure in wantonly slaying any of his
animal *brethren*. The phrase sounded strange to
me, but I found that he had previously adopted it
in that fine invocation commencing his poem of
Alastar, which shows how completely he fraternized
with universal nature :—

> Earth, ocean, air, beloved brotherhood !
> If our great mother have imbued my soul
> With aught of natural piety to feel
> Your love, and recompense the boon with mine :—
> If dewy morn, and odorous noon and even,
> With sunset and its gorgeous ministers,
> And solemn midnight's tingling silentness ;—
> If Spring's voluptuous pantings when she breathes
> Her first sweet kisses, have been dear to me ;
> If no bright bird, insect, or gentle beast
> I consciously have injured, but still loved
> And cherished these my kindred ;—then forgive
> This boast, beloved brethren, and withdraw
> No portion of your favour now.

Never, never shall I forget my last wandering
with the poet, as we stretched far away from the
haunts of men, beneath the high over-arching
boughs, which, forming around us a Gothic temple,
with interminable cloisters, still opening as we
advanced, seemed to inspire him with the love and
the worship of nature, and to suggest a fuller dis-
closure of his religious views than he had hitherto
imparted to me. Becoming gradually excited as he
gave way to his sentiments, his eyes kindled, he
strode forward more rapidly, swinging his arms to
and fro, and spoke with a vehemence and a rapidity
which rendered it difficult to collect his opinions on
particular points, though I have a clear recollection
of their general tendency. However absurd and
untenable may be the theory of atheism, he held it

to be preferable to that nominal theism, which in fact is real demonism, being a deification of man's worst passions, and the transfer to an imagined fiend of that worship which belongs to an all-loving God. He quoted Plutarch's averment, that even atheism is more reverent than superstition, inasmuch as it was better to deny the existence of Saturn as king of heaven, than to admit that fact, maintaining at the same time that he was such a monster of unnatural cruelty as to devour his own children as soon as they were born; and in confirmation of the same view he quoted a passage from Lord Bacon, asserting the superiority of reason and natural religion. Any attempt at an impersonation of the Deity, or any conception of Him otherwise than as the pervading spirit of the whole illimitable universe, he held to be presumptuous; for the finite cannot grasp the infinite. Perhaps he might have objected to Coleridge's grand definition of the Creator, as a circle whose centre is nowhere, and whose circumference is everywhere. Without asserting the absolute perfectibility of human nature, he had a confident belief in its almost limitless improvability; especially as he was persuaded that evil, an accident, and not an inherent part of our system, might be so materially diminished as to give an incalculable increase to the sum of human happiness. All the present evils of mankind he attributed to those erroneous views of religion in which had originated the countless wars, the national hatreds, the innumerable public and private miseries that make history a revolting record of suffering and crime. Every national creed and form of worship since the world began had successively died away and been superseded; experience of the past justifies the same anticipation for the future; the feuds and schisms and separations in our own established faith are the rents and cracks that predict the approaching downfall of the temple. Now, if mankind, abandoning all those evanescent symptoms, could be brought universally to adopt that religion of Nature which, finding its heavenly revelation in man's own heart, teaches him that the best way to testify his love of the Creator is to love all that he has created; that religion, whose three-leaved Bible is the earth, and sea, and sky—eternal and immutable Scriptures, written by God himself, which all may read and none can interpolate, there would be a total cessation of the *odium theologicum* which has been such a firebrand to the world; the human race, unchecked in its progress of improvement, would be gradually uplifted into a higher state, and all created beings, living together in harmony as one family, would worship their common Father in the undivided faith of brotherly love and the gratitude of peaceful happiness.

Utopian dreams, perchance, visionary yearnings, too great and glorious ever to receive their consummation upon earth; but who shall describe the profound emotion with which I listened to them? As we wandered alone through the vast natural cathedral of the woods, our feet falling inaudibly upon the turf, so that all around was hushed, as if the earth itself were listening to the rapt enthusiastic voice, while through the leafy openings overhead the blue sky seemed to smile benignly down upon him, who can wonder, although I was so many years older, that a solemn reverence began to mingle with my admiration of the singular youth by my side? When I gazed upon his beaming countenance, and saw his fragile frame excited by his theme until his bosom appeared to be " heaving beneath incumbent deity "; when I recalled his exquisite genius, his intellectual illumination, his exuberant philanthropy, his total renunciation of self, the courage and grandeur of his soul, combined with a feminine delicacy and purity, and an almost angelic amenity and sweetness, I could almost fancy that I had been listening to a spirit from some higher sphere, who had descended upon earth to inculcate a self-realizing confidence in the lofty destinies of mankind, and to teach us how we might accelerate the advent of a new golden age, when all the different creeds and systems of the world would be amalgamated into one—and liberated man would bow before the throne of his own aweless soul, or of the power unknown.

During the poet's residence in Italy, I corresponded with him regularly on the subject of his poems, generally to make the same unfavourable report as to their sale, and often to receive the same reply, that since he found the public refused to sympathize with his effusions, he should cease to emit them; but the injustice of the outer world had turned his thoughts inwards; he found in the muse both a recipient for his blighted affections, and a vent for his aspiring hopes; and he wrote on, in spite of neglect, and in defiance of abuse. Remembering his school-boy's vow, he determined to fulfil his mission. I had frankly confessed my opinion that his writings, too subtle and mystical, and even too imaginative for the public taste, would have a better chance of success if they exhibited a greater variety of human character, and a more intelligible object. Mrs. Shelley says:—" More popular poets clothe the ideal with familiar and sensible imagery. Shelley loved to idealize the real, to gift the mechanism of the material universe with a soul and a voice, and to bestow such also on the most delicate and abstract emotions and thoughts of the mind." When this is extended to a long and not very intellible allegory, the writer must content himself with an "audience fit, though few."   Confessing his preference of idealism to reality, Shelley says in one of his letters, " The Epipsychidion is a mystery: as to real flesh and blood, you know that I do not deal in those articles; you might as well go to a gin-shop for a leg of mutton as expect anything human or earthly from me."

The " Œdipus Tyrannus; or Swellfoot the Tyrant," was transmitted to me in manuscript, with a request that I would get it anonymously published. Though I thought it unworthy of Shelley's genius, which was little adapted to satire, and still less to political pleasantry, I complied with his request, little suspecting the dilemma in which it would involve me. Scarcely had it appeared in the bookseller's window, when a burly alderman called upon me on the part of "The Society for the Suppression of Vice," to demand the name of the author, in order that he might be prosecuted for a seditious and disloyal libel. On my denying its liability to this accusation, and refusing to disclose the writer's name, I was angrily apprised, that unless I consented to give up the whole impression to the Society, an action would instantly be commenced against the publisher, who stood by the side of the alderman in deep tribulation of spirit. To save an innocent man from fine and imprisonment, and the chance of ultimate ruin, I submitted to this insolent dictation of the Society, and made holocaust of " Swellfoot the Tyrant " at the Inquisition Office, in Bridge Street, Blackfriars.

Much as Shelley was maligned by strangers, none of those who knew him personally had ever spoken of him except in terms of unbounded admiration and affection.   Perhaps no one formed a juster estimate of his character, and no one was more competent to judge, than Lord Byron, who thus describes him :—

"He was the most gentle, most amiable, and *least* worldly-minded person I ever met; full of delicacy, disinterested beyond all other men, and possessing a degree of genius, joined to simplicity, as rare as it is admirable. He had formed to himself a *beau ideal* of all that is fine, high-minded, and noble; and he acted up to this ideal, even to the very letter. He had a most brilliant imagination, but a total want of worldly wisdom."

CHAPTER XVII

1825—1832

The declining years of Robert Smith—His verse-work—
Family marriages—Death of his second wife—His last illness
and death.

In his declining years Robert Smith lived a quiet
and useful life, devoting himself to his children and
grand-children, and unostentatiously associating
himself with every good work that came to hand.
He observes :—

A retired village life as mine will henceforth be,
can afford but little occasion for remark of any kind.
If I cannot attain to *Otium cum dignitate*, I must
endeavour at all events to escape its opposite extreme, *Tedium vitæ.*

After living at Champion Hill, Camberwell, and
Leyton in Essex, he finally settled down for the
remainder of his days at St. Anne's Hill, Wandsworth.

Beneath his grave and business-like demeanour
lay a fund of quiet wit and humour, which, whenever
an opportunity offered, found vent in versification.
Thus, when his wife's young niece, who was very
musical, was staying with them, he scribbled her the
following lines :—

I.

Praise, undeserved, the poet says,
  Is satire in disguise ;
But commendation that is just
  No poet will despise.

II.

Thus, " Laura, you are much improv'd
  In manners and in learning ; "
Now, you will readily admit
  That uncles are discerning.

III.

Turn to your music-book, you'll find
  Rules and instructions plenty,
Selected for the pupil's use,
  By Paddon and Clementi.

IV.

Give to these rules a wider field,
  A metaphoric meaning,
So as to make them rules of life,
  Weeding as well as gleaning.

V.

That every thought, and word, and deed.
  May properly avail,
Order it rightly, then sum up
  In " Diatonic scale."

VI.

Neither too ♯ nor yet too ♭
  Be ♮ " Piano " ;
True to your " Time," your ⌢ your ♩
  In " Basso " or " Soprano."

VII.

Though you have ♪ ♪, "fret," and *tr.*
　With | upright, don't ⌣
And, should you take a crabbed ∿
　"Finale," no :𝄢:.

VIII.

Whene'er you feel "con furia" rise,
　Restrain it from ⬎
This do in "amorosa" style,
　Dolce ⬍.

IX.

So manage "Cadence," "Air," and "Grace"
　(You play in "Minor" key)
As that the "Dominant"[1] produce
　A "Perfect-Harmony."

X.

'Twixt Chittagong[2] and Bedford Square[3]
　How vast the difference found !
There, all is dismal, dreary waste,
　Here, highly cultur'd ground.

In 1821, his eldest grand-daughter, Maria (familiarly called Mira), had married the Rev. J. Channing Abdy, curate of St. George the Martyr, Southwark, whose father, the Rev. W. J. Abdy, rector of St. John's, Horsleydown, died in 1823. The living being vested in the Crown, his son applied to the Lord Chancellor for it. He succeeded in his application contrary to all expectation, clerical etiquette being rather against the bestowal of a

---

[1] Her governess.
[2] Her birthplace.　　　[3] Her boarding-school.

living upon the son of a late incumbent. Abdy's most formidable rival was a certain Dr. Sampson, to whom Robert Smith, triumphing in his son-in-law's victory, addressed the following stanza :—

> Sampson, thy hopes upon St. John's,
>   An Abdy raised, and can extinguish ;
> Fathers had merit, so have sons,
>   And there are patrons who distinguish
> Whatever emanates from Eldon [1]
> Must of necessity be well done.

Maria Abdy later in life contributed to the *New Monthly* and *Metropolitan Magazines* and several of the fashionable annuals many poems of considerable merit, which were collected and printed for private circulation. After presenting one of these volumes to Horace Smith's friend, Mrs. S. C. Hall, she received the following letter of acknowledgment :—

My dear Madam,

A thousand thanks for the charming gift you sent me. I have read the poems with great pleasure ; some few are old friends. It was most kind of you to remember me in this way.

I know you are very busy, for I often see your name, and you must permit me to add, never without pleasure and advantage.

I am glad you like my young friend Toulmin. She is a very charming and valuable person, and not at all tinted with that awful bluism which disfigures so many literary ladies.

I think a cousin of yours is one of Mr. Hall's dear friends, Mr. E. M. Ward ; what a noble artist and estimable man he is.

[1] The Lord Chancellor.

I see Horace Smith's name very frequently in print, but of late I have not had time to read much —to my sorrow.

I assure you I sympathize very affectionately with you in your sorrow,[1] for I know what your sensitive nature must endure.

Very faithfully,
Your obliged,
ANNA MARIA HALL.

The Rectory, Old Brompton,
    18*th March,* 1826.

Mira Abdy had been married nearly nine years before she was blessed with any offspring. At last a boy was born; and when Robert wrote to Mira's mother (his daughter) congratulating her upon having become a grandmother, he enclosed these lines :—

Nonumque prematur in Annum.

I.

So Mira fancies that " prematur "
Applies alike to Art and Nature,
  At least, that it admits a " may be ";
She therefore waits " nine years " the time,
Then stereotypes her prose and rhyme,
  And publishes——a little baby !

II.

O what a theme for spleen and wonder !
" Who ever heard of such a blunder ?
  'Tis all a hoax—a fib—no better."
Nay, ladies, nay, all general rules
Have their exceptions, in the schools,
  And Mira seems to be " confined " by letter.

---

[1] Her husband's death.

III.

What comforts new, what honours too
To Father, Mother ! Me, and you !
  Mira is well ! the child alive !
To all of us the scene is new,
" Great grand-dad," I, at eighty-two,
  You, " Grand-mamma " at fifty-five.

IV.

To guard, however, against jeers,
  As to mere words—or meaning,
Tell Mira, that nine months (not *years*)
  Are quite enough for weaning.
And here I close my scrawl, God bless
Mamma and babe ! Adieu.

The marriages of his other grand-daughters came later on. In 1826 Elizabeth Cadell was married to Mr. William Oliver, a solicitor of No. 2 Tudor Street, New Bridge Street, Blackfriars, who attained considerable eminence in his profession, and lived for many years at Wimbledon.

On the 16th September, 1828, Rosa,[1] another Cadell grand-daughter, was united to Mr. Burgess, at that time a clerk in the Victualling Office, and the following year her sister Sophia married Mr. Henry Leman.

The last family wedding Robert Smith attended was that of Joanna Cadell.[2]

June 4th, 1831.—On this day [he says] my grand-daughter, Joanna Cadell, was married at St. Pancras

---

[1] After the death of Mr. Burgess, she married the Hon. R. Edwardes, uncle of the late Lord Kensington.

[2] The author's mother.

Church to Mr. Henry Beavan, an attorney in Sackville Street, Piccadilly. My daughter and myself went into a glass coach to the *déjeuner*, given on this occasion by Mr. Cadell.

Up to the age of 77, Robert Smith had been troubled with very few ailments, except an occasional severe cold, the result of constant exposure in travelling. Then, almost without any warning, and while his wife was confined to her room by a bad attack of pleurisy, he was seized with a fit of apoplexy. He was never again the hearty, robust old gentleman that he had been; and the gout inherited from his mother began to show itself in a peculiar form of cutaneous affliction, most tedious and tormenting, his eyesight began to fail, and his strength visibly declined. His intellectual faculties were as bright as ever, and when the weather permitted he always drove out in his carriage to see his daughters, the eldest of whom, Maria, came to keep house for him just before his wife's death in 1828, which, after several years of illness, happened as suddenly as that of his first wife in 1804.

Robert Smith was now more and more dependent upon his children and grand-children, who were devoted to him.

Weak as he was physically, his mind was wonderfully alert, and being asked by his granddaughter, Eliza Smith, to compose something for her album, he wrote as follows :—

> Oh, what is Cupid, with his bow and darts,
>   Compar'd to Phillis, and her strange demands !
> The little archer only aims at hearts,
>   She takes our hearts—then asks us for our hands.
> But will no Damon check the wild career,
>   And strive, at least, to shorten the research ?
> Now dare to turn the tables on the fair,
>   By asking *her* to sign *his* "album" in the Church ?

At last the summons came.   His daughter, continuing the family journal, writes :—

September 27*th.*—On this day my father breathed his last ! He had fallen into a kind of stupor attended by difficulty of breathing.   He died quite easily, without pain or struggle.

Thus passed out of the world, at the age of eighty-five, one of the most upright, kind, unselfish, and excellent of men.

With characteristic unostentation, he left instructions that he might be buried " with as little ceremony and in as simple a manner as possible," in All Saints Churchyard, Wandsworth.

CHAPTER XVIII

James and Horace Smith as Wits and Humorists.

HORACE SMITH, writing of his brother James, says :—

He was one of the most agreeable companions imaginable, and it was difficult to pass an evening in his company without feeling in better humour with the world ; such was the influence of his inexhaustible fund of amusement and information, his lightness, liveliness and good sense. He was not very witty or brilliant, nor even very ready at repartee. Indeed, I am pretty sure that most of the best things recorded of him were *impromptus faits à loisir ;* but no man ever excelled him in starting pleasant topics of conversation, and sustaining it ; nor was it well possible for a party of moderate dimensions, when he was of it, to be dull. The droll anecdote, the apt illustration, the shrewd remark—a trait of humour from Fielding, a scrap of song from the *Beggars' Opera,* a knock-down retort of Johnson's, a couplet from Pope or Dryden—all seemed to come as they were wanted, and, as he was always just as ready to listen as to talk, acted each in turn as a sort of challenge to the company to bring forth their budgets, and contribute towards the feast.

He was rather fond of a joke at the expense of his own branch of the legal profession, and always gave a peculiar emphasis to any line in his songs that referred to an attorney, as for instance :—

> Mr. Barker's as mute as a fish in the sea,
>   Mr. Miles never moves on a journey,
> Mr. Gotobed sits up till half after three,
>   *Mr. Makepiece was bred an attorney;*
> Mr. Gardener can't tell a flower from a root,
>   Mr. Wilde with timidity draws back,
> Mr. Ryder performs all his journeys on foot,
>   Mr. Foote, all his journeys on horseback.

Yet James Smith had the greatest respect for his profession and instinctive reverence for legal dignitaries.   An invitation to dine with a judge afforded him more gratification than would a command to banquet with Royalty itself.

In his day [continues Horace Smith] it was customary on emergencies for the judges to swear affidavits at their dwelling-houses. James was desired by his father to attend a judge's chambers for that purpose, but being engaged to dine in Russell Square, at the next house to Sir George Holroyd's, one of the judges of the Court of King's Bench, he thought he might as well save himself the disagreeable necessity of leaving the party at eight o'clock, by dispatching his business at once; so a few minutes before six, he boldly knocked at the judge's, and requested to speak to him on particular business. The judge was at dinner, but came down without delay, swore the affidavit, and then gravely asked what was the pressing necessity that induced James Smith to disturb him at that hour. As Smith told the story, he raked his invention for a plausible

excuse, but finding none fit for the purpose, he
blurted out the truth—"The fact is, my lord, I am
engaged to dine at the next house—and—and—"—
"And, sir, you thought you might as well save your
own dinner by spoiling mine?"—"Exactly so, my
lord, but—"—"Sir, I wish you a good evening."

Though he brazened the matter out, he said he
never was more frightened in his life.

The following well-known anecdote of James Smith
is thus related in full by his brother Horace:—

The many bodily infirmities of Charles Mathews,
and more especially the sad accident that lamed him
for life, had tended to irritate a temper which his
extreme sensitiveness sometimes rendered touchy,
though his nature was always kind and genial.
Among his little *prandial* peculiarities was a ve-
hement objection to mock-turtle soup, on account
of some unwholesome ingredient with which, as he
asserted, it was usually thickened. Once I met him
at a party where several servants in succession having
offered him a plate of his "pet abhorrence," he at
length lost patience, uttered an angry, "No, I tell
you!" and petulantly tossing up his elbow at the
same time, upset a portion of the rejected compound
upon his sleeve. Next day, I again encountered him
at dinner, when he related what had occurred, exclaiming, "I am delighted beyond measure that my
coat is spoiled; I have locked it up; I wouldn't have
it cleaned for twenty pounds; call to-morrow, and I'll
show you the sleeve; it stands of itself, stiff as the
arm of a statue. You wouldn't believe me when I
told you on good authority, that the lawyers sold all
their parchments to the pastry-cooks to make some
villainous stuff called glaize or gelatine, or in plain

English, *glue*, out of which they manufacture jelly, or sell it to our poisoning cooks, who put it into their mock-turtle to make the gruel thick and slab."

" I have heard of a man eating his own words," said James Smith, "but if your statement be true, a man may have unconsciously eaten his own *acts* and *deeds*."

" He may, he may ! " cried Mathews. " Egad, my friend, I thank you for the hint, it explains all about my confounded indigestion.   Doubtless I have some other man's *will*, which renders it so insubordinate to my own will ; I myself love roast pork and plum-pudding, but this alien will, transferred from some lawyer's office to my intestines, will not allow me to digest them.   You have heard of the fellow with a bad asthma who exclaimed, ' If once I can get this troublesome breath out of my body, I'll take good care it shall never get in again,' and I may well say the same of this parchment usurper who has taken possession of my stomach.   How he got there is the wonder, for years have elapsed since I swallowed glue—I mean jelly or mock-turtle."

But for felicitous impromptu, the anecdote of James Smith told by the Rev. Julian Young, son of the famous actor, Charles Mayne Young, possibly bears the palm.   Mr. Young says :—

When Jesse was preparing for the press his *Gleanings in Natural History*, James Smith one day unexpectedly burst in upon him.   The moment he saw him, he said, "My dear Smith, you have come in the very nick of time, as my good genius, to extricate me from a difficulty.   You must know that to each of my chapters I have put an appropriate heading.   I mean by that, that each chapter has prefixed to it a quotation from some well-known author suited to the subject treated of, with one exception. I have been cudgeling my brains for a motto for my chapter on *Crows and Rooks*, and cannot think of one.   Can you?"—"Certainly," said he, with promptitude, "here is one from Shakespeare for you! 'The cause (caws), my soul, the cause (caws)!'"

The following is one of James Smith's humorous compositions :—

At a certain election dinner at Cambridge, the Mayor sat at one end of the table and Sir Peter Pawsey, a gentleman of good estate in Lincolnshire, at the other.   Sir Peter's son, a raw, long-legged lad from Harrow, was also at table. After dinner, the general buzz that frequently occurs in a mixed party was succeeded by a momentary silence.   "Here is one of those awkward *pauses* that one sometimes meets with at table," observed the Mayor to a doctor of civil law on his right.   The conversation went on, and in about ten minutes another cessation of talk suddenly took place.   "Here is another of those awkward *pauses* at table," repeated the mayor to the doctor.   "Not half so awkward as a Cambridge mayor," bellowed Sir Peter Pawsey, casting a furious glance at the astonished chief magistrate.   The fact was, the baronet had pocketed the first supposed personal affront, which he had taken to himself; but the second, glancing as it seemed to do, upon his darling and only son, was too much for his temper's endurance.

James Smith was in the habit of sending Lady Blessington occasional epigrams, complimentary scraps of verse, or punning notes, like this :—

The newspapers tell us that your new carriage is very highly varnished. This, I presume, means your wheeled carriage. The merit of your personal carriage has always been, to my mind, its absence from all varnish. The question requires that a jury should be *impannelled*.

The following is an epigram by James Smith upon a village physician and a vicar who often walked arm in arm together—

D.D. AND M.D.

How D.D. swaggers, M.D. rolls !
  I dub them both a brace of noddies ;
Old D.D. has the cure of souls,
  And M.D. has the cure of bodies.

Between them both, what treatment rare
  Our souls and bodies must endure !
One has the cure without the care,
  And one the care without the cure.

James Smith was great at " taking off" the foibles of the Cockneys of his day, his descriptions being most faithful. *Mrs. Dobbs at Home*, which appeared in the *New Monthly Magazine*, is perhaps the least known of these. It is rather a long poem, but the opening lines are worth repeating :—

What ! shall the *Morning Post* proclaim
For every rich or high-born dame
From Portman Square to Cleveland Row,
Each item no one cares to know ;
Print her minutest whereabouts,
Describe her concerts, balls, and routs,
Enumerate the lamps and lustres,
Show where the roses hung in clusters,
Tell how the floor was chalked, reveal
The partners in the first quadrille—

> How long they danced, till, sharp as hunters,
> They sat down to the feast—from Gunter's ;
> How much a quart was paid for peas,
> How much for pines and strawberries,
> Taking especial care to fix
> The hour of parting—half-past six ?
> And should no bard make proclamation
> Of routs enjoyed in humbler station ?
> Rise, honest Muse, in Hackney roam,
> And sing of " Mrs. Dobbs at Home."
> He who knows Hackney, needs must know
> That spot enchanting—Prospect Row,
> So called because the view it shows
> Of Shoreditch Road, and when there blows
> No dust the folks may one and all get
> A peep—almost to Norton Folgate.
> Here Mrs. Dobbs at number three
> Invited all her friends to tea.

Concerning aldermen and city magnates generally, James was always good-humouredly sarcastic ; as for instance :—

THE CLAPHAM CHALYBEATE

Who has e'er been at Clapham must needs know the pond
    That belongs to Sir Barnaby Sturch ;
'Tis well stock'd with fish ; and the knight's rather fond
    Of bobbing for tench or for perch.

When he draws up his line to decide if all's right,
    Moist drops o'er his pantaloons dribble ;
Though seldom, if ever, beguiled by a bite,
    He now and then boasts of a nibble.

Vulgar mud, very like vulgar men, will encroach
    Uncheck'd by the spade and the rake ;
In process of time it enveloped the roach
    In Sir Barnaby's Lilliput lake.

Five workmen, well arm'd, and denuded of shoes,
    Now fearlessly delved in the flood,
To steal unawares on the Empress of Oaze,
    And cast off the insolent mud.

The innocent natives were borne from the bog,
    Eel, minnow, and toad felt the shovel,
And lizard-like eft lay with fugitive frog
    In a clay-built extempore hovel.

The men worked away with their hands and their feet,
    And delved in a regular ring ;
When lo ! as their task work was all but complete,
    They wakened a mineral spring.

" We've found a Chalybeate, sir," cried the men ;
    " We halt till we know what your wish is."—
" Keep it safe," quoth the knight, "till you've finished, and
        then—
    Throw it back with the rest of the fishes."

These are necessarily but samples of the poetic humour of James Smith. Of his racy conversation and *bons mots*, alas ! mere scraps remain on record.

My political opinions [he once said] are those of the lady who sits next to me, and, as the fair sex are generally " perplexed like monarchs with the fear of change," I constantly find myself conservative.

" Mr. Smith, you *look* like a Conservative," said a young man across the table, thinking to pay him a compliment. " Certainly, sir," was the prompt reply; " my *crutches* remind me that I am no member of *the movement party*."

We are enjoined upon grave authority [he once wrote] to put off the old man. I should be happy to do so if I could. At present I am flying in the face of scripture, and putting it *on*.

Alluding to the obelisk newly erected at the entrance of the Victoria Park in honour of Queen Victoria, he said :—

The people of Bath surpass the Athenian sage.
He merely chewed the pebbles; but, according to the
Morning Herald, at Bath the Victoria Column is in
everybody's mouth !

When one of James Smith's friends remarked that,
since he had obtained a pension, he had ceased to
write, James Smith replied—" I see you are a pen-
shunner."

He used to relate with great glee a story illustrat-
ing the general conviction that he disliked rurality.
He was sitting in the library at a country house,
when a gentleman proposed a quiet stroll into the
pleasure-grounds. " Stroll ! why, don't you see my
gouty shoe ? "—" Yes, I see that plain enough, and
I wish I'd brought one too, but they're all out
now."—" Well, and what then ? "—" What then ?
Why, my dear fellow, you don't mean to say that
you have really got the gout ? I thought you had
only put on that shoe to get off being shown over
the improvements."

Horace Smith's humour was of a different order
from his brother's. Shelley said of him :—

> Wit and sense,
> Virtue and human knowledge, all that might
> Make this dull world a business of delight
> Are all combined in Horace Smith.

His definition of wit is that it " consists in dis-
covering likenesses, judgment in detecting differ-
ences. Wit is like a ghost, much more often talked
about than seen. To be genuine it should have

a basis of truth and applicability, otherwise it degenerates into mere flippancy."

Here is an instance of his humour in verse :—

THE ENGLISHMAN IN FRANCE

A Frenchman seeing, as he walk'd,
  A friend on t'other side the street,
Cried " Hem ! " exactly as there stalk'd
  An Englishman along the road ;
One of those Johnny Raws we meet
  In every seaport from abroad,
Prepared to take and give offence,
  Partly, perhaps, because they speak
About as much of French as Greek,
  And partly from the want of sense.
The Briton thought this exclamation
Meant some reflection on his nation,
So bustling to the Frenchman's side,
" Mounseer Jack Frog," he fiercely cried,
" Pourquoi vous dire 'Hem !' quand moi passe ? "
Eyeing the querist with his glass,
The Gaul replied—" Monsieur God-dem,
Pourquoi vous passe quand moi dire 'Hem' ? "

The poet Keats greatly appreciated Horace Smith's wit, and in a letter to his brother and sister, remarks :—

Horace Smith said to one who asked him if he knew Hook, 'Oh, yes, *Hook and I* are very intimate.' There's a page of wit for you to put John Bunyan's emblems out of countenance.

In a letter to Cyrus Redding, Horace Smith says:—

You came down (to Brighton) last month to take a shower-bath or two ; if you want warm baths, now is your time ; and you will have nothing to pay, as the air will confer them gratuitously.

Should any of the articles I gave you for the Magazine prove objectionable, you can return them when any parcel is coming from Burlington Street. They are mere *hors-d'œuvres*, as the French *cartes* say, and do not deserve to be treated with any ceremony.

Here are a few amusing passages from Horace's writings :—

At some private theatricals given at Hatfield House, old General G—— was pressed by a lady to say whom he liked best of the actors. Notwithstanding his usual bluntness, he evaded the question for some time, but being importuned for an answer, he at length growled—"Well, madam, if you will have a reply, I liked the prompter the best, because I heard the most of him, and saw the least of him!"

He describes an alderman (for he did not admire the city fathers) as "a ventri-potential citizen, into whose mediterranean mouth good things are perpetually flowing, although none come out. His shoulders, like some of the civic streets, are widened at the expense of the corporation."
A saw he describes as " a sort of dumb alderman, which gets through a great deal by the activity of its teeth. N.B. A bona-fide alderman is not one of the ' wise saws ' mentioned by Shakespeare, at least in ' modern instances.' "

Once, when at Harrogate, observing some pilasters surmounted with the *Cornua Ammonis*, Horace ventured to ask the builder to what order they belonged.

" Why, sir," replied the man, putting his hand to his head, " the horns are a little order of my own."

Horace was rather severe upon barristers as a class, but qualified his strictures by remarking :—

All briefless barristers will please to consider themselves excepted from the previous censure, for I should be really sorry to speak ill of any man *without a cause.*

With *bons vivants* he had little sympathy :—

An epicure [he says] has no sinecure; he is unmade, and eventually dished by made dishes. Champagne falsifies its name when once it begins to affect his system; his stomach is so deranged in its punctuation, that his colon makes a point of coming to a full stop; keeping it up late ends in his being laid down early; and the *bon-vivant* who has always been hunting pleasure, finds at last that he has only been whipping and spurring, that he might be the sooner in at his own death !

Writing of epitaphs, he says :—

Sir Christopher Wren's inscription in St. Paul's Cathedral, " *Si monumentum requiris circumspice,*" would be equally applicable to a physician buried in a churchyard, both being interred in the midst of their own works.

Alluding to the depreciation of house property, Horace observes :—

What is the value of houses ? It is notorious that they are everywhere falling, especially the very old ones ; rents threaten to be all pepper-corns ; house-owners will not get salt to their porridge, even if they distrain upon their tenants, and make quarter-day a day without quarter.

The word "sack" is found in all languages—which a profound antiquary has explained by suggesting that it was necessary to have that primitive word, in order that every man, when he took his departure from the tower of Babel, might ask for his own bag.

Friendship, Horace Smith considered, cannot long exist among the vicious—

For we soon [he says] find ill company to be like a dog, which dirts those the most whom it loves the best. After Lady E. L. and her female companion had defied public opinion for some time, her ladyship was obliged to say, " Well, now, my dear friend, we must part for ever; for you have no character left, and I have not enough for two."

An umbrella is an article which, by the morality of society, you may steal from friend or foe, and which, for the same reason, you should not lend to either.

The world is a great inn kept in a perpetual bustle of arrivals and departures—by the going away of those who have just paid their bills (the debt of nature), and the coming of those who will soon have a similar account to settle.

CHAPTER XIX

Horace Smith's recollections of Sir Walter Scott, Southey, and Thomas Hill of Sydenham.

As I have before remarked, the Smiths—more especially Horace—could number amongst their acquaintances nearly all the celebrated men of their day; but space does not admit of more than a reference to a few of these.

In company with his friend, Mr. Barron Field of the Temple, who subsequently became Judge of the Supreme Court of New South Wales, Horace Smith journeyed to Edinburgh, where he had the honour of being introduced to Sir Walter Scott, an event of which he gives the following account: [1]—

On the 7th of July, 1827, having left Speir's Hotel in Edinburgh at an early hour, I proceeded to the Court-house, in which a few persons were already assembled, awaiting the arrival of the judges. At one extremity of a railed enclosure, below the elevated platform appropriated to their lordships, sat Sir Walter Scott in readiness for his official duties as clerk of the court, but snatching his leisure moments as was his wont, and busily engaged in writing, apparently undisturbed by the buzzing in the court, also the trampling feet of constant

[1] *A Greybeard's Gossip about his Literary Acquaintances.*

new-comers. The thoughts which another man
would have wasted by gazing vacantly around him,
or by "bald, disjointed chat," he was probably at
that moment embalming by committing to paper
some portion of his immortal works. Let me
frankly confess that his first appearance disappointed
me. His heavy figure, his stooping attitude, the
lowering grey brow, and unanimated features, gave
him, as I thought, a nearer resemblance to a plod-
ding farmer than to the weird magician and poet
whose every look should convey the impression that
he was "of imagination all compact." Quickly,
however, were his lineaments revivified and altered
when, upon glancing at a letter of introduction,
which my companion had placed before him, he
hastened up to the rail to welcome me. His grey
eyes twinkled beneath his uplifted brows, his mouth
became wreathed with smiles, and his countenance
assumed a benignant radiance as he held out his
hand to me, exclaiming, " Ha! my brother scribbler!
I am right glad to see you." Not easily, "while
memory holds her seat," will that condescending
phrase and most cordial reception be blotted from
my mind. On learning that I should be compelled
to quit Edinburgh in two days, my fellow-traveller,
Mr. Barron Field, having business at the Lancaster
Assizes, he kindly invited us to dine with him,
either on that day or the next, for both of which,
however, we were unfortunately pre-engaged.
Though the parties who had thus bespoken us were
barrister friends, from whose society I anticipated
no small pleasure, most willingly would I have
forfeited it, had I foreseen the great delight and
honour in which I might have participated.
" Positively, I must see something of you before you
leave ' Auld Reekie,' " kindly resumed Sir Walter.
" Suppose, you come and breakfast with me to-

morrow, suffering me to escape when I must make my appearance in court." To this proposition we gave an eager assent, and I need scarcely add that on the following morning we presented ourselves at his door, within a minute of the time specified.

Our host was dressed, and ready to receive us; his daughter, Miss Scott, presently made her appearance, shortly followed by her brother, Mr. Charles Scott. During our short meal, I can recall one remark of Sir Walter, which, trivial as it was, may be deemed characteristic of his jealousy in the minutest things that touched the good reputation of Scotland. I happened to observe that I had never before tasted bannocks, when he entreated me, and earnestly repeated the request, not to judge of them by the specimen before me, as they were badly made, and not well-baked. Our conversation chiefly turned upon Edinburgh, of which city, so grand and picturesque from its locality, so striking from the contrast of its old and new towns, I expressed an unbounded admiration. Our host, however, assured me that the Highland scenery would have been found more romantic and imposing, and expressed his wonder, considering the quickness, facility, and economy with which it might now [1] be explored, that I should lose so favourable an opportunity of proceeding further north, even if I did not pay my respect to the Hebrides.

A few months before my visit to Scotland, I had dedicated a little book [2] to Sir Walter, forwarding to him a copy in which I had endeavoured to express my great and sincere reverence for his character. ... From the breakfast-party I have been describing, my friend and myself were reluctantly tearing ourselves away, that our host might not be too late for the court, and already we had reached the hall,

[1] 1827.   [2] *Reuben Apsley.*

when Sir Walter, detaining me by the button, drew me a little on one side, as he said with a mystifying smile and tone:—

"Did it ever happen to you, when you were a good little boy at school, that your mother sent you a parcel in the centre of which she had deposited your favourite sweetmeat, whereof you had no sooner caught a glimpse than you put it aside that you might wait for a half-holiday, and carry it with you to some snug corner where you could enjoy it without fear of interruption?"

"Such a thing may have occurred," said I, much marvelling whither this strange inquiry was to lead.

"Well," resumed my colloquist, "I have received lately a literary dainty, bearing the name of —— (here he mentioned the title of the work I had sent him). Now, I cannot peruse it comfortably in Edinburgh, with the daily claims of the Court of Sessions, and a variety of other interruptions; but when I get back to Abbotsford, won't I sit down in my own snug study, and devour it at my leisure."

Sir Walter's time, I well knew, was infinitely too precious to be wasted in the perusal of any production from my pen; but the kindness of his speech, and the playful *bonhommie* of his manner, were not the less manifest, and not the less gratefully felt. He had politely invited me to visit him at Abbotsford when he should return to it, and though I could not avail myself of his courtesy, I determined to make acquaintance with the mansion which, solidly as he had constructed it, was destined to be the least enduring of his works. After another hasty ramble, therefore, over the most picturesque city in Europe, I bade it a reluctant adieu, and started for Abbotsford, fraught with abundant recollections and pleasant anticipations, most of which bore reference to Sir Walter Scott.

Not over pleasant, however, did I find the approach
to his mansion, for the river had been swollen by
heavy rains, the waters threatened to enter our
post-chaise, and the rocky ground sorely tried its
springs. Probably the old abbots never ventured
across the ford, to which they have bequeathed their
name, in a close carriage. The surrounding localities presented but small attraction, for, though the
far-extending scenery was enlivened by the river,
and its prevailing bareness was relieved by wide
plantations over the demesne, the latter were too
young at that period to assume any more dignified
appearance than that of underwood. By this time [1]
they have, probably, grown out of their sylvan
pupilage.

The building constituted a museum of relics so
rich in historical associations, many of them bearing
such immediate reference to some of his novels, that
almost every stone might literally be said to "prate
of his whereabout."

Small as was the armoury in the hall, it excelled
many a larger collection in curiosities, most of the
weapons having an historical or personal interest
attached to them. Some of these were donations
from individuals, but when Sir Walter became a
purchaser of such rarities, he must have laboured
under the disadvantage of raising the market price
against himself. The gun of an obscure marauder
could be of little value to any one; but when it was
known to have belonged to Rob Roy, the hero of a
popular novel, and was to be sold to the author of
the work, it acquired an adventitious enhancement,
which must have rendered its purchase much more
expensive. In the library I noticed a splendidly
bound set of our national chronicles presented by
George IV., one of the very few instances ever

<hr>

[1] 1848.

evinced by that monarch of a taste for books, or of any attention to an author. In one of his poems, Sir Walter cautions the reader that

> "He who would see Melrose aright
> Must view it by the pale moonlight;

but as I had been told that *he himself had never taken his own advice*, I proceeded to visit the abbey in the daytime, and in my next morning's drive over a dreary moor of forty miles to Otterburn, had abundant time to reflect upon all that I had seen and heard in the modern Athens, and in the residence of our age's most illustrious writer.

* * * * *

At Keswick, we visited the poet Southey. Not without emotion did I push back the swing-gate, giving access to the large rambling garden in which his house was situated; not without a reverent curiosity did I gaze upon the books of which his collection was so large that they overflowed their appropriate receptacles, and thickly lined the sides of the stairs up which we ascended.

* * * * *

In a handsome apartment, forming both a library and sitting-room, we found the laureate, surrounded by a portion of his charming family. Of trivial events I never retain the specific date, but the honour of an introduction to so distinguished a writer will excuse my recording that it occurred on the first day of July. I have not forgotten his telling me that I had chosen too early a period for visiting the Lakes, as the weather was seldom propitious at that season; and fully did the skies confirm his assertions, for it rained almost incessantly during the whole of my stay at Keswick. No clouds or mists, however, intercepted my sight of the laureate, and nothing could be more cordial than the reception I experienced. His quick eye and sharp intelligent features might have enabled him to pass for a younger man than he really was, had not his partially grizzled hair betrayed the touches of age. His limbs, too, seemed to share the activity of his mind, for in the course of our conversation, requiring reference to some particular book, he ran with agility up the rail-steps which he had rapidly pushed before him for the purpose, and instantly pounced upon it. One of his daughters assured me that he knew the exact position of every volume in his library, extensive as it was. That he possessed few, if any, which he had not consulted, is evident from the multifarious reading displayed in *The Doctor*, the volumes of which are but so many common-place books of uncommon reading.

We passed the evening at his house, the conversation generally taking a literary turn; though I cannot recall its particular subjects, I remember to have brought away with me an impression—perhaps an erroneous, perhaps a presumptuous one—that he betrayed occasionally more party spirit than was quite becoming. If I had not been too diffident in such a presence to disclose my own opinions, he might, perhaps, have reciprocated the thought. Old age has taught me to abjure all dogmatism; to distrust my own sentiments, to respect those of others wherever they are sincerely entertained. That so good, so kind-hearted a man as Southey should write with so much acrimony, not to say bitterness, whenever he became subject to a political or religious bias, has excited surprise in many persons who did not reflect that his residence in a remote country town, surrounded by a little coterie of admirers, whose ready assent confirmed him in all his prejudices and bigoted notions, must have had a perpetual tendency to arrest his mind and to prevent its moving forward with the general march of intellect and liberality.

As a public writer, for such might he be deemed from his intimate connection with the *Quarterly Review*, he should have resided in the metropolis. I have already noticed the injurious effect of a long expatriation upon manners; and though Southey never left England, his self-banishment from London imparted a degree of rigid austerity to his mind, and literally accounted for its want of urbanity. Wordsworth, all whose sympathies are with nature, rather than with towered cities and the busy hands of men, is in his proper element among lakes and mountains; but a critic and a writer, whose business it is "to catch the manners living as they rise," should always reside in a capital city.

Southey made another and a still more unfortunate mistake when he appropriated to himself the device of *in labore quies*—when he maintained and acted upon the theory, that change of mental labour is equivalent to rest, and if he alternated between history, poetry, and criticism, he would not require any relaxation or repose. For any man this would have been a perilous error, but for one whose sequestered life, however charming might have been his domestic circle, admitted little other social enjoyment and allowed hardly any varieties of amusement, a long course of such monotonous labour could not fail to grow doubly hazardous. But a few more years had been thus passed when the whole sympathizing world had occasion to deplore the truly melancholy results produced by this unmitigated over-exertion of the intellectual faculties, when, to use the words of his widow, the fiat had gone forth, and " all was in the dust ! "

In 1828, long before this calamity, I forwarded him

a little work,[1] of which he immediately acknowledged the reception in a truly gratifying letter. Most justifiably might I present a copy of it to the reader upon the sole ground that every unpublished writing from such a pen must be acceptable; but I will frankly confess that I have an additional motive, and that *laudari a laudato viro* is an honour which I cannot consent to forego, when I have such an excusable opportunity for claiming it :—

Keswick, Nov. 6, 1828.

DEAR SIR,
    The book, which your obliging letter of the 28th last announced, arrived yesterday afternoon, and, having this morning finished the perusal, I. can thank you for it more satisfactorily than if the gratification were still an expected one. You have completely obviated every objection that could be made on the choice of scriptural scenes and manners, and you must have taken great pains as well as great pleasure in making yourself so well acquainted with both. In power of design and execution this book has often reminded me of Martin's pictures, who has succeeded in more daring attempts than ever artist before him dreamt of. I very much admire the whole management of the love-story.

The only fault which I have felt was a want of repose. How it could have been introduced I know not, but it would have been a relief. There is a perpetual excitement of scenery and circumstances even when the story is at rest, and the effect of this upon me has been something like that of the first day in London after two or three years at Keswick. Young readers will not feel this, and as we advance in life, we learn to like repose even in our pleasures.

Do me the favour to accept a copy of my *Collo-*

---

[1] *Zillah, a Tale of the Holy City.*

quies when they shall be published (as I expect) in January. Though they contain some things which possibly may not accord with your opinions, there is, I think, much more with which you will find yourself in agreement, and the prints and descriptive portions may remind you of a place which I am glad to remember that you have visited.

My wife and daughters thank you for what will be their week's evening pleasure. So does my pupil and play-fellow, Cuthbert, who, I am glad to say, feeds upon books as voraciously as I did at his age.

Believe me, my dear sir,

Yours, with sincere respect,

ROBERT SOUTHEY.

One of the most amusing and hospitable of the Smiths' friends was Thomas Hill—the proprietor of the *Monthly Mirror*, to which, from 1807 to 1810, James was a constant contributor—"at whose hospitable board at Sydenham," says Horace Smith, "my brother and myself were frequent guests; generally encountering some of the popular wits, literati, and artists, and never quitting his cottage without the pleasant recollection of a cordial welcome, and much convivial enjoyment, among companions equally distinguished for their solid attainments and their social vivacity."

Cyrus Redding writes that—

Thomas Hill was a character long known wherever a quorum of literary men chanced to meet, that is if he could get admission into it. He had no literary tastes or acquirements. His manners were those of his business, a city drysalter. But what mattered all this if he himself thought it was otherwise, and in consequence of that idea, and having been once the proprietor of a little theatrical periodical, he took a fancy to those in the " literary line," as he would have phrased it. He imagined himself a Thames Street Mæcenas. To assume this character, he invited a number of literary men to his villa at Sydenham. Of the number were the two brothers Smith, Barnes, afterwards of the *Times*, George Colman, Mathews, Campbell, Hook, and others, who did not object to a jaunt of eight miles for a merry meeting.

He gave plain dinners and good wine, in exchange for which his guests used to play upon his idea of being a literary patron, to his infinite gratification. They often sat late, and got back to town at the dawn of morning, on their way giving improvisations, and reciting, literally, " rhymes on the road." Campbell, who lived at Sydenham, nearer the summit of the hill than the drysalter, used to accompany those townward bound, and take leave of them at a particular spot, flinging up his hat and wig in the air, when they parted, he to his two-o'clock bed, and the rest of the party, or a portion of them, to business rather than the blankets when they arrived home.

Horace Smith has left the following account of his Sydenham friend :—

In addition to Hill's besetting sin of imagining all his own geese, and all the geese of all his friends, to be swans, he was an inexhaustible quidnunc and gossip, delighting more especially to startle his hearers by the marvellous nature of his intelligence, not troubling his head about its veracity, for he was a great economist of truth, and striving to bear down and crush every doubt by ever-increasing vehemence of manner and extravagance of assertion.

P

If you strained at a gnat he would instantly give
you a camel to swallow; if you boggled at an im-
probability he would endeavour to force an impossibility down your throat, rising with the conscious
necessity for exertion, for he was wonderfully demonstrative, until his veins swelled, his grey eyes goggled,
his husky voice became inarticulate, his hands were
stretched out with widely disparted fingers, and the
first joint of each thumb was actually drawn backwards in the muscular tension occasioned by his
excitement.   Embody this description in the figure
of a fat, florid, round little man, like a retired
elderly Cupid, and you will see Hill maintaining a
hyperbole, not to say a catachresis, with as much
convulsive energy as if he believed it! And yet it
is difficult to suppose that, deceived by his own
excitement, and mistaking assertion for conviction,
he did not sometimes succeed in imposing upon
himself, however he might fail with his hearers;
otherwise he would hardly wind up, as I have more
than once heard him, by exclaiming—
"Sir, I affirm it with all the solemnity of a death-
bed utterance, of a sacramental oath."
Blinded by agitation and vehemence he could no
longer see the truth, and went on asseverating until
he fancied that he believed what he was saying.
This, however, was in the more rampant stage of the
disorder; there was a previous one, in which he
would look you sternly in the face, and in a tone
that was meant to be conclusive, and to inflict a
death-blow upon all incredulity, would emphatically
ejaculate, "Sir, I happen to *know* it!"
If this failed, if his hearer still looked sceptical,
he would immediately play at double or quits with
his first assertion, adding a hundred per cent. to it,
and making the same addition to the positiveness
with which he supported it, until he gradually

reached the rabid state, in which he would not condescend to affirm anything short of an impossibility, or to pledge anything short of his existence to its literal veracity.

*   *   *   *   *

His large literary parties were always given at his Sydenham Tusculum, which, though close to the roadside, and making no pretensions to be " a cottage of gentility," was roomy and comfortable enough within, spite of its low-pitched thick-beamed ceilings, and the varieties of level with which the builder had pleasantly diversified his floors. The garden at the back, much more useful than ornamental, afforded an agreeable ambulatory for his guests, when they did not fall into the pond in their anxiety to gather currants—an accident not always escaped. Pleasant and never-to-be-forgotten were the many days that I passed beneath that hospitable roof, with associates whose varied talents and invariable hilarity might have justified us in despising the triteness of the quotation, when we compared our convivial symposia with the *noctes cœnæque Deum.*

On those summer afternoons, we mounted the little grassy ascent that overlooked the road, and joyfully hailed each new guest as he arrived, well aware that he brought with him an accession of merriment for the jovial dinner, and fresh facetiousness for the wit-winged night ! Let it not be thought that I exaggerate the quality of the boon companions whom our Amphitryon delighted to assemble. If we had no philosophers who could make the world wiser, we had many a wit and wag who well knew how to make it merrier. Among those most frequently encountered at the jollifications were Campbell, the poet, then occupying a cottage in the village, and by no means the least hilarious of the party; Mathews, and sometimes his friend and his brother comedian, Liston; Theodore Hook; Edward Dubois, at that time editor and main support of the *Monthly Mirror*; Leigh Hunt and his brother John; John Taylor, the editor of the *Sun* newspaper; Horace Twiss;[1] Barron Field; John Barnes, who subsequently became editor for many years of the *Times* newspaper; and some few others.

Hill never married, and finally took chambers in James' Street, Adelphi, wherein he resided till his death.

At last [continues Horace Smith] the pale summoner, who knocks alike at the door of the cottage and the palace (the Latin original is too hackneyed for quotation) found his way to the book-groaning third floor in the Adelphi, and it was announced that poor Tom Hill was dead! The statement was not universally believed, for he had lived so long that many thought it had become, like his inquisitiveness, a habit which he could not shake off. For the last half-century at least, his real age had been a mystery and a subject of incessant discussion among his friends, none of whom could coax or cajole him out of the smallest admission that might throw light upon the subject. . . . My brother James once said to him, "The fact is, Hill, that the register of your birth was destroyed in the great fire of London, and you take advantage of that accident to conceal your real age."
But Hook went much further by suggesting that

---

[1] A nephew of Mrs. Siddons, and one of the executors of her will. He was an eminent lawyer and politician, and was Vice-Chancellor of the Duchy of Lancaster. He wrote the *Life of Lord Eldon*.

he might originally have been one of the little Hills
recorded as skipping in the Psalms. No counter-
statement that might at least reduce him to the level
of Jenkins or old Parr, was ever made by the ruddy
patriarch. Perhaps he did not know his real age—
at all events, he never told it; nor could others supply
the information which he himself would not or could
not furnish; for the Mæcenas of Queenhithe not
being *atavis edite regibus*, like his namesake of Rome,
there were no known relations, dead or living, who
could throw any light upon this chronological
mystery. It has been stated, on what authority I
know not, that he was only eighty-three when he
died.

CHAPTER XX

Horace Smith's Recollections of Charles Mathews and
Theodore Hook.

Between Mr. and Mrs. Charles Mathews and the
Smiths a cordial and lasting friendship existed,
accentuated in the case of James by most pleasant
business relations.

Shortly before Mathews left England for America,
Horace wrote to him, expressing himself strongly
against the contemplated trip :—

Brighton, 1822.

Dear Mathews,

You have no occasion for your friendly fear
that I must have been " first knocked *down*, and then
up by a bus or a cab," since I neither called a second
time at Ivy Cottage, nor availed myself of the box
you were so kind as to reserve for us. In fact, I
knew nothing of the latter friendly arrangement, as
I was compelled to leave London on Friday, and did
not receive your letter, which was sent after me,
until yesterday. Best thanks, nevertheless, for your
kind intentions; and you may well suppose that I
would gladly have seen you " At Home," both
theatrically and domestically, if I could. The mis-
translation you mention is absurd enough; but one
might easily find twenty worse cases in our highways

and byways; for the common people have a strange propensity to adapt foreign words to their own familiar notions, particularly in the signs of shops and public-houses. *L'Aiguille et Fil* (the needle and thread) after being corrupted, perhaps in France, into *L'Aigle et Fils*, has been faithfully imported by our haberdashers as the *Eagle and Child*. Every one knows the perversion of *Boulogne* mouth; and the arms of one of the city companies suspended from an inn at Hounslow with the motto of " God encompasses us" procured for the house the name of the Goat and Compasses,—a singular conjunction, which is now actually figured on the signboard in lieu of the original arms. I have told you (have I not?) of Mrs. Lennox's strange blunder in translating from the French an account of the siege of Namur, which is equalled, if not surpassed, by one of those hacks employed by Cave to *do into* English Du Halde's *Description of China*, most Hibernically fixing an important occurrence to the twenty-first day of the *new* moon, having confounded the French words *neuve* and *neuvième*.

I should not, perhaps, intrude the opinion, but since you ask me how I like your friend—as a companion, I must frankly answer, not over much. He is ready and fluent, but it seemed to me to be a quickness of words rather than ideas. Whatever subject was started, he appeared to think it necessary to be always eloquent, in which, as well as in some other respects, he reminded me of " that great man, Mr. Prig, the auctioneer, whose manner was so invariably fine that he had as much to say upon a ribbon as upon a Raphael."

Your receiving the thanks and applauses of —— for not knowing what you ought to have known touching his benefit, reminds me of an exploit of my own, when I was a boy at school, and was asked the Latin for the word "cowardice." Having forgotten it, I ventured to say that the Romans had none; which was fortunately deemed a *bon mot*, and I got praises and a laugh for not knowing my lesson.

So you really have serious thoughts of crossing the Atlantic, and picking Brother Jonathan's pocket of his dollars after you have thrown him into fits of laughter, and you speak of the project as calmly as if you were about to fly from a country where you had been unhappy and unsuccessful, and from people who did not appreciate you as you deserve. Why, you Mammonite, what is to become of *us* in your absence? You will be making a fortune at *our* expense, not that of the Yankees; and as to any pleasure in the trip, lay not that flattering unction to your soul. The voyage, like all other voyages, must be a monotonous, objectless, occupationless, idealess nuisance; and how limited must be the pleasure of land travelling, even in the finest country in the world, where there are no human, or at least no civilized associations—nothing to connect the past with the present! What are rocks, forests, after your first stare of admiration, where there are no ruins, no local traditions, no historical records to lift them out of their materiality, by associating them with the great names and great achievements of past ages? You remember what Johnson says about the plains of Marathon and the ruins of Iona. You may get stimulants to patriotism and piety in many other places than these [of the Old World]; but what elevating recollections can you conjure up in a new country? Johnson has given his opinion on this very subject (and I say *ditto* to the Doctor)— for when some one asked, "Is not America worth seeing?" he replied, "Yes, sir, but not worth going to see!" That you will make it worth your while *financially*, I don't doubt—that it will answer your expectations in any other respect, I *do* doubt; that you would do much better to remain quietly where you are, I am quite sure. My wish may be father to the thought, but that does not invalidate it. I and mine to thee and thine.

Ever yours,
HORATIO SMITH.

P.S.—I saw our witty friend, Dubois[1] in London, who told me an anecdote in which you figured. W—— (so said the wag) pressed you to act for his benefit in the afterpiece at Covent Garden, which you said you would willingly have done, but that you were engaged that night to perform in the afterpiece at the English Opera-House, and could not cut yourself in half. "I don't know that," replied W——, "for I have often seen you act in *two pieces.*" Is this true? or is it one of Dubois' own children?[2]

When Mrs. Charles Mathews was collecting material for her husband's Memoirs, she applied to James and Horace Smith for any letters of his that they might have preserved. The result was very disappointing. James wrote back:—

27, *Craven Street*, 1837.

MY DEAR MRS. MATHEWS,

I have looked among my letters for any papers I might have retained of your departed and lamented husband. I have only been able to find one, which he sent me from America. I forward it with this.

I have forborne to intrude upon you with condolences on account of your bereavement, looking as

---

[1] At one time editor of the *Monthly Mirror;* author of *My Pocket-Book,* etc.

[2] *Memoirs of Charles Mathews,* by Mrs. Mathews.

I do upon such tributes as useless.   You must
permit me, however, upon this occasion, to dilate a
little upon the subject.

Charles Mathews was one of my first theatrical
acquaintances, and (without disparagement to his
brethren of the sock and buskin), I will add, one of
my most valued friends.   He was really what the
poet (perhaps a little too warmly) denominates "the
noblest work of God"—an honest man.   Whatever
character he might be called upon to assume on the
stage, he never lost sight of his own.   This circumstance was properly appreciated by the world.   He
moved in the best circles of society, and was valued
not less for the originality of his talents than for the
excellence of his moral character.   His public admirers and his private friends are equal sufferers
from his premature departure.

Believe me to remain,
Yours with great esteem,
JAMES SMITH.

With Horace Mrs. Mathews was even less successful, but his reply gives a capital *résumé* of
Mathews' excellent qualities.   He wrote:—

Brighton, October 2, 1837.

DEAR MRS. MATHEWS,

    I am both sorry and ashamed to confess that
of the many letters received at various times from
the friend whose loss I shall never cease to deplore,
I do not retain a single line in my possession.

    I am sorry, because it prevents my complying
with your request; and ashamed, because my con-
science now reproaches me with not having attached
sufficient importance to his ever pleasant communi-
cations.   It is some consolation to know that I have
not served him worse than others, the fact being,

that I have always been glad to get rid of letters as fast as I could. While unanswered, I contemplate them as accusing angels; I hate them afterwards for the compunctuous visitings they awakened before I could summon resolution to reply to them; and with this feeling veiled under an affected dislike to the accumulation of papers, I commit them to the flames as soon as I can. For my offence in this instance I ought to stand in the pillory with the never-sufficiently-to-be-anathematized cook, who lighted her kitchen fire for several months with *unique* old plays taken from a trunk in her master's library.

"Alas! poor Yorick! . . . a fellow of infinite jest, of most excellent fancy. Where be your gambols now? Your songs? your flashes of merriment that were wont to set the table in a roar?" By how many thousands has this hackneyed quotation been uttered with reference to Mathews; but, alas! how few can feel it so deeply, so poignantly, so irrecoverably, as those who were of his own immediate circle, and could therefore appreciate the charm of his society, whether in his moods of inexhaustible sprightliness, or when the rich stores of his penetrating mind were suffered to flow forth in rational and instructive conversation never long unembellished with some amusing anecdote.

Not only do I find it impossible even now to reconcile myself to his loss; but at times, strange as it may sound, I can hardly believe in its reality. He was not of an age to justify any anticipation of such an event; he seemed so well in health and so full of glorious glee when I last saw him; it is so difficult to imagine that he who was all vitality, who was, as it were, the very life of life, should be snatched from the convivial circle and consigned to the cold dumb grave, that one may well be pardoned for striving, even against conviction, to avoid the pang of so heart-withering a thought! and when it forces itself upon one's belief, it brings with it the aggravating reflection that the loss is utterly irreparable. There was but one Charles Mathews in the world—there never can be such another! Mimics, buffoons, jesters, wags, and even admirable comedians, we shall never want; but what are the best of them compared to *him?* Hyperion to a Satyr! He was the only *original* imitator I have ever encountered, for while others satisfied themselves with endeavouring to *embody* their originals, he made it a study to *mentalize* them. I am obliged to coin a word, but my meaning is, that while he surpassed all competitors in the mere mimicry of externals, he was *unique* in the subtlety, acuteness, and truth with which he could copy the *mind* of his prototype; extemporizing his moods of thought with all those finer shadings of the head and heart that constitute the niceties of individual character. As this intellectual portraiture demands a much higher order of talent than corporeal mimicry, so it is enjoyed with a much more exquisite zest by those who can appreciate its difficulty. Others might produce the image, and elaborate a faithful likeness, but Mathews alone held the Promethean torch that could vivify and animate it. You and I know full well that in this manner his own suggestions, creations, and mental mockeries, were the very soul of his entertainments at the Strand Theatre, although they were written and methodized by others. For this the public gave him little credit, any more than for the extraordinary powers of memory evinced in these unrivalled performances, with their numerous songs, and the *ad libitum* patter between the verses, very often varied with each *encore*. I remember his telling me that in a single week at

Edinburgh he had given as many, I think, as four *different* " At Homes," and all without book, note, or memorandum,—an effort of memory which I apprehend to be totally without parallel.

À propos to his performances in " Auld Reekie," which I visited some years ago, I recollect Sir Walter Scott mentioned them to me in terms of the highest admiration, adding expressions of sincere respect and friendship for the individual apart from all public and professional claims. Perhaps, there has never been a comedian who, while he lived in the full roar of popularity on the stage, was so universally and so thoroughly respected in private life, as Mr. Mathews. This it is that has made his loss so deeply and so widely felt. What numerous friends he possessed in England, Scotland, Ireland, America, to say nothing of the community at large, and how truly we may affirm that in his instance, even more extensively than in that of Garrick, his death " has diminished the public stock of harmless pleasure, and eclipsed the gaiety of nations ! "

Tragedians, it has been observed, are generally sprightly and jocose, while comedians and professional jesters not unfrequently sink into dejection or even confirmed hypochondria—a tendency which may easily be explained upon the principle of action and reaction, for the efforts of both classes are very exhausting, and they can only unbend by taking an opposite direction to that which has fatigued them. We may sit in one posture, until, like the tailor in the pit of Dublin theatre, we are glad to stand up to rest ourselves. Our minds like our bodies seek relief in contraries—a fact which is exemplified in nations as well as individuals. The habitually vivacious French find relaxation in cold, stern, unimpassioned classical tragedies; the taciturn melancholy Englishman is solaced by fun. farce, and foolery. I don't think Charles Mathews exhibited in any marked degree this professional bent of mind; but when severed from home and his usual resources, he certainly did seem to require pretty constant excitement to keep him from stagnating, as he called it, though I myself liked his quiet moods not less than his joyous and hilarious triumphs. It was only the difference between still and sparkling champagne. Some like the effervescence more than the flavour of the wine, others the reverse; and Mathews, in his various moods, could charm and gratify every taste. But if I run on with the list of his various and high qualifications, I shall never have done; and I must, therefore, devote the slip of paper that remains to the assurance that I am, with sincere regard, dear Mrs. Mathews,

Yours faithfully,
HORATIO SMITH.[1]

Horace Smith, contrasting the wit and humour of his friend Theodore Hook with that of Charles Mathews, says:[2]—

Far different was the effect produced by the unvaried and irrepressible ebullience of Theodore Hook's vivacity, which was a manifest exuberance from the conjunction of rampant animal spirits, a superabundance of corporeal vitality, a vivid sense of the ludicrous, a consciousness of his own unparalleled readiness, and a self-possession, not to say an effrontery, that nothing could daunt. Indulging his natural frolicsomeness rather to amuse himself than others, he was not fastidious about the quality of his audience, whom he would startle by some outrageous horseplay, or practical joke, if he found

---

[1] *Memoirs of Charles Mathews.*
[2] *A Greybeard's Gossip about his Literary Acquaintances.*

them too stupid for puns, jests, and songs. Thus you were always sure of him; he required no preparation, no excitement, he was never out of sorts, never out of spirits, never unprepared for a sally, however hazardous.

*　　　*　　　*　　　*　　　*

The century must have been young when I first met him at the house of the late Nat Middleton the banker, then living in Charles Street, St. James's Square. A large dinner-party was assembled, and before the ladies had withdrawn, the improvisatore was requested to favour the company with a song; his compliance was immediate and unembarrassed, as if it were an affair of no difficulty; and the verses, turning chiefly upon the names of the guests, only once varied by an allusion to some occurrence of the moment, were so pointed and sparkling, that I hesitated not to express my total disbelief in the possibility of their being extemporaneous, an opinion which some "good-natured friend" repeated to the singer. "Oh, the unbelieving dog!" exclaimed the vocalist. "Tell him if I am called upon again, he himself shall dictate the subject and the tune, which of course involves the metre; but it must be some common popular air." All this took place, and the second song proving still more brilliant than the first, I made a very humble palinode for my mistrust, and expressed the astonishment and delight with which his truly wonderful performance had electrified me. Not without difficulty, however, had I been enabled to believe my own ears, and several days elapsed before I had completely recovered from my bewilderment, for, as an occasional rhymester, I could well appreciate the difficulty of the achievement.

Some months after this encounter, while on my way to call upon a friend in Bedford Square, I was overtaken by so sudden a storm of thunder, lightning, and rain, that I took shelter in the doorway of a house in Charlotte Street, where I had hardly ensconced myself, when a figure ran helter-skelter to my side, seeking, as I imagined, the same protection as myself. It proved, however, to be Theodore Hook, who, after expressing his pleasure at our unexpected meeting, told me that the house was his father's, and, opening the door with a latch-key, asked me to put into the paternal port until the storm was over; an invitation which I readily accepted, and was ushered into a small back drawing-room, his own peculiar sanctum, which an associate of his thus describes:—"The tables, chairs, mantelpiece, piano, were all covered with a litter of letters, MS. music, French plays, notes, tickets, rhyming dictionaries; and not a seat to be had." Such was his plight at the time of my induction, with the addition of a half-finished bottle of wine, of which, after offering me a glass, he tossed off a large bumper, so early were sown the seeds of that propensity which gained upon him so lamentably in after-life! The day was sultry, the windows had been left open, so had the piano, at which Hook seated himself, and looking up at the sky, while he accompanied himself on the instrument, he sang in rhyme an extemporaneous defiance of the still raging storm, in terms so daring and unmeasured, that while I was surprised by his cleverness I was infinitely astounded by his outrageous audacity. We all know that a thunderstorm, the merely fortuitous strife of the elements, is produced by the collision of air-driven clouds; but the certain destructiveness and uncertain direction of the death-fraught electric spark, and the lingering delusion, not unassociated, perhaps, with our boyish recollections of the Jupiter Tonans, that these terrific fulminations are the voice of an offended deity, are calculated to awaken a feeling of vague solemnity, even in the minds of the most reckless. Not such, however, was its effect upon Hook, who, as the storm died away, a result which he attributed to his own menaces, began to imitate the retiring thunder on his instrument.

"Are you not afraid of the fate of Salmoneus?" I inquired.

"No, but the storm is afraid of me," he replied; and at the same time throwing down one of his gloves as a gauntlet, he sang a challenge to the clouds, inviting them to return and renew the contest, if they were not satisfied with the defeat they had already sustained.

Let not any one accuse him of intentional profaneness; it was the mere outburst of boisterous temerity, proceeding from intoxication of animal spirits, and a desire to astonish his auditor, in which latter object he certainly succeeded.

Retaining his seat at the piano, after the conclusion of his strange escapade, he asked me whether he should give me an extempore opera scene with imitations of the principal performers, or a Sadler's Wells burletta, such as was then currently performed in that suburban theatre. The latter won my preference, and most complete, as well as entertaining, was the performance. The morning song of Patty the dairymaid, as she sallied forth to milk her cows, the meeting, and the duet with her rustic lover, Hodge; the scolding of the cross old mother at her staying away so long from the cottage; her vindication by the good-tempered father—all given, music as well as words, in an unpremeditated trio; the advent of the squire—his jovial hunting-song— his dishonourable proposals to Patty, and their indignant rejection—his quarrel with Hodge, who upbraids him with his base attempt—his ignominious retreat, and the marriage of the happy pair, announced by a merry peal from the village bells, were all presented with such a perfect imitation of the Sadler's Wells libretto, as well as of the characters introduced, that his promptitude and versatility filled me with an indescribable amazement.

A rollicking buffoonery, and puns, and jests, and extemporaneous songs, and practical jokes of the most matchless impudence, were Hook's predominant characteristics; but he occasionally indulged a quiet drollery, not less laughable than his witty flashes. I once met him at a dinner-party, where his spirit seemed to be rebuked by the presence of two solemn-looking elderly noblemen, until, the subject having turned upon Shakespeare, one of the company observed that the only individual of all his acquaintance who thought that illustrious poet over-rated, was Perry, of the *Morning Chronicle.*

"This excites no surprise in me," said Hook, very gravely. "You must recollect that the bard has gone out of his way and substituted one beverage for another, for the express purpose of passing him by, and showing him a slight."

"Beverage! Slight! What *can* you mean?" demanded two or three voices.

"Why, in that well-known line—'To suckle fools and chronicle small beer'—is it not manifest that he *ought* to have written—Chronicle *Perry?*"

Sheer as was its absurdity, the address of the remark, and the dry seriousness with which it was propounded, shook the commoners with laughter, and even elicited a smile from the peers.

Often have I sat upon tenter-hooks for fear of the consequences, while Hook has been playing off his pranks with an impertinence that could hardly fail to be detected and resented; and more than once have I known him to be indebted to his legs for his escape. When supping with him one night at the

Hummums, he made such a point-blank attack by mimicry and every species of annoyance upon a corpulent respectable-looking country gentleman sitting in the same box, that at length he turned fiercely round upon his tormentor, exclaiming—

"What the devil do you mean by this impertinence?"

"My dear sir," replied Theodore, blandly, "my meaning can be explained to your entire satisfaction if you will allow me to say one word to you at the door of the coffee-room."

"Well, sir, well," growled the stranger, "I do expect entire satisfaction, and am ready to hear what you have got to say."

With which words he stalked to the door, which he had no sooner reached, than Hook resumed—

"You are to understand, sir, that I have laid a wager with my friend that I can run to the pit-entrance of Drury Lane Theatre faster than you can. Mind, we are to start when I clap my hands;" which signal he instantly gave, and took to his heels with a speed that soon carried him out of sight of his fat and fuming victim.

By the same safe but not very dignified expedient, did he extricate himself from a still more perilous dilemma at Sydenham. One Sunday afternoon, a party of us were strolling through the village just as the inhabitants were returning from church, when Hook, having suddenly turned-down his shirt-collar, pushed back his curly hair, and assumed a puritanical look, jumped into an empty cart by the roadside, and began to hold forth in the whining tones of a field preacher. Gathering ourselves in front to listen to him, we formed the nucleus of a congregation, which presently included a score or two of open-mouthed labourers and country crones. So enthusiastic and so devout were the sham preacher's manner and matter, that he commanded the deep attention of his audience, until, with a startling change of voice and look, he poured forth a volley of loud and abusive vulgarities, jumped from the cart, and ran across the fields, pursued by a couple of incensed rustics, who soon, however, abandoned a chase which they found to be hopeless. That we might not be suspected of any participation in this gross and inexcusable outrage, of which, indeed, all of us were really innocent, and many of us completely ashamed, we joined in the fierce indignation of the bystanders, fully assenting to their prediction that the perpetrator would inevitably come to be hanged in this world, and be provided with particularly warm quarters in the next. . . . An absence of several years from England, and my subsequent residence in a provincial town, so completely separated me from Hook, that though I often heard of his "sayings and doings," I only caught infrequent personal glimpses of him. Rumour had apprised me that he had been living too fast in a financial sense; and his bloated, unhealthy appearance gave me painful assurance at every fresh interview that the remark was equally applicable to his social habits. The last time I had the pleasure of dining in his company was in the year 1840, at the London residence of the late Lady Stepney. At this period his customary beverage was brandy and champagne in equal portions with an infusion of some stimulating powder, which he generally carried about with him. Appetite for food seemed to have nearly failed him, but he sought compensation in champagne, and I could perceive little or no diminution of his customary vivacity and his witty sallies. Willingly taking his place at the piano in the drawing-room, he commenced, "by particular desire of several persons of distinction," with the favourite mock cathedral chant of "The Little Birds do sing;" after which he was prevailed upon to treat us with an extempore song, which proved as prompt, sparkling, and felicitous, as the best effusion of his best days.   In the midst of it, Sir David Wilkie stole into the room, making his salutations in a whisper, lest he should disturb the singer, who was so far from being disconcerted that he immediately introduced him to the company as

> "His worthy friend, douce Davy Wilkie,
> Who needn't speak so soft and silky,"

since his entrance, instead of interrupting him, had supplied him with another verse.   A minute or two afterwards, a particle of candlewick fell upon the arm of Miss B——, an incident which the vocalist instantly seized, by addressing the lady, and declaring that it excited no surprise in him whatever—

> "Since he knew very well, by his former remarks,
> That wherever she went she attracted the sparks."

In this impromptu style, his tumbler being duly replenished, he continued to delight and astonish his auditors, until, at the warning of the tell-tale clock, striking the little hours, they tore themselves reluctantly away.

Poor, dear, fascinating, mirth-dispensing, body and mind-afflicted Theodore Hook!   From such scenes, from courtly bowers, and festive halls, and lordly saloons, where flattery, homage, worship, a living apotheosis, were lavished upon him by starred and gartered grandees, jewelled peeresses, bright-eyed belles, and the *élite* of the *beau-monde*, the miserable merry-andrew dragged himself to his unblessed home, utterly exhausted both in frame and mind, to bewail, in bitter compunction, his ruined prospects, his ever-increasing embarrassments, his waning health, his wasted life, and the felt approaches of that death which would leave his creditors unpaid, his children and their mother utterly destitute ! The firework had been played off; it had flashed and sparkled, and scattered light and cheerfulness around, delighting all by its ever-changing and ever-charming forms and hues; and nothing now was left but the darkened, unsightly frame-work of the wheel, worn, wasted, and shattered by its own brilliant gyrations under an artificial and self-consuming impulse. A few weeks before the dinner-party at which I had seen him *lionizing* in all his glory, and apparently sharing the happiness that he conferred, he had made the following entry in his diary—

"January 1st, 1840.—To-day another year opens upon me with a vast load of debt and many incumbrances. I am suffering under constant anxiety and depression of spirits, which nobody who sees me in society dreams of; but why should I suffer my own private worries to annoy my friends ? "

He died the next year, and was buried in Fulham churchyard; but few mourners, and none of any rank or fame, following him to the grave. Not they ! More deeply would they have regretted the loss of a favourite living dog than of their dead lion ! The popular player, mountebank, and buffoon had taken his benefit in the way of invitations, banquets, jollifications, metropolitan revels, and the run of rural castles, when a man of genius and pleasantry was wanted to enliven the dulness of the guests; and the sacrificers had now nothing further to do with or for their victim. No, nor for *his* victims! the produce of his books and other effects, about £2500, having been surrendered to the Crown as the privileged creditor, and his children and their mother being thus left penniless, a subscription was opened for their assistance, to which the King of Hanover generously transmitted £500, probably in grateful remembrance of the able assistance he had received from Hook's pen, when a malignant and groundless outcry was raised on account of the suicide of Sellis, His Majesty's German servant. Some of the friends of the deceased in middle life came forward with liberal donations; but few, very few, of those who had either profited as politicians by Theodore Hook's zeal and ability, or courted him in their lofty circles for the fascination of his wit, were found to show any feeling for his unfortunate offspring.

The practical jokes of Theodore Hook, especially in the early portion of his career, were sometimes senseless; and in these "questionable freaks," as he dubs them, Horace Smith confessed that he occasionally participated.

There is a local tradition amongst the oldest inhabitants of Fulham, that Hook, who was in the habit of driving about that remote suburb in a curricle, one evening drew up at the door of the Golden Lion, a tavern dating back to the time of Henry VII., and engaged "mine host" in earnest "horsey" controversy. Presently, leaving his companion to continue the discussion, in which the landlord, who prided himself upon his knowledge of horseflesh, had become intensely interested, he entered the house, and, knowing his way about, contrived, unperceived, to enter the cellars, where he deliberately turned on the taps and removed the spigots from the casks not in use, until the entire stock of ale and porter was flowing away in streams. The astonishment and indignation of the owner, who, after seeing Hook drive away, found his cellar flooded with malt-liquor, may be imagined; and a pretty stiff bill for damages reminded Hook that "pranks" were sometimes rather costly forms of amusement.

JAMES SMITH.

CHAPTER XXI

The personal appearance of James Smith—His habits—His social circle—His clubs—His love of London—Revisits Chigwell school—His last illness and death.

THE personal appearance of James Smith was decidedly striking. In his prime—when *Rejected Addresses* was published (1812)—he was considered to be one of the handsomest men about town. Tall, straight-limbed, and well-proportioned, blue-eyed, and fresh complexioned, his hair growing well back from a noble and intellectual forehead, the manly beauty of his person was evident, even in the unlovely dress of that period, with its heavily-lapelled, deep-cuffed coats, tight-fitting pantaloons, and stiff cravats that perpetually seemed to threaten apoplexy or strangulation. His manner was that of a polished well-bred gentleman, combined with a singular fascination of address. No one could better appreciate courtesy in others than he who possessed it in a marked degree. Later in life, depressed and enfeebled by ill-health, his natural animation somewhat failed him ; but no amount of suffering could extinguish the cheerfulness of his countenance when in congenial society, or dim the merry twinkle in his eyes that from long ̇usage had contracted an habitual look of drollery, ever ready, at the prompting of anything, animate or inanimate, to find articulate utterance in some witty saying. Even his painful malady he made the subject of a now well-known epigram—

> The French have taste in all they do,
>   While we are left without;
> Nature to them has given *goût*,
>   To us has given gout.

He was a confirmed bachelor. His father used often to expostulate with him, instancing his own happy experience of matrimony—but in vain. After one of these attempts to shake his son's resolution, the good old gentleman made the following entry in his Journal :—

September 4, 1829.—I went with my daughter Maria in a fly to call upon my son James, in Austin Friars. The gout has made ravages upon his health and personal comfort, but his spirits, I understand, have not much fallen off. I wish that he had taken to himself a prudent wife with good connections and a sufficiency of fortune to comfort him in his declining years ! This wish I have often expressed to himself and to his brother Leonard, who also has preferred a bachelor's life to that of a married man.[1]

James Smith's celibacy [says Horace] proceeded rather from too discursive than too limited an admiration of the sex. To the latest hour of his life, he exhibited a marked preference for the young, the

[1] Leonard subsequently married a Miss Lane, a West Indian cousin, and died suddenly, January 14th, 1837, leaving no children.

intelligent, and the musical ; and never concealed his dislike of a dinner-party composed exclusively of males.   It will be seen that even in the many hours of solitude and sickness that threw a shade over the closing scenes of his life, he does not appear even to have regretted his bachelorship.

Many were the jokes he made against his unmarried state, one of which he wrote in his niece's album—

> Should I seek Hymen's tie,
> As a poet I die—
>   Ye Benedicts, mourn my distresses !
> For what little fame
> Is annexed to my name
>   Is derived from *Rejected Addresses.*

His habits were most methodical and regular; but, the day's labours over, he was ready for any gaiety and recreation.   He almost lived in the theatres, and the passion that survived all others was his devotion to the drama.   Having excellent judgment, he was often consulted by actors upon matters of their own art; and so infallible was his memory that they frequently applied to him for the dates of half-forgotten plays they themselves had figured in.

Being pre-eminently sociable he was a great diner-out, and, although never a *bon vivant*,[1] possessed a keen appreciation of the niceties of gastronomy, and was a good judge of wine.   So wide was his circle of acquaintances that no dinner-party of any importance was considered complete without his lively presence and amusing conversation.

[1] Though he was not fastidious, he had a particular aversion to certain popular dishes, such as venison pasty, rabbit pie, calves' head and bacon, tripe, mutton broth, and mackerel.

His favourite *salon* was that of Lady Blessington, the beautiful, accomplished, but wayward leader of fashion, at Seamore Place, Curzon Street, and at Gore House, Kensington, where he met all the celebrities of the day—Thomas Moore, Walter Savage Landor, Sir Edward Bulwer Lytton, Samuel Lover, Benjamin D'Israeli, etc., etc.   At these assemblies, crippled as he was, and forced to wheel himself about in a kind of invalid chair, he had always something pleasant and witty to say to everybody, his best *bons mots* and brightest smiles being reserved for his fascinating hostess.

Perhaps, his most intimate friend was Count D'Orsay, who, he always declared, was unrivalled in his combination of good sense and gaiety.   On one occasion, James Smith met the Countess Guiccioli at Gore House, and after dinner they became very confidential, exchanging reminiscences of Lord Byron, Shelley, and Leigh Hunt, whom she had met in Italy, and for the remainder of the evening they enjoyed an uninterrupted *tête-à-tête*.   Shortly afterwards, on setting down James Smith at his house in Craven Street, D'Orsay remarked, " What was all that Madame Guiccioli was saying to you just now ?"

" She was telling me her apartments are in the Rue de Rivoli, and that if I visited the French capital she hoped I would not forget her address," replied James.

" What !   It took all that time to say that !   Ah ! Smeeth, you old humbug ! that won't do."

James Smith thus describes a dinner at the future Lord Lytton's :—

Saturday, December 23, 1838.—I dined with E. L. Bulwer, at his new residence in Charles Street, Berkeley Square, a splendidly and classically-fitted up mansion. One of the drawing-rooms is a fac-simile of a chamber which our host visited at Pompeii,—vases, candelabra, chairs, tables to correspond. He lighted a perfumed pastille modelled from Mount Vesuvius. As soon as the cone of the mountain began to blaze, I fancied myself an inhabitant of the devoted city; and, as Pliny the Elder, thus addressed Bulwer, my supposed nephew—

"Our fate is accomplished, nephew. Hand me yonder volume; I shall die as a student in my vocation. Do you then hasten to take refuge on board the fleet at Misenum. Yonder cloud of hot ashes chides thy longer delay. Feel no alarm for me. I shall live in story. The author of *Pelham* will rescue my name from oblivion." Pliny the younger made me a low bow.

Occasionally James Smith joined the family dinner parties of his friend and medical attendant, Dr. Paris,[1] of Dover Street, Piccadilly, whose eldest son, Mr. Tom Paris, recalls the fact that in his mother's drawing-room, James Smith used to sing *The Last Shilling* and other humorous songs; " we children," he says, " standing round and in a measure held in check by his commanding presence, and his odd way of changing from a laugh to a grave expression with

---

[1] Dr. Paris was a physician of considerable eminence, famous for the extent and accuracy of his chemical knowledge, and for his popular lectures on *Materia Medica*. In 1844 he became President of the Royal College of Physicians, and was annually re-elected until his death in 1856.

a solemn stare at the young faces still laughing. I can see him now in my mind's eye."

James Smith wrote the following lines to his favourite physician on his birthday:—

> Namesake of Helen's favourite boy,
>   Who shunn'd the martial fray,
> May all your days be days of joy,
>   Like this, your natal day.
> My votive glass, not pledged by stealth,
>   I fill at Bacchus' shrine ;
> And thus, convivial, drink your health,
>   Whose skill establish'd mine.

To Mr. Tom Paris he sent the following epigram—

"ON TOM'S FIRST TAIL COAT

> At the loss of your jacket, Tom, cease to repine,
>   Let some younger Harrow boy nab it.
> Your form you have alter'd, and I have changed mine,
>   We both are the creatures of *habit*."

At Ivy Cottage, Fulham, James Smith was the ever welcome guest of Charles Mathews ; and he was frequently to be seen at the hospitable board of Mr. Francis Fladgate, a solicitor, of Essex Street, Strand. Fladgate, who was a fellow-member of the Garrick Club, and had pronounced dramatic tastes, lived in an unpretending but very comfortable house in Brompton, not far from Thurloe Square, where he gave the most delightfully informal little dinners, at which were present such men as Planché, Harrison Ainsworth, the Kembles, Count D'Orsay, and the Rev. R. H. Barham, of *Ingoldsby Legends* fame, whose daughter,[1] from quite an early age, generally went with her father when he dined out, and has a delightful recollection of the bright conversation and gaiety that characterized these gatherings.

Fladgate was a most interesting man, his memory well stored with anecdotes of the older Kean, Kemble, and other great lights of the stage; and as recently as 1888, when Henry Irving produced *Macbeth* at the Lyceum, Fladgate gave his friends at the Garrick a most vivid delineation of how the part had been acted by the old school, and forcibly described John Kemble's method of representing the " Stranger."

W. Jerdan says that Fladgate was one of the Sydney Smith species of wits (who are rare), and was so prolific in piquant sayings that, if all were remembered, they might fill a volume. When Elliston was in treaty to become the lessee of Drury Lane Theatre, he gave way to more than his usual excitements, and, consulting his legal adviser at all hours in no very proper state, was thus addressed by Fladgate—" Hang it, sir, there is no getting through any business with you, who come to me fresh drunk every night and stale drunk every morning."

As might be expected from his habits and disposition, James Smith was what Dr. Johnson said of Boswell—a " very clubbable man," and belonged to no less than three clubs, something to be rather proud of in the first forty years of the present century. In the year 1800 there existed only about half-a-dozen of

---

[1] Lady E. A. Bond, widow of the late Principal Librarian of the British Museum.

these convenient resorts, and at the time of James Smith's death (1839), there were but twenty-one, with which contrast the number contained in the most recent list of principal London clubs. First of his clubs in importance was the Athenæum. He was one of the original members whose names appear in the private printed list, dated 22nd June, 1824, other members in that year being—The Earl of Aberdeen, Lord Abinger, Lord Blessington, Sir Francis Burdett, Thomas Campbell (the poet), Sir Astley Cooper, the Rt. Hon. John Wilson Croker, Isaac D'Israeli, Henry Hallam (the historian), Sir Henry Holland, Charles Kemble, Samuel Rogers (the poet), Horace Twiss, J. M. Turner, R.A., the Duke of Wellington, Sir A. Westmacott, R.A., Sir David Wilkie, R.A., Roger Wilbraham, Rev. Thos. Malthus, Dr. Magee, Bishop of Dublin, the Earl of Mansfield, Charles Mathews, Thomas Moore (the poet), William Mulready, R.A., Viscount Palmerston, Sir Thomas Lawrence, P.R.A., C. R. Leslie, R.A., and H.M. Leopold, King of the Belgians.

In August and September of 1831 private meetings were held at Drury Lane Theatre, and subsequently at No. 3, Charles Street, to consider the founding of a new club, to be called after the immortal Garrick, "for the purpose of bringing together the patrons of the drama and its professors, and also for offering literary men a rendezvous." The prime movers in the matter were Sir Andrew Barnard the banker, Francis Mills, Esq., Samuel J. Arnold, Esq., Samuel Beazley, Esq., Lord Kinnaird, the Earl of Mulgrave, and Sir George Warrender, Bart. The first general meeting was held at Charles Street, when it was decided that the number of members should be limited to three hundred, the first hundred to consist of the founders and their friends; the second hundred, of those who might be introduced and guaranteed by three members; and the third hundred to be balloted for in the usual way.

James Smith was among the fortunate second hundred, and his name was enrolled October 1st, 1831.

Probatt's private hotel, No. 29, King Street, Covent Garden[1]—long since demolished—was taken on lease, and with a few alterations, made sufficiently commodious. It was open for members on the 5th of February, 1832, and on the 13th an inaugural dinner was given, when one hundred and eight members and friends were present and H.R.H. the Duke of Sussex occupied the chair. A charmingly appropriate song, written by the Rev. R. H. Barham,[2] was admirably sung by Braham.

The following is an extract from the list of the principal members of the Garrick in 1835 :—

The Marquess of Anglesea, K.G., the Earl of Chesterfield, the Duke of Devonshire, K.G., the Earl of Mulgrave (President), the Hon. Fulke Greville, Lord Arthur Hill, Captain Gronow, M.P., the Rev. R. H. Barham, Thomas Forbes Bentley, John Murray, Samuel Rogers, Sir John Soane, James Sheridan

[1] From King Street, the Club removed to its present house in Garrick Street.

[2] Not, as W. Jerdan relates, by James Smith.

R

Knowles, Richard Brinsley Sheridan, William Jerdan, F.S.A., Nathaniel and Anthony Rothschild, P. N. Talfourd (barrister), Francis Fladgate (solicitor), W. M. Thackeray, J. R. Planché, Theodore Hook, Clarkson Stansfield, Charles John Kean, Charles Kemble, William Macready, Charles Mathews, Charles Mayne Young, John Braham, Captain Marryat, etc., etc.

Of such talented and respectable "good fellows" was the club composed; yet *Fraser's Magazine* for November 1834[1] scurrilously attacked James Smith, and the members of the club generally, in language which I reproduce only to show to what depths a leading periodical could descend in those days:—

There sits James Smith with his feet pressing a soft cushion, his elbows dropped by the arms of an easy chair, his hand resting on a crutch, his hair departed from his head, his nose tinged with the colours of the dawn, and his whole man in a state of that repose which indicates that he has had much work in his way while sojourning in this world, and that, like Falstaff, he is taking his ease in his own inn, the *Garrick*—a club of gentlemen which in a great measure would answer the description given by that worthy knight of his companions in arms, as being principally composed of "gentlemen of companies, slaves as ragged as Lazarus—discarded, unjust serving-men, younger sons of younger brothers, revolted tapsters and ostlers trade-fallen." Among them sits James Smith, regaling them with jokes, which, if they are not quite so good as Falstaff's, have at least the merit of being as old. . . . But let him have his praise. His single talent was a good talent,

---

[1] *Gallery of Literary Character*, No. 54.

and there is no reason why he should wrap it up in a
napkin.   We have already alluded to the universal
diffusion of his name among us English folk, and its
trite and ordinary sound in our ears.   It is, perhaps,
more congruous on that account with the station
which he has chosen to hold in our literature.   His
place there is of the Smiths, Smithish.   In his own
magazine essays, it is a favourite pastime to represent
Mr. Deputy Higgs of Norton Folgate apeing the
great, and very much disparaged for the parody.   To
Scott, to Southey, to Wordsworth, to Byron, Smith
is what this Norton Folgatian is to the gentlemen of
White's.   He is, therefore, well named ; and let him
not repine at his “ compellation,” as in former days,
when, walking in Oxford Street with Wilson Croker,
he observed over a shop door, “Mortimer Percy,
tailor.”   “ Is it not too hard,” said James, then fresh
from all the honours of the *Rejected Addresses* about
him, “ that two such grand and aristocratic names
should be the lot of a tailor, while two wits and
gentlemen are moving about the street, afflicted with
the names of Croker and Smith ? ”

> “ No—the name is right— ;
> And may the Garrick hail with loud acclaims,
> For many a year, the gouty jokes of James.”

Among the relics and mementoes preserved at the
Garrick is a crutch-cane, presented to the club
by R. G. Clarke, Esq., in 1855, once the property of
gout-afflicted James Smith, to whom it had been left
by General Phipps, a member of Lord Mulgrave's
family, who had purchased it at Venice.

But James Smith's favourite as well as earliest
club, was the Union in Trafalgar Square, to which he
was elected on the 11th of February, 1823, his proposer

and seconder being General Phipps and Mr. Pascoe
Grenfell, M.P. This club was founded in 1821, for
politicians of whatever party, mercantile and professional men, together with what James Smith described
as "gentlemen at large." The army and navy element was then more pronounced in the club than it is
at present, and there were more peers of the realm.
Amongst James Smith's contemporaries were Lord
Athlone, Viscount Gage, Viscount Torrington, the Earl
of Buckinghamshire, the Hon. F. Bertie, the Rt. Hon.
W. Huskisson, Sir J. M. Doyle, Sir Henry Rycroft,
Sir T. Hislop, Sir E. Antrobus, Sir J. Fellows, etc.,
etc.

In his latter years, when infirmities were upon
him, James Smith found the Union most convenient,
it being only a couple of hundred yards or so from
Craven Street, a distance that he could just manage
to compass by means of his crutch-sticks. He used
to go there at about three o'clock in the afternoon,
and at six o'clock, when the drawing-room became
deserted, he adjourned to the dining-room, where he
usually dined off haunch of mutton or lamb chops,
when in season, restricting himself to a single half-
pint of sherry. Then he would convey himself to the
cozy library on the first floor, and read until nine,
call for a cup of coffee and a biscuit, continue reading
until eleven, and home to bed.

Craven Street, Strand, is one of those old-fashioned
thoroughfares peculiar to the locality, which lead to
the river. No. 27, where James Smith lived in the
evening of his life, is a three-storeyed house, near the

bottom of the street, on the left-hand side from the Strand. It has a curious miniature bow-window on the drawing-room floor, and appears to be unaltered. This modest establishment was carefully presided over by a housekeeper, of whom he wrote:—

May, 1838.—Mrs. Glover reminded me on Tuesday, that on that day she had just been twenty-four years in my service. What a lapse of time! How different was I then from that which I am now! then a rollicking, lively, fresh-coloured man of the town, running from dinner to rout, and from tavern to opera; and now quiet and contented, with all my social eggs in one basket. May the basket never break!

Although a confirmed metropolitan in his tastes, with little or no liking for "grinding the gravel," as he used to call an excursion out of his beloved London, he went for many successive summers to Mulgrave Castle in Yorkshire, on long visits to Earl Mulgrave (the present Marquis of Normanby's grandfather). Nearer home, he frequently stayed at Sheen, near Guildford, at his friend's the Rev. Torre Holme, to whom he bequeathed his well-known portrait by Lonsdale, of Berners Street.

For Chigwell, the scene of his school-days, he retained a great affection, and after a lapse of fifty years revisited it, jealously noting every change that had taken place. He writes—

Strange that a village should survive,
For ten years multiplied by five,
   The same in size and figure.

> Knowing nor plenty nor distress—
> If foiled by fortune, why no less ?
> If favoured, why no bigger ? [1]

Time had not effaced the image of Nancy, the pride of Chigwell Row, who so distracted the elder Chigwellians in church, for Smith took the trouble to seek her out.   He writes :—

> I pass the Vicar's white abode
> And pondering gain the upward road,
>   By busy thoughts o'erladen,
> To where ' the pride of Chigwell Row '
> She lives—a handsome widow now,
>   As erst a lovely maiden ! [2]

Could James Smith resume this life and look in at his old school, he would find there a " Smith " dormitory, so called in honour of the authors of *Rejected Addresses*, and on each side of the library fireplace he would come face to face with presentments of himself and his brother Horace.   In the *Chigwell Kalendar*, he would, amongst many important entries, come across the dates of his birth and death, also those of his brother.   In short, he would find that it is the tradition of the school to be " very proud " of having had a share in the education of the Smiths, *par nobile fratrum*.

James Smith's patience in suffering was remarkable.   He bore his ever-increasing attacks of gout with great fortitude, seldom alluding to his malady, and checking all reference to it on the part of others. In the presence of visitors he tried to throw off even

---

[1] *Chigwell Revisited.*   [2] *Ibid.*

the appearance of invalidism. When he required medical advice, he used to dispatch the following characteristic bulletin to Dr. Paris.

27, *Craven Street.*

Feverish! please call upon,
Yours truly,
James Smith.

He would not permit even his nearest relations to nurse him. The faithful Mrs. Glover was the only person from whom he would accept assistance.

In the early part of 1839 he was seized with acute influenza, which, combined with a very bad attack of gout, so completely upset him that his life was almost despaired of. He recovered, however, for the time, and joined his brother Horace at Tunbridge Wells, where, though quite crippled, he seemed to rally in an extraordinary manner, regaining all the buoyancy of his youth, singing, jesting, and laughing with his nieces from morning to night.

Alas! the candle was only flickering in its socket prior to extinction. With the last days of the year, though his pain was much lessened, he knew that he was approaching his end, which he regarded with philosophic resignation. As Christmas Day drew near, he rallied for a short period, and thought himself justified in accepting an invitation to dine with Dr. Paris on that festive occasion; but in the meantime, his malady assumed a fatal form, locating in the vital organs, and at two o'clock on the morning of December 24th he quietly passed away in the sixty-fifth year of his age.

At his own request, he was buried with the utmost privacy in the vaults of St. Martin's Church. No commemoration tablet marks the house where he died, nor does "storied urn or animated bust" any-where recall his name. But he is not forgotten ; and if it be a merit to have added to the world's store of wit, and to have contributed to the innocent happiness of hundreds, James Smith lived to some purpose, and we should "keep his memory green."

CHAPTER XXII

APPARENTLY contented with the success of his contributions to the *Rejected Addresses*, and wanting all motive for serious effort, James Smith henceforth produced only what may be regarded as fugitive pieces.

He contributed to the *New Monthly Magazine* from its commencement in 1821; and he composed miscellaneous sketches, etc., in prose and verse, which, after his death, were brought together and published by his brother. He also wrote the text for Charles Mathews' entertainments, the most important of which were *The Trip to France* and *The Country Cousin.* For these he received the handsome sum of £1000. They were written in the years 1820—1822; but long before, as Mrs. Mathews relates in her *Memoirs of Mr. Charles Mathews*, James Smith had been the collaborator of that gifted comedian. Says Mrs. Mathews:—

In the course of this winter, 1808, Mr. Mathews conceived the idea of performing *An Entertainment;* yet, doubting the possibility of one pair of lungs

being able to furnish strength sufficient for three
consecutive hours' exertion, "the occasional assistance of Mrs. Mathews in the vocal department" was
called in as a make-weight, and as the entertainment was only intended to be represented in Yorkshire, where I had been always received with
partiality, such an auxiliary was not altogether
insignificant to the end desired.

Our friend, Mr. James Smith, kindly undertook
to write some songs suitable to Mr. Mathews'
peculiar powers; and to link together certain descriptions which he had heard him give, of eccentric
characters, manners, and ventriloquy. So excellent
was the whole, that it proved brilliantly successful;
and this first effort of actor and author, after ten
years became the foundation of that extraordinary
series of *At Homes* upon which my husband's
great professional reputation was perfected. Among
the songs, *The Mail Coach* and *Bartholomew Fair*,
which Mr. Mathews afterwards sung till all playgoers
were familiar with them, were the most popular;
and though introduced so long ago, and on every
possible occasion, they were as full of point and
attraction in the year 1818, as if then heard for the
first time. . . . How deeply my husband considered
himself to be indebted to Mr. Smith for connecting
and applying in so masterly a manner the matter
which was before him, and for the humorous songs,
written so admirably to display the original powers
of the singer, may be imagined. *The Mail Coach*
and *Bartholomew Fair* were the first of their class,
and might be said, like the two bags of gold, to be
the fruitful parents of many more, well known to
the public as belonging peculiarly to Mr. Mathews.

For this invaluable service Mr. Smith declined
anything like payment, and would at length only
allow my husband to present him with some trivial

remembrance. Mr. Smith's acknowledgment of this trifle offers so agreeable an evidence of his liberal feelings, and his friendship for my husband, that I cannot resist inserting it here.

> "*Basinghall Street,*
> *July* 8, 1808.

MANY thanks, my dear sir, for your present. Your kindness has caused you to overrate my poor abilities; though you do no more than justice to the alacrity with which I endeavoured to serve one for whose private worth and professional talents I entertain so high an esteem. I barely supplied the outline; your initiative skill supplied the colouring and finish.

Had I leisure for the undertaking, I certainly should endeavour to exhibit your powers in a more dramatic form, and transplant my weak pen from the lecture-room to the stage; but other avocations prevent such an attempt.

It is rather a novel case, that the 'pursuit of the law' should save a man from damnation.

With best compliments to Mrs. Mathews, believe me,

> Dear sir, very truly yours,
> JAMES SMITH.

TO CHARLES MATHEWS, ESQ."

Quite different was it with Horace Smith, who, although he postponed all serious effort until he retired from business, could not keep his pen quite idle. The hankering after dramatic fame ever strong within him, he wrote, in 1813, a five-act comedy entitled *First Impressions, or Trade in the West;* also a farce called *The Absent Apothecary,* the fate of which production, he says, effectually cured him of his aspiration to become a play-writer.

The authorship of the former had been carefully kept from all but his friend, Mr. Barron Field, at whose chambers he had agreed to dine on the night of its first representation. Mr. Langsdorff, an *attaché* of the Bavarian embassy, was present, but he did not divine the reason for drinking success "to the new play." After dinner the three went together to Drury Lane Theatre, and took their places in the pit.

All went smoothly [says Horace Smith] until the delivery of a claptrap speech by one of the actors, to the effect that money raised in England for a single charity, often exceeded the revenues of a whole German principality. "*Vot is dat?*" whispered Langsdorff to the author; "*does he loff at de Jair-mans? den, I shall damn his blay.*" Whereupon, in spite of Field's protestations, he set up a low hiss, which presently awakened sympathetic though not very alarming echoes in various parts of the house. Every playgoer knows that a sound of this sort, like a snowball, gathers as it rolls, and that even an individual goose seldom fails to obtain sympathizing responses from his own flock. At first no particular effect was produced, but the unpacified German, con-tinuing to renew the experiment, succeeded at length in establishing a decided opposition.

The unfortunate author, sitting upon thorns, but endeavouring to look particularly comfortable, when the fate of the comedy seemed doubtful, sought to avoid suspicion by venturing now and then on a gentle sibillation, delivered *sotto voce*, more in sorrow than in anger, and with the natural tenderness of a father correcting his own child. But, as the clamour became louder, and the failure of the play appeared more certain, his anxiety to escape detection was pushed to such nervous excess that he even commenced a vociferous cry of " *Off! Off!* " Presently, however, a change came over the spirit of the house ; two or three scenes in succession had won manifest favour, and when the author, still more excited by some fresh but very partial signs of disapprobation, would have renewed the cry which Langsdorff was ever ready to commence, it was put down by still louder and more clamorous exclamations of " *Silence ! turn them out ! turn them out !* " Peremptory as was the mandate, the playwright gratefully obeyed it, and even his German neighbour was compelled to hold his tongue ; the piece was given out for repetition without a dissentient voice. It was acted twenty nights successively , and though possessing but little merit, it could claim the distinction of being the first instance (since the days of the Countess of Macclesfield and Savage) where the condemnation of the offspring has been eagerly sought by its own parent.

But Horace Smith was not cured of his craving for fame as a playwriter, until the following episode occurred. He was about to bring out a farce, the great success of which was so confidently predicted by the performers during the rehearsals, and more especially by his friend Tom Dibdin, himself an experienced dramatist, that the author, in an unlucky hour, consented to the insertion of a notice in the *Morning Chronicle*, assigning to him the authorship of the forthcoming piece, entitled *The Absent Apothecary*.

Horace Smith, however, had his own misgivings on the subject. Writing to his friend Horace Twiss, he says :—

DEAR TWISS,

Black Fate hangs o'er me, and the avenging gods. Will you witness my damnation to-morrow night, which they desire me to expect?

I wish you would go, you are a good laugher, though I do not promise that you *ought* to laugh.

Yours truly,

H. SMITH.

Tuesday night.

That he might witness his anticipated triumph in comfort without being seen, Mr. Raymond gave him admission to his own private box at Drury Lane, which adjoined the corner of the two-shilling gallery, where the playwright took his seat. From the commencement there was a furious contest between the supporters and the assailants of the new piece; and during a lull in the uproar, Smith heard a savage-looking fellow in the gallery close to his elbow, exclaim to a friend of the same stamp, "I say, Jack, if I could get hold of the precious ass that wrote the rubbish, I'm blessed if I wouldn't take and chuck him right over." Not having the least wish to be thrown overboard by the gallery gods, the author quietly left the box and stole down-stairs, believing that, if discovered, he would be torn in pieces by the dissentients, so furious had they become.

On reaching the outside of the theatre, and finding himself shrouded in friendly darkness, he felt as if he had just saved his life, and was hastening away, when an irresistible desire to learn the fate of his bantling drew his step backwards to the stage-door. Nobody being there, he crept in, unobserved, and stealing to the rear of the building, where a solitary lamp just served to make the darkness visible, stationed himself beneath it, listening to the loud conflict that agitated the invisible audience. While thus occupied, two scene-shifters approached his retreat, and recognizing him, for they had frequently seen him at the rehearsals, one said to the other in a pitying and patronizing tone, "Tell you what, mate; I shouldn't mind betting a pot of porter that this here farce looks up a'ter all."

Far from being consoled by the opinion of these discriminating critics, the author felt so humiliated by their commiseration that he again left the theatre, and betook himself to the coffee-room of the *Hummums*, where his brother had appointed to meet him and communicate the final decision of the audience. Soon did the herald appear, but with a sinister and flushed expression. *The farce had been most unequivocally condemned!*

Next morning, as he was threading his way

through unfrequented streets for fear of encountering any of his acquaintances, his eye glanced upon a play-bill before which he stood transfixed, for it announced a second performance of *The Absent Apothecary*. There it was in huge red letters, which appeared to grow in size as he rubbed his eyes and looked again and again. Then he ran to Golden Square, where lived the stage-manager, whom he luckily found at home.

"Surely, sir, this must be some dreadful mistake," was his ejaculation as soon as he recovered breath enough for speech.

"No, indeed, my friend, no mistake whatever; all right, all right."

"All right! I thought my unfortunate farce was unequivocally condemned last night?"

"So it was. With all my experience, I have seldom seen a hostile opinion so very decidedly and generally expressed."

"In the name of heaven, then, why have you announced it for repetition?"

"On that very account; for the public will be so very indignant at seeing it brought forward again, that they will come by hundreds to confirm their sentence—there will be a famous uproar as soon as it begins—I shall then go forward as manager, and pledge myself to its withdrawal, and by this means, you see, we shall be sure of a bumper."

"And so for your bumper house, for which I don't get a farthing, I am to undergo a second martyrdom?"

The manager gave a shrug of the shoulders, not less significant than Lord Burleigh's celebrated shake of the head.

Horace Smith took his departure, vowing that he would never again attempt to write for the stage; and he kept his word.

In 1825, when Horace Smith returned from Versailles, some of his miscellaneous pieces were collected, and, under the title of *Gaieties and Gravities*, were published by Henry Colburn.

After a brief sojourn in London he went to Tunbridge Wells, where he lived for three years at Mount Edgcombe Cottage, and wrote *Brambletye House*, published by Henry Colburn in 1826. In this historical novel, he availed himself of romantic incidents connected with the Cromwellian and Restoration period of English history, and largely helped in developing a taste for that particular style in tales of adventure.

It is of course a truism that Sir Walter Scott had previously, in 1822, introduced it in *Peveril of the Peak*, and when Horace Smith forwarded to Scott a copy of *Brambletye House* he modestly admitted that his intention in writing that book was to follow in the footsteps of the Master of romance.

Brighton, 5, Hanover Crescent,
July 4, 1826.

Sir,

As I never proposed any other object to myself, in my novel of *Brambletye House*, than to produce a humble imitation of that style which you

s

have so successfully introduced into the department of literature, I was so far gratified by the sale of the first two editions, as it proved that I had made some little approach towards my model. The call for a third I believe to be mainly attributable to the generous notice which you condescended to take of me in the Preface to *Woodstock*, for which I should sooner have taken the liberty to address you with my thanks, but that I waited to request your acceptance of a copy. Requesting you to do me the favour of now accepting it, I have the honour to be, with the most unfeigned admiration of your talents,

Sir,

Your obliged and obedient humble servant,

HORATIO SMITH.

Scott, on the other hand, in the Preface to which Horace Smith alludes, gracefully states that *Brambletye House* might, to a certain extent, claim priority over his own work :—

"Hawks," we say in Scotland, "ought not to pick out hawk's eyes," or live upon each other's quarry; and, therefore, if I had known that, in its date and in its characters, this tale was likely to interfere with that recently published by a distinguished contemporary, I should unquestionably have left Doctor Rochecliffe's manuscript in peace for the present season. But before I was aware of this circumstance, this little book was half through the press; and I had only the alternative of avoiding any intentional imitation by delaying a perusal of the contemporary work in question.

Some accidental collision there must be, when works of a similar character are finished on the same general system of historical manners, and the same historical personages are introduced. Of course, if such have occurred, I shall be probably the sufferer. But my intentions have been at least innocent, since I look on it as one of the advantages attending the conclusion of *Woodstock*, that the finishing of my own task will permit me to have the pleasure of reading *Brambletye House*, from which I have hitherto conscientiously abstained.

Sir Walter kept his word to the letter; in his Diary we read:—

25, *Pall Mall, Oct.* 17, 1826.

I read with interest during my journey, *Sir John Chiverton* and *Brambletye House*. . . . They are both clever books;—one in imitation of the days of chivalry—the other (by Horace Smith, one of the authors of *Rejected Addresses*) dated in the time of the Civil Wars, and introducing historical characters.

Later, in the same Diary, Sir Walter Scott admits, with amusing naïveté, his own undetected sins as regards *cribbing*, while condemning its undisguised practice by others.

October, 1826.

Another thing in my favour is that my contemporaries steal too openly. Mr. Smith has inserted in *Brambletye House* whole pages from De Foe's *Fire and Plague of London*. Steal! foh! a fico for the phrase—Convey, the wise it call! When I convey an incident or so, I am at as much pains to avoid detection as if the offence could be indicted at the Old Bailey.[1]

---

[1] Lockhart's *Memoirs of the Life of Sir W. Scott*, 1837.

In his excursions about Tunbridge Wells, Horace Smith came across a ruined mansion in Ashdown Forest, Sussex, that had been dismantled by Cromwell's troops. Years afterwards it had been set fire to by a half-crazy woman; and as there happened to be an unsuspected store of gunpowder in the cellars, the house was blown up. Horace Smith took this spot as the scene of his book, to which it gave the title, and introduced the incident of the explosion. The romanticism inseparable from the Elizabethan and Carolian age always had a peculiar fascination for him; and his friend, Cyrus Redding, was right in regarding a visit they paid together to Penshurst as the determining cause of Horace Smith's adoption of this interesting style.

Brambletye House long retained its popularity, and has frequently been republished. *À propos* of this novel, Horace Smith, writing to Mr. S. C. Hall in reference to a MS. he had sent to the *New Monthly Magazine*, says:—

October 17, 1831.
10, *Hanover Crescent.*

I am sorry you should deem the smallest apology necessary for returning my MS., a duty which every editor must occasionally exercise towards all his contributors. From my domestic habits and love of occupation I am always scribbling, often without due consideration of what I am writing, and I only wonder that so many of my frivolities have found their way into print. With this feeling, I am always grateful towards those who save me from committing myself, and acquiesce very willingly in their decisions. In proof of this, I will mention a fact of which I am rather proud. Mr. Colburn had agreed to give me £500 for the first novel I wrote, and had announced its appearance, when, a mutual friend who looked over the MS. having expressed an unfavourable opinion of it, I threw it in the fire, and wrote *Brambletye House* instead. Let me not omit to mention, to the credit of Mr. C., that, upon the unexpected success of that work, he subsequently presented me with an additional £100.

Yours very truly,
HORATIO SMITH.

Robert Smith criticized *Brambletye House* in his *Journal* as follows :—

(1829) I have omitted to notice in its proper place that early in the present year my son Horace published a little work in three duodecimo volumes, called *Brambletye House, or Cavaliers and Roundheads.* It has hit the public taste, and has had a great run.

For my own part, I do not much relish these "historical novels," in which truths are so much mixed up with fiction as to confound the unsuspecting reader. Besides, Horace has too often erred in giving to some of his characters the vulgar habit of swearing, etc., a fault which will not fail to give offence to *serious* characters, without having in it anything to *please* the light and thoughtless. I have hinted to him my opinion upon this defect; though I do not perceive that any of his critical reviewers have noticed it.

Stimulated by the success of *Brambletye House,* its author produced in the same year *The Tor Hill,* also published by Henry Colburn. This deals with the Reformation period, and the scene is laid in the neighbourhood of Glastonbury Abbey. Although interesting,. it bears traces of hasty writing, and deserves the verdict pronounced by its author's father:—

Towards the present month (October), my son Horace published another book in three volumes duodecimo, called *The Tor Hill*. In my opinion, it comes out too soon after *Brambletye House*. Authors should take sufficient time for digesting their plans and correcting errors. In this respect Horace has forgotten the advice of his Latin namesake, *Nonumque prematur in annum*. He has not taken as many months.

There was no second edition of *The Tor Hill*, but it was translated into French by Defauconpret of Paris.

Reuben Apsley, an historical novel of the time of James II., followed in 1827; and in the course of the next year came *Zillah, a Tale of the Holy City*. They were both brought out by Colburn, and of the latter work there were two editions and a French translation.

Horace Smith, in a letter to Cyrus Redding, says (in the postscript):—

Will you tell Colburn, when you see him, that *Zillah* is the most appropriate name he could choose for my novel? I find that lady was the mother of Tubal Cain, the first of the Smiths, and, of course, the founder of my family. Perhaps the circumstance was in his eye when he pitched upon *Zillah*.

Zillah is an admirable presentation of the momentous incidents that occurred at Jerusalem during

the three years preceding the capture of the Holy
City by Herod (about 37 B.C.).

It was violently attacked in the *Quarterly Magazine*, and its detractors maintained that it was but
an imitation of Croly's *Salathiel*. This assertion
was ridiculous, as the two books were written
simultaneously ; but as *Salathiel* appeared first, the
publication of *Zillah* was deferred, Horace Smith
remarking in his advertisement—

Considering that the scene is often identical, and
the area nearly so, there are perhaps not so many
coincidences between the two novels as might have
been expected; and though the author of the present
work, willing to avoid any immediate comparison,
still less any appearance of competition, with the
powerful writer of *Salathiel*, postponed its publication, he has not thought it necessary to make any
alteration in its pages beyond a few trifling omissions.

After *Zillah* came *The New Forest* (1829), a work
dedicated to William Heseltine of Turret House,
Lambeth ; to the following year (1830) belongs
Walter Colyton, a tale of the Revolution of 1688,
the scene being laid near Bridgwater in Somerset.
To 1830 belongs also *The Midsummer Medley* (a
series of comic tales), and *Festivals, Games, and
Amusements, Ancient and Modern*, which went
through two editions in England, and one in New
York. In 1832 appeared *Tales of the Early Ages*,
and, in 1835, *Gale Middleton*. *The Tin Trumpet*,
published under a pseudonym in 1836, was repro-
duced in 1869 by Bradbury, Evans, and Co., with

the author's real name attached by permission of the family. This, an amusing and well-thought-out medley, alphabetically arranged, is one of his best works.

In 1838 came *Jane Lomax*, a tale of modern times, based upon the commission of a fraud, on which James Smith makes the following criticism:—

But there is another legal objection. Lomax[1] was, if I remember right, appointed executor under the will. He must in that capacity have possessed the *probate*, and could not make a copy. Again I have my doubts whether Lomax's crime was capital. It did not consist in forging the testator's handwriting, but in putting before him a false or substituted will for his signature; a fraud punishable, perhaps, with transportation; but not a forgery. The interest, at the close, would have been much better worked-up by a trial at law, or an indictment at the Old Bailey —Lomax in the dock, trembling as the proofs accumulated, and urged to "flare up" by his indignant helpmate. The will might have been set aside, and the man from abroad might have married the virtuous daughter. The wind-up with two old maids is an anti-climax.

People who write works of fiction are not bound to know the law, but in forming their catastrophes they should apply to those who do. I could have helped my brother to as pretty a law scene as you shall see on a summer's day.

In 1840 Horace Smith edited *Oliver Cromwell*, an historical novel, wherein the Lord Protector's portrait is drawn, to use the words of the preface, by

---

[1] The perpetrator of the fraud.

"a friendly hand." His interest in Cromwell had been greatly increased by the fact of his having handled and examined the Protector's skull, in the possession of a medical man whom he knew, who was not only quite satisfied as to its identity, but believed—and persuaded Horace Smith to believe—that it had been blown· down from the porch of Westminster Hall, and picked up by the sentry, who disposed of it to the Russell family.

In 1841 Horace Smith wrote *The Moneyed Man, or, The Lesson of a Life*, which went through two editions; and in 1842 he edited *Masaniello, an Historical Romance*. In 1843 he produced *Adam Brown, the Merchant*, and in 1844 *Arthur Arundel, a Tale of the English Revolution*. In the latter year appeared *Imitations of Celebrated Authors, Charles Lamb*, etc., two of the pieces in the book being by Horace Smith. In 1845 he penned his last work, *Love and Mesmerism;* and in 1846 his *Poetical Works*, collected for the first time, were published in two volumes.[1]

Although best known as a writer of prose fiction, Horace Smith established a reputation as an able, graceful, and above all, a natural poet. His verse is remarkable for variety in style and subject, and, as one might expect, is tinctured by a tendency to the humorous. He excelled in the class of versification midway between the serious and the comic, of which

[1] *Amarynthus the Nympholet, a Pastoral Drama, with other Poem,* (1821), has been mentioned in the notice of Shelley, Chap. XV.

his *Address to a Mummy in Belzoni's Exhibition* is a good example.

One of the stanzas runs thus:—

> Perchance that very hand now pinioned flat,
>   Has hob-a-nobbed with Pharaoh, glass to glass;
> Or dropp'd a half-penny in Homer's hat;
>   Or doff'd thine own to let Queen Dido pass;
> Or held, by Solomon's own invitation,
> A torch at the great temple's dedication.

His life-long friendship with Campbell aroused his deepest feelings on the occasion of the poet's funeral in Poet's Corner, Westminster Abbey, when the pall was held by six noblemen, and noted men of every shade of varying opinions stood round the grave.

Thus sings Horace Smith of Campbell's burial:—

> Around his grave in radiant brotherhood,
>   As if to form a halo o'er his head,
> Not few of England's master-spirits stood,
>   Bards, artists, sages, reverently led
>   To waive each separating plea
>   Of sect, clime, party, and degree,
> All honouring him on whom Nature all honours
>   shed.

Altogether, in prose and verse, Horace Smith published more than fifty volumes.

CHAPTER XXIII

1826—1849

MOST of Horace Smith's novels were written at Brighton, where, after leaving Tunbridge Wells in 1826, he resided until his death.

He could hardly have made a better selection than Brighton, for, until the railway from London began to bring down visitors by thousands and tens of thousands, it was a delightfully quiet place, yet justly boasting of society as bright and interesting as any to be found throughout the kingdom. In the season (summer) there was a fair amount of gaiety: public balls and assemblies; breakfast, tea, and card-parties; performances at the theatre; bands of music on the Steine; everywhere liveliness sufficient to compensate for the comparative dulness of the town during the rest of the year.

The city man of to-day, comfortably breakfasting in the Pullman car, as the train conveys him from Brighton to the scene of his work at the rate of some five-and-forty miles an hour, finds it hard to realize that, not so very long ago, such a thing was an unheard-of possibility. A couple of hours at the outside now takes him from his sea-side home to his city office, and ten shillings covers the cost of a first-class return ticket.

In 1827 private travelling was a luxury, and when old Robert Smith drove his wife down from Wandsworth to Brighton to see his son Horace, the expenses on the road there and back amounted to not less than £20 10s. 8d.,[1] and, as they slept at Crawley, the journey occupied about twenty-four hours each way. Few persons could afford either this expenditure or this delay. The coach was much quicker, but slow enough from our point of view; and even the Government contract speed with John Palmer in 1836 for the mails was but six miles an hour, subsequently increased to ten and a half. Nevertheless, during the " twenties," " thirties," and "forties," there were many admirably appointed, well-horsed, and well-driven private coaches that did the distance from Brighton to the Metropolis in five or six hours along good roads, and, so far as it was possible, the service was perfect. It must have been well patronized, as sixteen coaches ran daily throughout the year, and it is recorded with pride that, on one day in October 1833, nearly five hundred visitors arrived by these popular conveyances.

The average fare, fifteen shillings (inside passengers), seems low, but to this were added numerous

---

[1] The charge of an uncomfortable post-chaise was about two shillings per mile with many extras.

tips, the cost of hackney-coaches to and from the point of arrival and departure, and last, but not least, the expense of eating and drinking—a necessity, as the start was usually at seven or eight o'clock in the morning. Good opportunity was afforded for refreshment at " The Cock," Sutton, Croydon, Reigate, Crawley, and Hand-Cross, when excellent gingerbread, and Hollands that had not always been interviewed by the Excise, could be had. At Staplefield Common—a few miles nearer Brighton—a grand halt as a rule was called for a more substantial repast, which generally took the form of rabbit-pudding. Mrs. Glasse (1765) does not give any recipe for this famous local delicacy, although she mentions various strange meat puddings, one being composed of salt-pork, and another of a mixture of sheep's liver chopped up fine with suet, sweet herbs, nutmeg, pepper, and anchovy.[1]

Soon after he went to Brighton, Horace Smith became the tenant of No. 10, Hanover Crescent, a group of two-storeyed houses, facing the Level, and close to where the road to Lewes begins. The crescent stood in what was in those days the most northerly suburb of the town, and was almost rural. To the east and north were the open downs, unbuilt upon, and the walk to the sea-front by way of the Level

[1] I am able to give, for the benefit of my lady-readers, the following recipe for *mutton-pudding :*—Use the short bones from the neck, or what is commonly called the skirting. Add mushrooms, when in season, a sweet crust, and boil in basin. *Sometimes a rabbit is put with the mutton.*

and the North Steine might, without much exaggeration, have been described as " countrified."

At that time there existed no sea-wall, Marine Parade, Junction Parade, Madeira Road, or King's Road in the well-kept form we know. There were no tastefully-laid-out gardens or marine lawns; the Pavilion was a royal residence, and the grounds were strictly private and inaccessible; therefore, the Chain Pier was the favourite place for promenaders.

Arundel Terrace, Kemp Town, was the ultima thule of Brighton in the east. To the west, the old battery, with its flagstaff, cannons, and pyramids of shot, was a conspicuous object, and always attracted the young folks. About half-a-mile beyond, Brunswick Square, or, at the furthest, Adelaide Crescent and Palmyra Square, marked the western boundary of Brighton proper. From the fields to the north of the Square might be seen, a mile or so off, the outlying village of Hove, the intervening space dotted with farms and a few houses. Neither Cliftonville nor Prestonville had been thought of by the most speculative of builders. St. Peter's Church on the Level was approaching completion and consecration. The Royal York was the fashionable hotel; the Albion had not long been opened; the Old Ship, and the New Ship adjoining, were flourishing concerns; but the famous old Castle Tavern had been pulled down a few years before. Huge caravansaries, such as the Métropole and the Grand, were unknown.

The population of Brighton was about 40,000, and

its vast extension, especially towards the setting sun, was a thing of the future; yet who shall say that some prophet, regarded by his friends as a harmless lunatic, did not foresee with the eye of faith the "Queen of English watering-places" spread out beyond even its present limits, embracing Portslade, Southwick, and intervening open spaces, until the river Adur at New Shoreham alone checked the advance of brick and mortar?

In those pre-railway days (*i. e. ante* 1841), when everybody knew everybody, there were many interesting and original characters to be found at Brighton. First in importance, perhaps, was the Master of the Ceremonies, who, for the modest salary of £1000 a-year, presided at all the fashionable balls given at the Old Ship. Lieut.-Colonel John Eld had been appointed, in 1828, to this responsible post, and held it until his death in 1855, when the office of M.C. was abolished. He used to keep a book at the Libraries (as did also Dickens's immortal Angelo Cyrus Bantam, Esq., M.C. of Bath), in which the residents and visitors, who aspired to be fashionable, were supposed to enter their names. In the case of strangers, a formal introduction to the M.C. gave them an *entrée* to all entertainments over which he held sway. But customs were already quickly changing. Lady patronesses with "vouchers" supplanted this method of introduction; and, by the time the railway appeared, Colonel Eld's duties had become nominal. He was a singular man, and as he walked down the parade in his characteristic dress, of which a well-starched neck-cloth was a prominent feature, he looked, as he probably felt himself to be, "master," not only of the "ceremonies," but, potentially, of all Brighton.

Though not a resident, Sir St. Vincent Cotton, the prince of amateur whips, was as well known as anybody. He was a Cambridgeshire baronet, and a descendant of Cotton, the collector of MSS. He lost two fortunes at the gambling-table, inherited a third, and settled down at Madingley Hall, near Cambridge. His coach, the " Age," its horses and its fittings, were unique; even the horse-cloths were edged with broad silver lace !

One of the *habitués* of Bedford's Club House on the South Parade on the Steine, carried on by a Mr. Wiick, formerly in the establishment of the Prince Regent, was General Sir William Keir Grant, an old traveller and thorough man of the world, who had lost his right arm in a duel. He was overflowing with curious anecdotes and traveller's tales. Once he called upon a newly-married couple on their return from their honeymoon trip to Italy, and asked the fair but inexperienced bride how she liked Venice. " I was very much delighted," she replied, " but, to be sure, we timed our arrival most unluckily, for, only fancy, the place was flooded all the week we were there, and we had to go about in a boat ! "

Of Brighton clergymen (barring the Rev. F. W. Robertson), the two Andersons, James and Robert, were perhaps the most notable. Robert Anderson was of a very shy, retiring disposition, and his staid, still demeanour did little to betray the strong under-current of humour in his character. He loved to relate the following anecdote. It appears he had occasion to superintend the outside repairs of his chapel, when, amongst other improvements, a coating of mastic had been applied with good effect. One of his churchwardens, a highly respectable but rather illiterate individual, was much struck by the improved appearance of the frontage, and in a most impressive and eulogistic manner, thus expressed himself:—" I'll tell you what, Mr. Anderson, now that you have finished masticating your chapel, I shall follow your example, and masticate my house !"

Local journalism was well represented by Mr. William Fleet, for whom Horace Smith always had a sincere regard. Mr. Fleet was the proprietor and editor of the *Brighton Herald*, founded in 1806 as the advocate of rational liberal principles. In its youth it was distinguished as the paper *par excellence* for its quickness in making known to the public some of the most important events in European history. The *Herald* was the first to proclaim the escape of Napoleon from Elba. The news of the French Revolution of 1830 was received by the *Herald* in advance of all other journals ; and " slips " were forwarded from its office to the London *Times* the same night. Eighteen years later, the earliest announcement of Louis Philippe's arrival at New-haven as a fugitive, was made by this well-informed paper.

As regards professional men, Brighton was always well supplied, and in 1849 there must have been quite seventy-five physicians, etc., in practice, many of them eminently skilful.

Of solicitors there were not many, Brighton being a non-litigious town.

Art was represented by Sir Martin A. Shee, who, in 1850, was President of the Royal Academy.

In characters in the humbler walks of life Brighton was rich, and to Horace Smith they formed a constant and amusing study.

Male "bathers" and female "dippers"—successors of the Smoaker brothers, Mrs. Cobby, and Martha Gunn, queen of the bathing-machines—still existed, and did a roaring trade in the season. The bathing-women, in quaint costume, continued the practice of presenting their cards to visitors arriving by coach at Castle Square.

Mr. Matthews, the pier-master, was a well-known figure; and everybody who used the Pier made the acquaintance of the Rattys, *père, mère, et fille* (originals of the type that Dickens sketched), who were in rough weather frequently washed out of their rooms at the toll-house, always to return, however, with renewed energy to minister to the wants of their patrons and friends.

Then there was "Jonathan," the celebrated billiard-player, who used to exhibit his skill in one of the streets leading from the Marine Parade to James Street, where, too, could generally be seen a curious well-dressed little man, who went by the *soubriquet* of "Badger"—why, no one seemed to know.

In a small cottage standing on a common, midway between Kemp Town and Eastern Terrace, dwelt a singular character named Murray, who, because of his reticence concerning his early career, was assumed to have been a smuggler.   He did a splendid business in the sale of agate, pebbles, and all those curios with which a visitor returning from the sea-side deemed it the correct thing to load himself.

Everybody in Brighton knew Sake Deen Mahomed, a native of the East, who introduced into the town the art of shampooing. His private baths were largely patronized, and his fame was enshrined in verse by James Smith, and in prose by Horace. The former, in an *Ode to Mahomet, the Brighton Shampooer*, thus addresses him :—

> O thou dark sage, whose vapour bath
> Makes muscular as his of Gath
>   Limbs erst relax'd and limber ;
> Whose herbs, like those of Jason's mate,
> The wither'd leg of seventy-eight—
>   Convert to stout *knee* timber,
>
> Sprung, doubtless from Abdallah's son,
> Thy miracles thy sire's outrun,
>   Thy cures his deaths outnumber ;
> His coffin soars 'twixt heav'n and earth,
> But thou, within that narrow berth,
>   Immortal, ne'er shall slumber.[1]

Lastly, among other "originals" at Brighton, I will single out a vendor of brandy-balls, who, clad in spotless white, and wearing a kind of fez which

---

[1] He lived to be a centenarian.

enhanced his Jewish appearance, with a long curl of
black hair plastered down on each side of his face,
used to perambulate the quieter squares and terraces
every evening at dusk, singing in a melodious voice
of the mysterious confection, which, it may be pre-
sumed, was of home manufacture. He was a constant source of wonderment, especially to young
children.

As early as 1830, the *bourgeois* element had begun
to show itself amongst the visitors to Brighton.
Horace Smith, describing the visit of a certain Clio
Grub, puff provider for Warner's blacking, tells us
that

> To Brighton he went and secured a retreat
> In the pebble-built house of a narrow back street,
> With a staring bow-window to let him explore
> What was passing in either bow-window next door.

And he represents the civic visitant to Brighton as
singing—

> On the Downs you are like an old jacket
>   Hung up in the sunshine to dry ;
> In the town you are all in a racket,
>   With donkey-cart, whiskey, and fly.
> We have seen the Chain-Pier, Devil's Dyke,
>   The Chalybeate Spring, Rottingdean,
> And the Royal Pagoda, how like
>   Those bedaub'd on a tea-board or screen !

But it is James Smith who has left us the best
description of a London tradesman's experience in a
Brighton lodging-house of that period. It is contained
in a letter supposed to be written by the " cit.'s "
daughter, Louisa Thompson, to a friend in London:—

We have got a nice lodging in North Street, commanding a romantic view of all the passengers inside and out, as they alight from the New York Safety Coach. All the beauty and fashion of Brighton pass our door. Munden [1] went by yesterday leaning on his stick, and Incledon [2] this morning. The latter talks of leaving us, because Mr. Munn, of the Golden Cross Inn here, would not let him amuse the Royal Catch and Glee Club, by singing all the parts in *Glorious Apollo*. Mr. Munn offered him either treble, second, or bass, but the veteran determined to have all or none. If we do not return with a stock of health, which, properly invested, shall last us for life, it will be no fault of papa's. Before it is well daylight, he thumps at our chamber-doors with his stick, and calls out, "Come girls, come girls, nobody lies a-bed at the sea-side." No sooner are we down than he walks us off up the East Cliff as hard as we can trot, and in the course of our walk is sure to encounter three or four fat, red-faced men of his acquaintance (all papa's acquaintance are fat and red-faced); and when the elderly worthies have arrived opposite the Snake Houses, they stand open-mouthed to catch the sea-air, for all the world as if they were singing *Come if you dare* to those horrid Roman Catholics, the French, on the opposite coast, at a place they call Dip, because people go there to bathe. . . . Papa asked young Withers to dine with us to-day. He drove up in such a dashing fly! The dinner was very bad; a sprawling bit of bacon upon a tumbled bed of greens; two gigantic antediluvian fowls, bedaubed with parsley and butter, a brace of soles that perished from original inability to flounder into the ark, and the fossil remains of a dead sirloin of beef. I had no appetite, and had

---

[1] The actor. [2] The well-known singer.

just impressed our visitor with a notice of the delicacy of my stomach, when Mrs. Anderson bawled out from the bottom of the table, " Sir, you should have seen her at luncheon peg away at the prawns ! "

Horace Smith seldom let slip an opportunity to recommend to his friends the watering-place he found so congenial.

Writing to Charles Mathews in 1828 from Hanover Crescent, he says :—

Don't pretend to be indifferent to excitement, you know you cannot live without it. Almost all professors (like the house-painters and chimney-sweepers) have their own peculiar diseases, the histrionic malady being an insatiable craving for stimulants of some sort, and the most successful performers being generally the most subject to the complaint. I have elsewhere said :—

> That if one tolerable page appears
>   In Folly's volume, 'tis the actor's leaf,
> Who dries his own by drawing others' tears,
> And raising present mirth makes glad his future years.

But this must have been said for the sake of the rhyme, for my reason knew well enough that, even if it were true as to tragedians (which I doubt), the *comic* actor generally saddens himself by enlivening others, a fact which has been abundantly confirmed from the day of the celebrated Italian *Buffone* down to our own. This may seem rather hard, as he reverses the fate of many a poet, who dies to live, while the performer—

> His life a flash, his memory a dream,
> Oblivious, downward drops in Lethe's stream,

as soon as ever the breath is out of his body. You must recollect, *amico mio*, that he has his apotheosis while he is living, and a glorious one it is. Take, for instance, "Mathews at Home"; his theatre crowded to the ceiling, himself the focus of thousands of riveted eyes, and holding such an absolute power of fascination over the passions of his audience that at a single bidding they shall either melt into tears or burst into roars of irrepressible laughter, while the whole building seems to vibrate with their tumultuous applause. Is not this an apotheosis? and is there any mortal society, or resource, that will not appear stale, flat, and unprofitable, after such a deification? This is the feeling, coupled with the lassitude occasioned by over-exertion, both mental and bodily, that creates the craving for stimulants, which the sufferers have too often sought in the bottle, the dice-box, or in reckless dissipation. How natural, I had almost said how venial, is the mistake, and yet how little indulgence does the public evince even for errors of its own creation. We are like weak mothers, who spoil their children and then whip them for being spoilt. . . . It is the want of this hobby that makes you so fidgety and nervous when you are absent from home; and Brighton only finds more favour in your eyes than other places, because it is more gay and stimulant, and offers more numerous substitutes for the museum. How often have I heard you exclaim, "There is nothing out of London like Brighton in the season. The whole town is a fair. If I· lean out of my window at the Old Ship, I nod or chat to every fifth man that passes. If I mount my little white nag, and ride from Kemp Town to Brunswick Terrace, I am sure of half-a-dozen invitations to dinner. This I call enjoying life. . . ."

Writing to Mathews in the same year, Horace Smith says :—

Our fiery friend, " the Copper Captain," saw you last Wednesday, told you he was coming to Brighton, and yet you neither charged him with message or missive for me. How is this ? Are you in a pet with my last letter ? with my last letter wherein I took you sharply to task for asserting that you did not require excitement more than other men ? Luckily, you were never sulky—to little fumes and peevish outbreaks you will hardly deny your liability ; but as these never last longer than " one with moderate haste may count a hundred," do let me hear from you soon, " if thou lovest me, Hal."

To put you in good humour again, I must tell you that Mahommed yesterday pointed out to a friend of mine a suspended crutch, which he averred to have been yours, and that he had enabled you to throw it away by shampooing you ! There ! if this assertion of your restored equigravity does not restore your equanimity, nothing will ! So don't get into a passion, or you never will get out.

The following is a letter, on the subject of his novel, *Walter Colyton*, to his old friend, Thomas Hill (see Chapter XIX.) :—

Brighton, 19th March, 1830.

My dear Hill,

I have not had any further proof to send up till to-day, or I should have sooner written to thank you for your negotiation with Mr. Bentley, whose letter enclosing a note at four months date, came to hand only this morning. Of course I closed with them, but I certainly thought they ought not to have grudged me a trifling addition, hearing as I did, and from no doubtful authority either, that they gave others £500 *a volume*. However, I am satisfied, and if the work succeeds tolerably, I suppose they will do something better for me next time. With renewed thanks for your kindness, I am,

My dear Hill,

Yours very truly,

HORATIO SMITH.[1]

THOMAS HILL, ESQ.,
1, *James Street, Adelphi.*

A few days afterwards, he writes to Mrs. Heseltine[2] in quite a different vein :—

*Brighton, 10, Hanover Crescent,
22nd March, 1830.*

MY DEAR MRS. HESELTINE,

Pray don't let my young folks interfere with any of your arrangements, but as all times will be equally convenient for my father to receive them, I beg you will send them away whenever it suits you.

In return for inflicting two brats upon you, I have two favours to request—*wizzard :*—To prevent Eliza's head from entirely reposing on her knees, I am provided with a sharp pitchfork, which every now and then I dig in pretty deep under her chin, and to compel her to practice her shakes of a morning, to which she has an utter repugnance, I am obliged to stand over her with a cudgel and occasionally fell her to the earth. If you will perform for me these truly parental offices, I can only say that I shall be most happy to return them *fourfold* upon Amy whenever she comes to see us. Sending an agonizing pinch to all the children, Mrs. Cole, and Miss

[1] Bodleian Library MSS.   [2] Chapter XII.

Heseltine, and begging you to accept the same for yourself, I am,

Dear Mrs. Heseltine,
Yours very truly,
HORATIO SMITH.

To Mr. S. C. Hall, he writes:—

Brighton, 10, *Hanover Crescent*,
2*nd December*, 1835.

MY DEAR SIR,

Altho' my temporary absence from home may in some degree plead my excuse, yet I take shame to myself for not having sooner thanked you and Mrs. Hall for the *Amulet*[1] and its companion, a present which was the more acceptable both to me and Rosalind because we had somehow fancied that you had talk'd of discontinuing the Works. Both are very delightful books, and I sincerely hope that this year's sale may answer your expectations, and ensure their continuance.

Mrs. Abdy's copy was immediately forwarded to her. Altho' I trust that Mrs. Hall will never again have the plea of Rheumatism for visiting Brighton, I shall be delighted to find that some other motive may bring you both back to us, and I can answer that my petticoat inmates will be not less gratified than myself.

At this season we could make up some pleasant parties, but *at all times* you and Mrs. Hall will be most welcome to me and mine.

Yours very truly,
HORATIO SMITH.

P.S.—If you can put your hand on a long-winded

---

[1] A kind of Christmas annual, beautifully illustrated, issued from 1826 to 1836.

poem I sent some months ago for the *N. M. Mag.*, entitled *The Jews at Babylon*, please return or destroy it. It is about to appear in another form.[1]

In Brighton, as in all watering-places, the tide of fashion set in westward, and, about the year 1840, Horace Smith's "feminine surroundings" induced him to remove from Hanover Crescent to Cavendish Place—now the centre of the four-mile sea-front, the glory of Brighton and Hove.

Their house, No. 12, is to be found a little way up on the right-hand side, as you approach it from the King's Road. There is a fine view of the sea from its crescent-shaped windows; and, with its old-fashioned casement, it looks as it may have done any time during the last three-quarters of a century.

Here the Smiths loved to entertain their friends, and delighted in planning amusements for them—a ride on the Downs, an excursion to Devil's Dyke, Rottingdean, or to the castle at Bramber, to Old Shoreham with its fine Norman church, and to quiet little Lancing beyond.

Their Sunday afternoon receptions, when the representatives of art, letters, and science fore-gathered, were "the most rooted institutions in Brighton after the Chain Pier"—

> When each by turn was guide to each,
> And Fancy light from Fancy caught—
> And Thought leapt out to wed with Thought
> Ere Thought could wed itself with Speech.

[1] Bodleian Library MSS.

So notoriously hospitable were the Smiths that not only the celebrated men and women of the day resident in Brighton—and there were many—but all visitors of note found their way to the table of Horace Smith.

Amongst his congenial fellow-townsmen were Captain James Morier, traveller and novelist, the author of *Hajji Baba of Ispahan*, etc.; Dr. Mantell, the geologist; Mr. Moses Ricardo, scientist and working-man's friend; Mr. and Mrs. Montefiore; Charles Young, the actor (who had retired to Brighton); Captain and Mrs. Heaviside, well-known in fashionable circles, and residing in Brunswick Square; the Rounds, of Brunswick Terrace; J. J. Masquerier, the painter of *La Belle Alliance*, which, together with his portraits of Miss O'Niel and Miss Mellon, are in the collection of the Baroness Burdett-Coutts.

Amongst the Brighton visitors who were made free of No. 12 were Samuel Rogers; Sydney Smith; Dr. Lardner, an eminent scientific man, and editor of the *Encyclopædia* which bears his name; Charles Kean, the actor, between whom and Horace Smith there existed much sympathy and warmest friendship; Copley Fielding, the water-colour painter of landscapes; Julian Fane, poet and diplomatist (then quite a young man); H. T. Buckle, the historian of civilization; Macaulay; Professor Owen; Jesse; Harrison Ainsworth; Dickens, and Thackeray.

Of the last named, Rosalind Smith used to relate how one day he popped in, and flinging himself down on a couch with an expression of great despair, implored the "girls" to tell him a "nursery tale," "anything however trivial," to divert his mind and help to remove his anxiety, for he had (as was customary with him when in Brighton) put off his monthly contribution to a certain periodical, until but a couple of days were left for the work. Rosalind says that their nonsense comforted him, that he went away from Cavendish Place "like a giant refreshed with new wine," and accomplished his task easily, though nobody had a sight of him in the meantime.

As to the origin of *Pendennis*, Herman Merivale tells the following story :—"Such a Brightonian as Thackeray was led naturally to his frequenting their rooms (the Smiths'). It was to them that he confided how he was bound to produce the opening chapters of *Pendennis* within a few days, and had no plot and no idea wherewith to start one. Shade of Trollope, how shocking ! So then and there, they told him a true anecdote of Brighton life. 'That will do,' said he, and went home and began the novel which, afterwards, in defiance of all the laws of self-respecting composition, developed into a work which has its merits still. In return for the favour, he christened his heroine *Laura*, after a younger sister.

"It may be imagined with what interest the story was followed. . . . When first he visited the ladies after it was finished, the original Laura received him indignantly. 'I'll never speak to you again, Mr.

Thackeray; you knew I always meant to marry Warrington.'   In the same spirit, spoke Lady Rockminster, when she accepted the young couple— 'It is all very well, but I should have preferred "Bluebeard"' (her name for Warrington), which proves to my mind that ladies do not always know what is good for them.

"Worth recording, too, is the story of Thackeray going to see the Miss Smiths when he was about to give his *George the Fourth* lecture in the town, and expressing his relief that it was not to be in the Pavilion as at first proposed—'I didn't like,' he said, 'the idea of abusing a man in his own house.'"[1]

Of Charles Kean's father a characteristic story was related to Horace Smith by a tradesman whose memory went back to the days when travellers in china and glass used to come with samples all the way to Kent and Sussex from Staffordshire, in their "carriage and pair."   One of these commercials, he said, happening to meet Edmund Kean at Maidstone, challenged him to drink as much brandy-and-water hot as he could himself.   The traveller, seasoned vessel though he was, succumbed to the twenty-sixth tumbler, but Kean just managed the twenty-seventh, and won the wager!

Horace Smith had always been a great admirer of the celebrated actress, Miss Mellon, and when he met her as the Duchess of St. Albans at Brighton after a lapse of many years, he penned some stanzas to her, beginning :—

[1] *Life of W. M. Thackeray,* by Merivale and Marzials.

> Lady ! that sweet and cordial voice,
>   Unalter'd since I heard it last,
> Hath made my weaken'd heart rejoice
>   With recollections of the past.

Her rare qualifications were summed up thus :—

> The lively wit without alloy,
>   The mind acute, the spirit's flow—
> The kindly heart that welcomes joy,
>   Yet melts at every tale of woe.
> These honours which thou ne'er can'st waive,
>   These that no monarch could decree,
> Prove that 'twas Nature's self who gave
>   Thy Patent of Nobility.

Every winter at the beginning of the season, the Duchess came to St. Albans House, Brighton, to the joy of all, for she was the most liberal patroness of the tradespeople, the benefactress of the poor, and the disburser of unbounded hospitality to the upper classes. She used to hold what she called *omnium gatherums*, at each one of which, it is said, the oil and candle bill usually amounted to £20—a large sum in those days.

She was a woman (in appearance fat and somewhat red-faced) whom exaltation in rank could not spoil or wean from simplicity of habits.

After one of her gorgeous festivities, whereat all the delicacies of the season were profusely provided, when the guests had left, she turned to her sole remaining companion, and said, "Now I'm going to enjoy myself," and sat down in an unceremonious manner to a cold chicken and a bottle of stout.

Later on, the Smiths were fortunate in their

friendship with the Duchess's heiress, Miss Burdett-Coutts (now the Baroness), who, when at Brighton, always calls upon Horace Smith's eldest and only surviving daughter, to talk over the memories of the past. The Smiths were her frequent guests in London, and Masquerier's excellent portrait of Horace Smith (which forms one of the illustrations of this volume) hangs upon the walls of Holly Lodge, Highgate.

The Rev. F. W. Robertson, the great preacher of Trinity Chapel, I mention last of all, because he did not arrive at Brighton till 1847, not long before Horace Smith died, whom he had consequently few opportunities of meeting. His first sermon there was a memorable one; his text: " The Jews require a sign, and the Greeks seek after wisdom, but we preach Christ crucified," etc. As the Rev. Stopford Brooke says—" It at once awoke criticism and interest. As his peculiar views developed themselves, many of the old congregation left the church. Their places were rapidly filled up. Thoughtful and eager-minded men came in by degrees from all parts of Brighton, attracted not only by his earnest eloquence, but by his original thought and clever reasoning."

Amongst these was Horace Smith, who was in fullest touch with the broad and enlightened views on religion and politics that characterized the famous preacher, and, had he lived but a few years longer, he might have been the means of helping to stem the torrent of cruel and unjust sectarian persecution that awaited Robertson.

The man who in the past had stood by the side of the greatly misunderstood Shelley would most surely have undertaken the same noble office for the maligned incumbent of Trinity Chapel.

For some time before this period, Brighton society had become exceedingly gay, and at all brilliant functions, public and private, the daughters of Horace Smith were conspicuous—Eliza, the eldest, notoriously witty and amusing; Rosalind, the beautiful, overburdened with eligible offers of marriage, though dying unmarried in 1893; and Laura, the youngest, who married Mr. John Round, of West Bergholt, Essex, and died in 1864.

One of the most striking of the gay assemblies at that time, was a fancy dress ball, at which Dr. Lardner appeared as a courtier, and the lovely Mrs. Heaviside as a *dame de cour* of the Louis XVI. period, both attracting much attention. Unfortunately, the charms of his fair partner in the dance proved too much for the philosophy of the learned professor, and he fled with her *viâ* London to Paris, whither they were followed by the outraged husband. A sound horse-whipping of the culprit and a duel (without serious result) are said to have followed, with ultimately a divorce in the House of Lords.

This regrettable affair to a certain extent broke up the pleasant "inner circle" which had led the fashion in Brighton, and of which the Horace Smiths were such prominent members.

I must not close this sketch of Brighton and its

association with Horace Smith, without expressing my indebtedness to Mr. Charles Fleet, Mr. D. Burchell Friend, Mr. John Haines, and other townsmen, for many valuable facts relating to the past history of the flourishing and ever popular watering-place in which they reside.

HORACE SMITH.

CHAPTER XXIV

The declining years of Horace Smith's life—His last illness
and death—His personal appearance, tastes, opinions, character
and disposition—The end.

AT the close of the year 1840, Cyrus Redding,
resuming his correspondence with Horace Smith
after a lapse of many years, noticed that his handwriting " varied considerably from the very neat
text it had before displayed," which he regarded as
an evidence of failing health.

The following year, Horace Smith had a severe
attack of laryngitis, and on his recovery wrote the
following letter to one of his sisters :—

Brighton, 10th October, 1841.

MY DEAR ADELAIDE,

I know that Maria is rather prone to make
mountains of molehills, and, lest you should suppose
that I was going to give you all the slip, I think it
right to let you know that I am proceeding very
favourably, that I am again downstairs, and mean to
be better than ever in a very few days. It was an
attack of acute inflammation in the Larynx, owing
to a cold, and came on so suddenly in the night, as
to be very alarming from its appearance, and feeling
of suffocation ; but we soon got a medicine man who

bled me till I fainted, and when I recover'd I had recover'd my voice, and breathed with perfect ease! Unluckily a bad cough supervened which threw me back, but that yielded to active remedies and further reduction; and here I am nearly as well as ever, though not looking *quite* so rosy in the gills.

My imprisonment comes at an unlucky moment, the place being full of friends whose society I was anxious to enjoy, particularly that of Sir Charles and Lady Morgan, and Lady Stepney. Old Lady Holland, who has got Byham House just opposite, and who always had a romantic attachment to me (!!!), keeps us supplied with game and all sorts of goody-goodies, but I cannot now partake in them or join her parties, which I regret, as the last I joined was a very delightful one. All the world has been here; but the railroad is getting so completely out of vogue, that I suspect we shall soon lose many of our visitants.

All unite in kindest regards to yourself and Gom,[1] with,

Dear Adelaide,
Yours affectionately,
HORATIO SMITH.

From this time, his inclination, as well as his capacity, for literary labour sensibly declined. It was the evening of his life, and thenceforth he did little beyond writing a couple of novels, editing a romance, gathering together scattered poetical works, and contributing some entertaining biographical narratives to the *New Monthly Magazine.* But his life was never an idle one; it was one scene of active benevolence and thoughtfulness for the pleasure and

---

[1] Her husband, Mr. Gompertz.

happiness of others. The Mechanics' Institution, the Literary Society, the Mantellian Institution, and Phillips' School of Science, never lacked his help in any possible way towards their advancement. His services were always at the disposal of the charities; and when the Savings' Bank became seriously involved, he put forth his energies during the investigation that followed, to such an extent as to still further impair his health.

He used to take his family up to London for the early season, when they generally occupied a furnished house, No. 16, Cumberland Street, Regent's Park. His daughters indulged in a perpetual round of gaiety. They met all the celebrities of the day, and were rather awed once, so they declared, at finding themselves in the presence of no fewer than " five real live editors " !

Visits to town were varied by trips to Harrogate, Bath, Tunbridge Wells, and Cheltenham. From the latter place, Horace Smith sent his niece, Maria Abdy, the following *Address to the Queen*, which had excessively tickled his fancy. It was got up by some few deaf and dumb young men (residents of Cheltenham) after the attempt upon Her Majesty's life by Edward Oxford—

Cheltenham, 15th June, 1840.

Our dear Victoria,
　　We hope you will not be angry with us for sending you a letter. We think you were very frightened. All the deaf and dumb are very very displeased with the Edward Oxford. We love you

very much because you are a fine young Lady Sovereign. We were very much happy on your birthday. A gentleman gave us some cakes, ginger pop, oranges, lemonade, and nice things. We drank your Majesty's very good health. We cannot drink beer, ale, wine, brandy, gin, rum, porter, etc., etc., two of us are teetotallers. We think you like Prince Albert very much. He is a very handsome young gentleman. We all love him too much. He came from Germany. He wears very nice mustachios. He is an officer soldier. We saw his picture in the booksellers' windows. We are very thankful to God because he did not let the wicked villain kill you. The English ladies and gentlemen are all rejoice about it. We all love the Queen and the Lords and fine gentlemen M.P.'s. We pray for you every Sunday at church. We hope you will be very religious young lady, and say your prayers every morning and night, and read the Bible, and go to heaven when you die.

Your very loyal deaf and dumb.

To the same niece he wrote a letter in which he expresses his inability to perpetrate any more rhymes :—

Brighton, 12 Cavendish Place,
7th March, 1846.

MANY thanks, my dear Mira, for your very acceptable Volume, from the perusal of which I anticipate great pleasure, especially as a great proportion of the poems will be new to me. You seem to write with greater fluency and facility than ever, and must find it a very charming resource, to say nothing of the position which it gives you among the honoured Lady writers of England. At my age I can hardly expect the Muse to smile upon my advances, and my only inspiration in the composition of the *Murderer's Confession* was the struggle with such an unmanageable metre.

At present I feel as if I should never perpetrate any more rhymes, but I am collecting all my former offences in two little volumes, which I will send you when the procrastinating Mr. Colburn thinks fit to bring them out.

I don't see *Gulliver*, but shall certainly extend his travels to Brighton, that I may read the pieces you mention.

Mrs. Bib's Baby, in *Punch*, is very inferior to *Mrs. Caudle*, and cannot go on, I should think, much longer. We became very intimate with Ainsworth and his family, who passed the winter here, and gave a great many very gay parties.

Of Shirley Brooks I know nothing. Like that of Mademoiselle *Mars*, his name may be a *nom de guerre*. Mrs. Alaric Attila! I never! but I believe it's perfectly correct that when a person once ask'd her husband " What's your name ? " Echo answered—' Watts ! '

Please tell Mamma that Beavan lately sent me for perusal the Draught of a 50-folio document, to be signed on distributing my father's money! Heaven knows when the original will be completed ! I never pretend to understand Law proceedings.

Your affectionate Uncle,
HORATIO SMITH.

In a letter to his sister Clara, he confesses that old age is creeping upon him :—

Brighton, 12 Cavendish Place,
23rd July, 1846.

MANY thanks, my dear Clara, for your kind invitation, of which I would gladly avail myself, but that I really feel much too rheumatical and too sciatical to sleep out at this season of the year. In the spring I shall again be running up to London, and if you will then give me leave, I shall have much pleasure in taking a dinner and a bed at your house. *Entre nous*, I am feeling very old, and I am afraid of giving any excuse to the ailments that assailed me last winter.

When you see me, you will hardly know me, so very venerable have I become. My saucy girls (I am dreadfully chicken-pecked) say that if I did but look a few years younger I should look exactly like my father! Then my beak has assumed the colour of Aurora's fingers, and I am often overheard sorrowfully exclaiming—

> Alas!—how luckless is my lot!
> My nose is *red*—my books are not!

Notwithstanding all which calamitous circumstances, I am, with the united loves of my darling wife and my dad-flouting daughters,

My dear Clara,

Affectionately yours,
HORATIO SMITH.

The year 1849 opened with severe weather, and much sickness was prevalent; but Horace Smith wrote in excellent spirits to his sister Adelaide, the letter being almost the last she ever received from him :—

Brighton, 12 *Cavendish Place*,
7th *January*, 1849.

MY DEAR ADELAIDE,

I confess myself to be a most unnatural brother in having suffer'd the new year to become a week old without having written to wish you and Ephraim many happy returns : but I know you are both benevolent mortals, and will forgive a transgression for which so quick an apology is offer'd. There! isn't that prettily said, and won't you kiss and make it up? Tho' I haven't written to you, however, we often hear of you from various quarters, and I have been glad to learn that in a season of unusual sickness, you have both escaped without any very serious visitation. Long may we continue to receive equally favourable statements!

Pour nous autres, as the French say (why can't the fools speak English, like men?) we are as well as old age and sharp weather will allow. My wife, God bless her! wears exceedingly well—never very strong, but always bustling, cheerful, and affectionate, nor have *I* any cause of complaint, considering that I have now entered my seventieth year! Occasional menaces of Gout, but no actual visit—little bilious attacks, and bothering cramps at night, form the whole summary of my ailments, slight enough when I add that in general I sleep like a top, and that my spirits have no defect but that of being rather *boyish* for my advanced years.

My girls have not been very robust latterly, but they are seldom so well at this season of frequent Balls and late hours. People really seem to seek them out from all quarters, and invite them to every gay party. The Duke of Devonshire has just arrived, but there are so many *nobs* now in Brighton that we *snobs* can hardly expect to be invited this year to his Balls. We have got acquainted with the Moores, and with Lady Harriet thro' a Mr. Cole, who is, I believe, one of your neighbours. The Abdys have gone home. Maria is rather better than usual, but looking like the grandmother of Methusclah!

Adieu, beauty! not only as *was* but as *is*, for handsome is as handsome does. Accept for yourself and

Ephraim our united and most cordial love, and believe me ever

Your affectionate brother,
HORATIO SMITH.

Unfortunately the " menaces of gout " were much more serious than he thought. Later in the year, the family took a house at Tunbridge Wells, No. 6 Calverley Park, very charming, and in a most sequestered and beautiful part of the town, with private grounds and prettily laid-out gardens, where, so far as surroundings were concerned, peace and tranquillity reigned. But they had not long been there when alarming symptoms began to be apparent in Horace Smith's health. The inherited gout, hitherto dormant in his system, developed itself in the form of serious heart-troubles. His sufferings became very acute, but he met his approaching end with great resignation and serenity, even on his death-bed seeking to comfort his agonized wife and family. On the 12th of July, 1849, in the seventieth year of his age, Horace Smith passed into the unseen world, all that was mortal of him being laid to rest in the churchyard of Holy Trinity Church. " He died, as he had lived, loving and beloved, full of trust, joy, and hope."

In personal appearance, Horace Smith closely resembled his brother James, at any rate in early years, and in the beautiful drawing by Harlow (which forms the frontispiece to Mr. Murray's 1833 edition of *Rejected Addresses*) it is difficult to distinguish the one from the other.

Horace Smith had a particularly finely-formed head, likened by one of his friends to that of Socrates. He was tall and handsome, with a manly figure inclining to the robust. He had blue eyes, and regular features usually in repose, but moved to animation when anything amusing or good was said ; his discernment of humour, though more latent than that of James, was none the less keen. Frankness was stamped upon his countenance, and his general bearing was cordial, displaying much gentleness, but without the slightest trace of effeminacy or weakness.

As might be expected from the influences brought to bear upon him in childhood,[1] as well as from the mature conviction of his manhood, he was no friend either to Episcopalianism or to Sacerdotalism. He described bishops as " Protestant cardinals," and the system which they represent, as "a plethora of dignities and wealth, combined with an atrophy of merits and followers, which could never be symptoms of longevity in any Church, however firmly it may seem to be established." Consistently, therefore, he disapproved of the alliance of Church with State, which he designated an " unscriptural union." Of the Romish priesthood, he had but a poor opinion ; and on the subject of their celibacy he felt strongly, defining it as " a vow by which the priesthood in some countries swear to content themselves with the wives of other people !" On the other hand, he had a great horror of Protestant fanaticism—" the daughter of ignorance and the mother of infidelity "

[1] See Chapter IV.

—especially in the matter of strict Sabbath observance. Missions he did not approve of at all, as he considered that the missionary should begin by improving the temporal condition of the heathen, and that it was worse than useless to start by teaching the five points of Calvinism to barbarians unable to count their five fingers. Uniformity in religion he judged to be unobtainable. With intolerance he had no patience whatever, always quoting Pope's well-known lines—

> "For modes of faith let zealous bigots fight ;
> His can't be wrong whose life is in the right."

He advocated the total abolition of compulsory confessions of creed or faith, and the Test Acts he utterly condemned. The Reformation, he said, was not a struggle for religious freedom, but for Protestant intolerance instead of Catholic intolerance, and the struggle of modern Christians should be for emancipation from *all* intolerance.

"The right of examining what we ought to believe is the foundation of Protestantism, and to deny it is to revert to the Popish claim of infallibility."

In short, Horace Smith's religious views were the broadest—of the Maurice and Kingsley type ; and he firmly believed that there was a Providence ever watching over the destiny of mankind, but not a *particular* Providence for fanatics.

Death he beautifully defined as "the sleeping partner of Life, a change of existence." "Why" [said he] "should a long be less pleasant than a short sleep? Post-natal cannot differ from ante-natal unconsciousness; we were dead before we lived. Ceasing to exist is only returning to our former state, *speaking always in reference to this world.*"

In politics he was what we should call a Liberal-Conservative; though in his day he would more likely have been dubbed a Radical—even a Revolutionist, by most of the old high and dry Tory party. He was an intense admirer of Lord Brougham, and an out-and-out Reformer. He advocated the ballot, and delivered a speech at Brighton in favour of it. James Smith did not at all approve of this, and wrote to a friend, saying that Horace "had better abstain from politics altogether. It is his business as an author to please all parties." Horace believed in the elevation of the working-classes, and the abolition of the newspaper tax. He condemned the Poor Laws, and designated the Game Laws barbarous enactments. He disapproved of the privileges of either Peers or M.P.'s. He considered Public Opinion irresistible, and had firm faith in a *popular* government, which he compared to a pyramid, the firmest and most enduring of all forms.

His opinions on most subjects were marked by enlightenment. On the matter of education he held rather peculiar views; to him it appeared a game of cross-purposes, in which useless classics were taught at great expense in our public schools, and rapidly forgotten in after life. Of collegiate training he had a poor opinion; "the whole system," he said, "is a specimen of the moral, as some of their structures are of the architectural, Gothic."

He had no respect for ancestry, "a pedigree being," he declared, "generally the boast of those who had nothing else to vaunt;" thus he disapproved of primogeniture as being equally opposed to nature, reason, morality, and sound policy.

With that particular cant of art which substitutes a blind reverence for the painter—provided he be dead—for a judicious admiration of his paintings, he had no sympathy.

English law was to him merely hocus-pocus and chicanery; and lawyers, he said, "generally knew too much of law to have a very clear perception of justice."

War and military glory he held to be, the former an act of national madness, an irrational act confined to rational beings; and the latter, the sharing with plague, pestilence, and famine, the honour of destroying one's own species.

He had the greatest abhorrence of the grosser excesses of life, gluttony, drunkenness, swearing, etc. As a philosopher he was supremely optimistic. Human happiness, he thought, must be constantly augmenting; and the habit of exaggerating the misery of mankind was in his eyes a species of impiety, as being an oblique reflection on the benevolence of the Deity, while despondency was sheer ingratitude to Heaven.

Contentment was to him the best opulence; and of money, although more indispensable now than in

the days of the Greek philosophers, he used to say
that "a wise man would have it in his head rather
than his heart," but that poverty to the generous-
minded, desirous of relieving the wants of others,
was the greatest of evils.

On the subject of his own profession, he was full
of good sense. "Literary fame," he explained, was
"being partially known to-day, and universally forgotten to-morrow. It was more easily caught than
kept. If you do nothing, you are forgotten; and if
you write, and fail, your former success is thrown in
your teeth. He who has a reputation to maintain
has a wild beast in his house, which he must constantly feed, or it will feed upon him."

Some of Horace Smith's aversions were very distinctive. For instance, he greatly disliked the
practice of smoking and snuff-taking. To all forms
of fishing and angling he had the keenest antipathy,
going so far as to call an angler "a fish butcher, a
piscatorial assassin." Clubs he disliked, as being
founded upon selfishness and the cause of much
unhappiness between married people. All who wore
eye-glasses, except for the purpose of improving
their sight, he called coxcombs. Country cousins
he looked upon as periodical bores, who, "because
they happened to have some of your own blood in
their veins, think that they may inflict the whole of
their bodies upon you during their stay in town."
Although he lived for years by the sea, he could
never be brought to admire it, though he gave it
his profound respect. He said he did not care to

dwell upon the subject, even with his pen. He was particularly fond of rational conversation, though he detested mere argument on any topic. He maintained that Englishwomen were, in general, much better conversationalists than Englishmen were.

In his habits he was regularity personified. Punctually as the clock struck ten at night, unless visitors were present, he would retire, no matter what he was at the moment engaged upon. Day after day at Brighton he used, at a certain hour, to walk from his residence to Tupper's and Lucombe's Libraries, on the Old Steine; and afterwards, if the weather suited, would take a constitutional on the Grand Parade or the Chain Pier. In fact, he was decidedly methodical in all his actions.

In his dress he was particularly neat. He had no petty vices. In eating and drinking he was strictly moderate; in the former, his tastes rather tended towards the refinement of the French *cuisine* than to the prevailing solid diet of Englishmen.

He had a curious weakness for destroying all letters, however important; he looked upon them, when unanswered, as accusing angels, and he hated them, when replied to, as reminding him of his shortcomings. He loved trees, flowers, and gardens; the songs of birds delighted him. Music to him was a Divine voice. Drawing he thought, with Goethe, was one of the most moral of all accomplishments.

For all animals, particularly for cats, he had the greatest tenderness and sympathy. His love of children was most marked; he always went out of his way to amuse and entertain them, and they were quite fascinated by his really wonderful power of story-telling and mimicry. No wonder, therefore, that his popularity with all young people was immense.

Mrs. E. M. Ward, the well-known artist, retains an affectionate remembrance of this characteristic, and the delight that was caused in their home when "Uncle Horace" was expected. His arrival was the signal for a merry-making. Taking the children on his knees, he regaled them with fairy tales in extempore verse.

As Mr. S. C. Hall has said:—"Horace Smith was emphatically a good man; of large sympathy and charity, generous in giving even beyond his means, eminent for rectitude in all the affairs and relations of life, and I never heard him utter an injurious word of any one of his contemporaries, though our usual talk concerned them."

Horace Smith was, indeed, eminently lovable. Few could appreciate this somewhat rare quality better than Thackeray, who thus sums up the character of his friend:—"That good, serene old man, who went out of the world in charity with all in it, and having shown through his life, as far as I know it, quite a delightful love of God's works and creatures—a true, loyal, Christian man."

INDEX

ABDY, MARIA, 180–182, 293–295
Absent Apothecary, The, 252, 254–257
Adam Brown, 265
Alfred House Academy, 50–52
Anderson, the Rev. James, 272–273
—— the Rev. Robert, 272–273
Arthur Arundel, 265
Athenæum Club, 240

"Badger," of Brighton, 275
Banks, Sir Joseph, 68, 69, 71
Barham, the Rev. R. H., 238, 239
Bartholomew Fair, 250
Beavan, Henry, 184, 295
Blessington, Lady, 120, 236
Bond, Lady E. A., 239
Bramblelye House, 257–262
Brighton, 267-290
Brighton Herald, The, 273
Burdett-Coutts, the Baroness, 288
Burford, Peter Thomas, 42–44
Burgess, Hugh, 183
Busby, Dr. Thomas, 108, 110
Byron, Lord, 106, 107, 117, 176, 177

Cadell, Alderman, 83, 115
—— Elizabeth, 183
—— Joanna, 183
—— Rosa, 183
—— Sophia, 183
—— Thomas, 83, 115, 116, 184
Campbell, Thomas, 118, 266
Chigwell School, 42-47

Chigwell Village, 48, 245, 246
Christie, Mr., 152, 153
City Halls, 81, 82
City, the (1800 to 1810), 88, 89
Cobby, Mrs., 274
Cotton, Sir St. Vincent, 272
Country Cousin, The, 249
Covent Garden Theatre, Destruction of, 99
Cumberland, Richard, 97, 98
Curran, 77

Dodson, Clara, 129–132, 157–160, 295, 296
D'Orsay, Count, 120, 236
Drury Lane Theatre, Addresses for re-opening of, 104–106 ; some of the, 105–108
—— Destruction of, 99–102
—— New, the, 102–103
—— Re-building, Plans for, 102
—— Re-opening of, 106–108
Du Barry, Mdme., 17, 18, 20

Eld, Lieut.-Col., 271, 272
Elliston, Mr., 107

Family Story, A, 78, 79
Festivals, Games, and Amusements, 264
Field, Barron, 199, 252
First Impressions, 252, 253
Fleet, Charles, 290
—— William, 273
Fraser's Magazine, 242, 243
Friend, D. Burchell, 290

*

Fladgate, Francis 238 239
Ford, Miss, 133

Gaieties and Gravities, 257
Gale, Middleton, 264
Garrick Club, the, 240–244
—— David, 25, 26 ; Mrs., 107
George III., 72, 84
Gompertz, Adelaide, 291, 292, 296–298
Gordon Riots, Lord George, 29–33
Gunn, Martha, 274

Haines, John, 290
Hall, S. C., 119, 260, 261, 282, 283, 285, 305 ; Mrs., 181, 182
Harsnett, Archbishop, 43, 46
Heaviside, Mrs., 284, 289
Heseltine, William, 124–128; Mrs., 281, 282
Highgate Tunnel, the, 93-95
—— *The, or Secret Arch,* 95–97
Hill, Thomas, 134, 135, 208–213, 280, 281
Hook, Theodore, 120, 222–232
Hunt, Holman, 133, 134
Hunt, Leigh, 167

Imitations of Celebrated Authors, 265
Introduction, 1, 2

Jane Lomax, 264, 265
Jesse, Edward, 189, 190
Johnson, Dr., 40
"Jonathan," Brighton, 274

Kean, Charles, 121, 284
—— Edmund, 121, 286
Keats, John, 134–137, 154, 155
Keir Grant, Sir William, 272
Kemble, John, 74

Lang, Andrew, 153, 154
Lardner, Dr., 284, 289
Leman, Henry, 183
Lotteries, State, 82, 83
Louis XV., 16–21
—— XVI., 54, 56

Love and Mesmerism, 265
Lytton, Lord, 120, 236, 237

Magnus, Harry, 129
Mail Coach, The, 250
Marie Antoinette, 54–56
Masaniello, 265
Mansfield, Lord, 40
Mathews, Charles, 188, 189, 214–222, 238, 249–251, 278–280
—— Mrs., 217–222
Matthews, Mr., 274
Midsummer Medley, The, 264
Miller, John, 95, 98, 116
Moneyed Man, The, 265
Mulgrave, Earl of, 91, 145, 245
Murray (Brighton), 275
—— Mr. John, 115, 116, 118

"Nancy" of Chigwell, 47, 246
New College, Hackney, 49, 50
New Forest, The, 263

Oliver Cromwell, 265
Oliver, William, 183
Ordnance, Board of, 140–148
—— Parliamentary Election and, 144, 145

Paoli, "General," 21, 22
Paris, 13–15, 53–60, 157–161
—— Dr., 237, 238, 247
—— Tom, 237, 238
Patriotism in City, 72, 73
Perceval, the Hon. Spencer, 83, 90, 91
"Perdita" Robinson, 7
Poetical Works, 265

Ratty Family, the, 274
Redding, Cyrus, 162–166, 260, 262, 263, 291
Rejected Addresses, the Real, 104–108
Rejected Addresses, The, Murray, Mr. John, and, 115, 116, 118
—— Publication of, 114, 115, 116
—— Reviews of, 117, 118
—— Some of, 111–114

Rejected Addresses, written, How they came to be, 109, 110
Rennie, John, 93
Reuben Apsley, 262
Robertson, the Rev. F. W., 272, 273, 288, 289
Round, John, 289
Runaway, The, 79, 80

St. Albans, Duchess of, 286–288
St. James' Palace, Fire at, 99
Sake Deen Mahomed, 275, 280
Scott, John, 152, 153
—— Sir Walter, 111, 112, 199–204, 257–260
Shee, Sir Martin A., 274
Shelley, Percy Bysshe, 136–152, 154–156, 161, 167–177
Shenstone, the Poet, 70, 71
Smith, Clara, 129
Smith, Eliza (Tizey), 123, 124, 157, 289
Smith, Horace, *Absent Apothecary, The*, 252, 254–257
—— *Adam Brown*, 265
—— Alfred House Academy, at, 52
—— Ambition, his Literary, 122
—— Anecdotes of his brother James, his, 187–189
—— *Arthur Arundel*, 265
—— Aversions of, 303, 304
—— Birth of, 28
—— *Brambletye House*, 257–262
—— Brighton, at, 269, 278–286, 288–290, 292, 293; friends, his, 283, 284
—— Campbell, Thomas, his verses on, 266
—— Character and disposition of, 39, 89, 119, 122, 126, 139, 151, 156, 157, 284, 288, 289, 293, 299, 300–305
—— Chigwell School, at, 42–48, 52
—— Childhood of, 38–41
—— Children of, 123, 124, 156, 157, 284–286, 289
—— City counting-house, Clerk in, 71; early associations with the, 36, 37; merchant in the, 87–90; retires from business in, 156, 157; stockbroker in the, 92, 124–128
Smith, Horace, Death of, 298
—— Drama, his connection with the, 97–99
—— Education of, 42–48, 52
—— *Family Story, A*, 78, 79
—— *Festivals, Games and Amusements*, 264
—— Field, Barron, and, 199, 252
—— *First Impressions*, 252, 253
—— Fulham, at Elysium Row, 133, 134
—— *Gaieties and Gravities*, 257
—— *Gale Middleton*, 264
—— Hall, S. C., and, 119, 282, 283, 285, 305
—— Heseltine, Mrs., and, 281, 282; William, and, 124–128
—— *Highgate Tunnel, or Secret Arch, The*, 95–97
—— Hill, Thomas, and, 134, 135, 280, 281; his personal recollections of, 208–213
—— Hook, Theodore, his personal recollections of, 222–232
—— Humour in prose and verse, his, 194–198, 266, 276
—— Illness, his last, 298
—— *Imitations of Celebrated Authors*, 265
—— *Jane Lomax*, 264, 265
—— Kean, Charles, and, 121, 284
—— Keats, entertains, 134–136
—— Knightsbridge, at, 122, 123
—— Lang, Andrew, and, 153, 154
—— Letters to Abdy, Maria, 294, 295; to Dodson, Clara, 129–132, 157–160, 295, 296; to Gompertz, Adelaide, 291, 292, 296–298; to Hall, S. C., 260, 261, 282, 283; to Heseltine, Mrs., 281, 282; to Hill, Thomas, 280, 281; to Mathews, Charles, 214–217, 278–280; to Mathews, Charles, Mrs., 217–222; to Redding, Cyrus, 162–

166 ; to Shelley, 150–152, 155, 156, 161 ; Twiss, Horace, 254

Smith, Horace, Literary, dramatic and social circle, his, 119–121, 283, 284 ; works, his earliest, 78–80 ; his later, 251–266

—— London and elsewhere, trips to, 293

—— *Love and Mesmerism*, 265

—— Marriage, his, 122 ; his second, 132, 133

—— *Masaniello*, 265

—— Mathews, Charles, and, 214, 216, 217, 278–280 ; his personal recollections of, 214, 222 ; Mrs., and, 217–222

—— *Midsummer Medley, The*, 264

—— *Moneyed Man, The*, 265

—— *New Forest, The*, 263

—— *Oliver Cromwell*, 265

—— Opinions on Social and Political subjects, etc., his, 300–303

—— Paris, at, 157–161

—— Personal appearance of, 298, 299

—— *Poetical Works*, 265

—— Popularity with the gentler sex, his, 122

—— *Rejected Addresses*, and, 99, 103, 105, 109–112, 114–118, 122

—— *Reuben Apsley*, 262

—— *Runaway, The*, 79, 80

—— St. Albans, Duchess of, and, 286–288

—— —— Lines on the, 287

—— Scott, John, Duel, and, 152–154

—— —— Sir Walter, his personal recollections of, 199–204

—— Shelley, Percy Bysshe, and, 136–139, 149–152, 154–156, 161, 167, 168 ; his personal recollections of, 167–177

—— Southey, Robert, his personal recollections of, 204–208

—— Stock-Exchange, and, 124–128

—— *Tales of the Early Ages*, 264

Smith, Horace, Thackeray, W. M., and, 284–286

—— *Tin Trumpet, The*, 264

—— *Tor Hill, The*, 262

—— *Trevanion*, 80

—— Tunbridge Wells, at, 257, 260, 298

—— Twiss, Horace, and, 254

—— Versailles, at, 162–167

—— *Walter Colyton*, 263

—— *Zillah*, 262, 263

Smith, Horatio Shakespeare, 123, 124, 157

Smith, James, Alfred House Academy, at, 50–52

—— Ambition, his want of, 122

—— Articled to his father, 65

—— Athenæum Club, elected member of the, 240

—— Attorney, admitted as an, 72

—— Barham, the Rev. R. H., and, 238, 239

—— *Bartholomew Fair*, 250

—— Birth of, 24

—— Blessington, Lady, and, 120, 236

—— Bons-mots, etc., his, 193, 194

—— Book-keeping classes, attends, 52

—— Burford, Peter Thomas, and, 43, 44

—— Character and disposition of, 39, 43, 44, 46, 48, 147, 186–188, 233–237, 246-248

—— Chigwell, Revisits, 245, 246

—— —— School, at, 42–48

—— Childhood of, 38–41

—— City, his early association with the, 36, 37

—— Club-life, his, 239–245

—— *Country Cousin, The*, 249

—— Craven St., Strand, at, 27, 245, 247, 248

—— Dartmouth, at, 69

—— Death, his narrow escape from, 62, 63

—— Death of, 247, 248

—— D'Orsay, Count, and, 120, 236

Smith, James, Drama, his connection with the, 97–99
—— Education of, 42–52
—— Fame, literary, his illustration of the ephemeral nature of, 121
—— Fladgate, Francis, and, 238, 239
—— France, in, 60, 61
—— Fraser's Magazine, and, 242, 243
—— Garrick Club, elected member of, 241
—— Gravesend, etc., at, 68
—— Habits, his daily, 235
—— Housekeeper, his, 245, 247
—— Humorous compositions by, 190, 191, 276–278
—— Illness, his last, 247, 248
—— Isle of Thanet, in the, 69, 70
—— —— Wight, in the, 68
—— *Jane Lomax*, his criticism of, 264, 265
—— Jesse, Edward, and, 189, 190
—— Johnson, Dr., and, 40
—— "Leasowes," at, 70, 71
—— Legal profession, his respect for the, 187, 188
—— Letter to Mrs. Mathews, his, 217, 218
—— Lewes, at, 71
—— Literary and dramatic circle, his, 120, 121
—— —— Works, his earliest, 80, 81 ; his later (other than *Rejected Addresses*), 249, 250
—— London, his love of, 245
—— Lytton, Lord, and, 120, 236, 237
—— *Mail Coach, The*, 250
—— Mathews, Charles, and, 188, 189, 238 ; Mrs., and, 217, 218
—— Mansfield, Lord Chief Justice, and, 40
—— Matrimony, his indifference to, 122, 234, 235
—— Mulgrave, Earl of, and, 91, 145, 245

Smith, James, "Nancy" of Chigwell, and, 47, 246
—— New College, Hackney, at, 49, 50
—— Ordnance Board Solicitor, appointed joint-assistant to, 90, 91 ; sole assistant to, 145–148
—— Oxford, at, 71
—— Paris, Dr., and, 237, 238, 247 ; his letter to, 247
—— —— Tom, and, 237, 238
—— Perceval, Hon. Spencer, dines with, 83
—— Personal appearance of, 233, 234
—— Popularity with the gentler sex, his, 122
—— *Rejected Addresses*, and, 99, 109–118, 121, 122
—— Scotland, in, 65–67
—— Social circle, his, 119–121, 235–239
—— *Trip to France, A*, 249
—— Union Club, elected member of the, 244
—— Versification, his, 44, 45, 47–49, 51, 187, 191–193, 238, 275
Smith, Laura, 285, 286, 289
Smith, Leonard, 26, 42, 52, 234
Smith, Maria, 24
Smith, Robert, attorney, admitted as an, 22
—— —— Articled to an, 10, 11
—— Austin Friars, at, 92
—— Banks, Sir Joseph, and, 68, 69
—— Basinghall St., at, 36, 81
—— Birth and parentage of, 2
—— Board of Ordnance, his appointment to, 34 ; retirement from, 145, 146
—— *Brambletye House*, and, 261, 262
—— Brighton, at, 268
—— Cambridge, at, 87
—— Chantilly, at, 15
—— Compiègne, at, 16–21
—— Dartmouth, at, 69

Smith, Robert, Death, his narrow escapes from, 32, 33, 62, 63
—— Death of, 185
—— Declining years of, 178, 180–185
—— Du Barry, Madame, sees, 17, 18, 20
—— Education of, 3–5
—— Fen Court, at, 23
—— Frederick's Place, Old Jewry, at, 27
—— Freemason's Hall, at, 26
—— Garrick, David, and, 25, 26
—— —— Attends last appearance of, 26
—— Gordon Riots, and the, 29–34
—— Gravesend, etc., at, 68
—— Hanway, Mr., and, 25
—— Ireland, in, 73–77
—— Isle of Thanet, in, 69, 70
—— —— Wight, in, 68
—— London, early life in, 11, 12
—— —— First journey to, 7, 10
—— Louis XV., sees, 16–21
—— —— XVI. and Marie Antoinette, sees, 54–56
—— "Leasowes," at, 70, 71
—— Lewes, at, 71
—— Liverpool, at, 67, 68
—— Marriage, his, 22–24
—— —— His second, 86, 87
—— Mulgrave, Earl of, and, 91
—— Old Jewry, at, 35
—— Oxford, at, 71
—— Paoli, General, meets, 21, 22
—— Paris, at, 14, 15, 53–61
—— Patriotism, and, 72, 73
—— "Perdita" Robinson, meets, 7
—— Philanthropy, his, 24, 25
—— Recollections, his early, 3, 4, 7
—— Residences after retirement, his, 178
—— Royal Society, elected Fellow of the, 71

Smith, Robert, St. Paul's, at, 72
—— Scotland, in, 65–67
—— Society of Antiquaries, elected Fellow of, 35
—— —— Arts, elected Fellow of, 73
—— State Lotteries, and, 83
—— *Tor Hill, The*, and, 262
—— Versification, his, 5, 6, 179–183, 185
—— West Indies, goes to, 34, 35
—— Wife, death of his, 84, 85
—— —— second, 184
—— Mrs., 22–24, 84, 85
—— Mrs. (the second), 86, 87, 184
Smith, Rosalind, 156, 284, 289
Smith, Sophia, 26, 83
Smoaker, The Bros., 274
Southey, Robert, 112, 113, 204–208

Tales of the Early Ages, 264
Thackeray, W. M., 284–286, 305
Tin Trumpet, The, 264
Tor Hill, The, 262
Trevanion, 80, 132
Trip to Paris, The, 249
Twiss, Horace, 254

Union Club, The, 244, 245

Versailles, Horace Smith at, 162–167
Victoria, Queen, curious address to, 293, 294

Walter Colyton, 263, 280, 281
Ward, Charles William, 98, 99, 105, 109, 110, 116
—— E. M., R.A., 133, 181
—— Mrs., 305
Wellington, Duke of, 145, 146
White, Henry Kirke, 87

Young, the Rev. Julian, 189, 190

Zillah, 262, 263

NEW AND POPULAR NOVELS

In One Volume, crown 8vo, price 6s.

A PRINCE
From the Great Never Never

By MARY F. A. TENCH
Author of ' Where the Surf Breaks,' Etc.

NEW NOVEL BY G. M. ROBINS

In 1 vol., crown 8vo, price 6s.

Nigel Ferrard

By G. M. ROBINS (Mrs. BAILLIE REYNOLDS)
Author of ' Her Point of View,' Etc.

NEW NOVEL BY E. NESBIT

In 1 vol., crown 8vo, price 6s.

The Secret of Kyriels

By E. NESBIT
Author of ' Lays and Legends,' ' Grim Tales,' Etc.

NEW NOVEL BY CHRISTABEL COLERIDGE

In 1 vol., crown 8vo, price 6s.

The Main Chance

By CHRISTABEL COLERIDGE
Author of ' Waynflete,' ' The Tender Mercies of the Good,' Etc.

LONDON : HURST AND BLACKETT, LIMITED. (7

BOOKS FOR PRIZES AND PRESENTS

NEW CHRISTMAS BOOK

In 1 vol., 4to, price 2s. 6d.
With specially designed Cover lithographed in Nine Colours.

The Legend of The Christmas Rose

By A. O'D. BARTHOLEYNS
Illustrated by DELAPOER DOWNING.

NEW FAIRY TALE FOR CHILDREN

In 1 vol., crown 8vo, with Cover in Colours, gilt edges, price 3s. 6d.

The Pink Hen

By CUTHBERT SPURLING
With 14 Illustrations by DUNCAN TATE.

FAIRY TALES BY NETTA SYRETT
Illustrated by NELLIE SYRETT.
In 1 vol., large 8vo, handsomely bound, price 5s.

The Garden of Delight

By NETTA SYRETT
Author of 'Nobody's Fault,' Etc.

NEW STORY BY MISS DAVENPORT ADAMS
Illustrated by HARRY FURNISS.
In 1 vol., crown 8vo, extra cloth, gilt edges, price 4s.

Miss Secretary Ethel:
A Story for Girls of To-Day

By ELLINOR DAVENPORT ADAMS
Author of 'The Disagreeable Duke,' 'Little Miss Conceit,' Etc.

LONDON: HURST AND BLACKETT, LIMITED. (9

POPULAR WORKS BY POPULAR AUTHORS

THE NEW FICTION, and other Essays on Literary
Subjects. By H. D. TRAILL, Author of 'The New Lucian,'
'The Life of Sir John Franklin,' etc. 1 vol., crown 8vo,
price 6s.

IN CAMP AND CANTONMENT. Stories of Foreign
Service. By EDITH E. CUTHELL, Author of 'Only a Guard-
room Dog,' 'The Wee Widow's Cruise,' etc. 1 vol., crown
8vo, price 3s. 6d.

LADY HAMILTON AND LORD NELSON. By JOHN
CORDY JEAFFRESON. New and Revised Edition. Containing
Additional Facts, Letters, and other Materials. With
Portrait of Lady Hamilton. 1 vol., large crown 8vo, gilt
top, price 6s.

FAMOUS BRITISH WARSHIPS, and their Commanders.
By WALTER WOOD, Author of 'Barrack and Battlefield.'
With Portrait of Admiral Viscount Nelson. 1 vol., large
crown 8vo, price 6s.

THE TAME FOX, and other Sketches. By FINCH
MASON. With 6 Full-page Coloured Illustrations. 1 vol.,
large crown 8vo, price 7s. 6d.

BARRACK AND BATTLEFIELD. Tales of the Service
at Home and Abroad. By WALTER WOOD. 1 vol., large
crown 8vo, gilt top, price 6s.

THE REAL LORD BYRON. By JOHN CORDY JEAFFRESON.
1 vol., crown 8vo. With portrait of Lord Byron by T.
Phillips, R.A., engraved on steel, price 5s.

FIFTY YEARS OF MY LIFE IN THE WORLD OF
SPORT AT HOME AND ABROAD. By SIR JOHN DUG-
DALE ASTLEY, Bart. 1 vol., crown 8vo, with Portrait, price 6s.
Also in small crown 8vo, cloth, price 2s. 6d.

THE LAST OF THE BUSHRANGERS. An account of
the Capture of the Kelly Gang. 1 vol., crown 8vo, with eight
Full-page Illustrations, price 3s. 6d.

EDNA LYALL'S NOVELS

EACH IN ONE VOLUME CROWN 8vo—SIX SHILLINGS.

DONOVAN: A MODERN ENGLISHMAN.

"This is a very admirable work. The reader is from the first carried away by the gallant unconventionality of its author. 'Donovan' is a very excellent novel; but it is something more and better. It should do as much good as the best sermon ever written or delivered extempore. The story is told with a grand simplicity, an unconscious poetry of eloquence which stirs the very depths of the heart. One of the main excellencies of this novel is the delicacy of touch with which the author shows her most delightful characters to be after all human beings, and not angels before their time."—*Standard.*

WE TWO.

"There is artistic realism both in the conception and the delineation of the personages; the action and interest are unflaggingly sustained from first to last, and the book is pervaded by an atmosphere of elevated, earnest thought."—*Scotsman.*

IN THE GOLDEN DAYS.

"Miss Lyall has given us a vigorous study of such life and character as are really worth reading about. The central figure of her story is Algernon Sydney; and this figure she invests with a singular dignity and power. He always appears with effect, but no liberties are taken with the facts of his life."—*Spectator.*

KNIGHT-ERRANT.

"The plot, and, indeed, the whole story, is gracefully fresh and very charming; there is a wide humanity in the book that cannot fail to accomplish its author's purpose."—*Literary World.*

WON BY WAITING.

"The Dean's daughters are perfectly real characters—the learned Cornelia especially; —the little impulsive French heroine, who endures their cold hospitality and at last wins their affection, is thoroughly charming; while throughout the book there runs a golden thread of pure brotherly and sisterly love, which pleasantly reminds us that the making and marring of marriage is not, after all, the sum total of real life."—*Academy.*

A HARDY NORSEMAN.

"All the quiet humour we praised in 'Donovan' is to be found in the new story. And the humour, though never demonstrative, has a charm of its own. It is not Edna Lyall's plan to give her readers much elaborate description, but when she does describe scenery her picture is always alive with vividness and grace."—*Athenæum.*

TO RIGHT THE WRONG.

"We are glad to welcome Miss Lyall back after her long abstraction from the fields of prosperous, popular authorship which she had tilled so successfully. She again affronts her public with a very serious work of fiction indeed, and succeeds very well in that thorny path of the historical novel in which so many have failed before her. That 'glory of warrior, glory of orator, glory of song,' John Hampden, lives again, to a certain extent, in that dim half light of posthumous research and loving and enthusiastic imagination which is all the novelist can do for these great figures of the past, resurrected to make the plot of a modern novel."—*Black and White.*

LONDON : HURST AND BLACKETT, LIMITED.

(11

BEATRICE WHITBY'S NOVELS

EACH IN ONE VOLUME, CROWN 8vo—3s. 6d.

SUNSET

'We welcome such a story as "Sunset." It is slightly sentimental as one would guess from its title, but never mawkish, and it is illumined by flashes of humour, as well as by some occasional reflections that exhibit a close acquaintance with human nature.'—*The Times.*

'"Sunset" will fully meet the expectations of Miss Whitby's many admirers.'—*Globe.*

'Miss Whitby has always a story to tell. "Sunset" is as interesting in the telling as any that she has produced since "The Awakening of Mary Fenwick."'—*Daily Telegraph.*

THE AWAKENING OF MARY FENWICK

'We have no hesitation in declaring that "The Awakening of Mary Fenwick" is the best novel of its kind that we have seen for some years. The story is extremely simple. Mary Mauser marries her husband for external, and perhaps rather inadequate, reasons, and then discovers that he married her because she was an heiress. She feels the indignity acutely, and does not scruple to tell him her opinion—her very candid opinion—of his behaviour. Mary Fenwick and her husband live and move and make us believe in them in a way which few but the great masters of fiction have been able to compass.'—*Athenæum.*

ONE REASON WHY

'The governess makes a re-entry into fiction under the auspices of Beatrice Whitby in "One Reason Why." Readers generally, however, will take a great deal more interest, for once, in the children than in their instructress. "Bay" and "Ellie" are charmingly natural additions to the children of novel-land; so much so, that there is a period when one dreads a death-bed scene for one of them—a fear which is happily unfulfilled.'—*Graphic.*

PART OF THE PROPERTY

'The book is a thoroughly good one. The theme is fairly familiar—the rebellion of a spirited girl against a match which has been arranged for her without her knowledge or consent; her resentment of being treated, not as a woman with a heart and will, but as "part of the property;" and her final discovery, which is led up to with real dramatic skill, that the thing against which her whole nature had risen in revolt has become the one desire of her heart.'—*Spectator.*

IN THE SUNTIME OF HER YOUTH

'The careless optimism of the head of the family would be incredible, if we did not know how men exist full of responsibilities yet free from solicitudes, and who tread with a jaunty step the very verge of ruin; his inconsolable widow would be equally improbable, if we did not meet every day with women who devote themselves to such idols of clay. There is interest in it from first to last, and its pathos is relieved by touches of true humour.'—*Illustrated London News.*

MARY FENWICK'S DAUGHTER

'This is one of the most delightful novels we have read for a long time. "Bab" Fenwick is an "out of door" kind of girl, full of spirit, wit, go, and sin, both original and acquired. Her lover, Jack, is all that a hero should be, and great and magnanimous as he is, finds some difficulty in forgiving the *insouciante* mistress all her little sins of omission and commission. The whole is admirable.'—*Black and White.*

A MATTER OF SKILL

'The title story, showing how a stately girl is captured after a good deal of trouble, by a short and commonplace young man, is very amusing; and there are other sketches in which it is interesting to follow the wiles of Mother Eve ere she has come to years of discretion.'—*Academy.*

12)   LONDON: HURST AND BLACKETT, LIMITED.

The only Authorized Editions

OF

'JOHN HALIFAX, GENTLEMAN'

ILLUSTRATED EDITION

Illustrations by HUGH RIVIERE, large crown 8vo, extra cloth, gilt top, price 6s.

STANDARD EDITION

Crown 8vo, cloth, with frontispiece by SIR JOHN MILLAIS, Bart., price 5s.

TEWKESBURY EDITION

Crown 8vo, cloth, with portrait of Author by PROFESSOR HERKOMER, cloth, price 3s. 6d.

POPULAR EDITION

Crown 8vo, cloth, price 2s.

PEOPLE'S EDITION

In medium 8vo, cloth, price 1s.

In paper cover, price 6d.

LONDON: HURST AND BLACKETT, LIMITED. (13

MRS. CRAIK'S NOVELS

Each in One Volume, Crown Octavo, 3s. 6d.

JOHN HALIFAX, GENTLEMAN.

"The new and cheaper edition of this interesting work will doubtless meet with great success. John Halifax, the hero of this most beautiful story, is no ordinary hero, and this his history is no ordinary book. It is a full-length portrait of a true gentleman, one of nature's own nobility. It is also the history of a home, and a thoroughly English one. The work abounds in incident, and is full of graphic power and true pathos. It is a book that few will read without becoming wiser and better."—*Scotsman.*

A LIFE FOR A LIFE.

"We are always glad to welcome this author. She writes from her own convictions, and she has the power not only to conceive clearly what it is that she wishes to say, but to express it in language effective and vigorous. In 'A Life for a Life' she is fortunate in a good subject, and she has produced a work of strong effect. The reader, having read the book through for the story, will be apt (if he be of our persuasion) to return and read again many pages and passages with greater pleasure than on a first perusal. The whole book is replete with a graceful, tender delicacy; and in addition to its other merits, it is written in good careful English."—*Athenæum.*

CHRISTIAN'S MISTAKE.

"A more charming story, to our taste, has rarely been written. Within the compass of a single volume the writer has hit off a circle of varied characters, all true to nature— some true to the highest nature—and she has entangled them in a story which keeps us in suspense till the knot is happily and gracefully resolved; while, at the same time, a pathetic interest is sustained by an art of which it would be difficult to analyse the secret. It is a choice gift to be able thus to render human nature so truly, to penetrate its depths with such a searching sagacity, and to illuminate them with a radiance so eminently the writer's own."—*The Times.*

A NOBLE LIFE.

"This is one of those pleasant tales in which the author of 'John Halifax' speaks out of a generous heart the purest truths of life."—*Examiner.*

"Few men, and no women, will read 'A Noble Life' without finding themselves the better."—*Spectator.*

"A story of powerful and pathetic interest."—*Daily News.*

THE WOMAN'S KINGDOM.

"'The Woman's Kingdom' sustains the author's reputation as a writer of the purest and noblest kind of domestic stories. The novelist's lesson is given with admirable force and sweetness."—*Athenæum.*

"'The Woman's Kingdom' is remarkable for its romantic interest. The characters are masterpieces. Edna is worthy of the hand that drew John Halifax."—*Post.*

A BRAVE LADY.

"A very good novel, showing a tender sympathy with human nature, and permeated by a pure and noble spirit."—*Examiner.*

"A most charming story."—*Standard.*

"We earnestly recommend this novel. It is a special and worthy specimen of the author's remarkable powers. The reader's attention never for a moment flags."—*Post.*

MISTRESS AND MAID.

"A good, wholesome book, as pleasant to read as it is instructive."—*Athenæum.*

"This book is written with the same true-hearted earnestness as 'John Halifax.' The spirit of the whole work is excellent."—*Examiner.*

"A charming tale charmingly told."—*Standard.*

LONDON : HURST AND BLACKETT, LIMITED.

MRS. CRAIK'S NOVELS

Each in One Volume Crown Octavo, 3s. 6d.

YOUNG MRS. JARDINE.

"'Young Mrs. Jardine' is a pretty story, written in pure English."—*The Times.*

"There is much good feeling in this book. It is pleasant and wholesome."—*Athenæum.*

"A book that all should read. Whilst it is quite the equal of any of its predecessors in elevation of thought and style, it is perhaps their superior in interest of plot and dramatic intensity. The characters are admirably delineated, and the dialogue is natural and clear."—*Morning Post.*

HANNAH.

"A powerful novel of social and domestic life. One of the most successful efforts of a successful novelist."—*Daily News.*

"A very pleasant, healthy story, well and artistically told. The book is sure of a wide circle of readers. The character of Hannah is one of rare beauty."—*Standard.*

NOTHING NEW.

"'Nothing New' displays all those superior merits which have made 'John Halifax' one of the most popular works of the day."—*Post.*

"The reader will find these narratives calculated to remind him of that truth and energy of human portraiture, that spell over human affections and emotions, which have stamped this author as one of the first novelists of our day."—*John Bull.*

THE UNKIND WORD.

"The author of 'John Halifax' has written many fascinating stories, but we can call to mind nothing from her pen that has a more enduring charm than the graceful sketches in this work. Such a character as Jessie stands out from a crowd of heroines as the type of all that is truly noble, pure, and womanly."—*United Service Magazine.*

STUDIES FROM LIFE.

"These studies are truthful and vivid pictures of life, often earnest, always full of right feeling, and occasionally lightened by touches of quiet genial humour. The volume is remarkable for thought, sound sense, shrewd observation, and kind and sympathetic feeling for all things good and beautiful."—*Post.*

A WOMAN'S THOUGHTS ABOUT WOMEN.

"A book of sound counsel. It is one of the most sensible works of its kind, well written, true-hearted, and altogether practical. Whoever wishes to give advice to a young lady may thank the author for means of doing so."—*Examiner.*

"These thoughts are worthy of the earnest and enlightened mind, the all-embracing charity, and the well-earned reputation of the author of 'John Halifax.'"—*Standard.*

"This excellent book is characterised by good sense, good taste, and feeling, and is written in an earnest, philanthropic, as well as practical spirit."—*Post.*

HIS LITTLE MOTHER.

"'His Little Mother' is the story of a sister's self-sacrifice from her childhood until her early death, worn out in her brother's and his children's service. It is a pathetic story as the author tells it. The beauty of the girl's devotion is described with many tender touches, and the question of short-sighted though loving foolishness is kept in the background. The volume is written in a pleasant informal manner, and contains many tender generous thoughts, and not a few practical ones. It is a book that will be read with interest, and that cannot be lightly forgotten."—*St. James's Gazette.*

www.ingramcontent.com/pod-product-compliance
Lightning Source LLC
Chambersburg PA
CBHW031130120726
47905CB00006B/1631